Yoga Studies in Five Minutes

Religion in 5 Minutes

Series Editors
Russell T. McCutcheon
University of Alabama
Aaron W. Hughes
University of Rochester

Published

Religion in Five Minutes
Edited by Aaron W. Hughes and Russell T. McCutcheon.
Atheism in Five Minutes
Edited by Teemu Taira
Buddhism in Five Minutes
Edited by Elizabeth J. Harris
Hinduism in Five Minutes
Edited by Steven W. Ramey
Indigenous Religious Traditions in Five Minutes
Edited by Molly Bassett and Natalie Avalos
Pagan Religions in Five Minutes
Edited by Suzanne Owen and Angela Puca
The Old Testament Hebrew Scriptures in Five Minutes
Edited by Philippe Guillaume and Diana V. Edelman

Forthcoming

African Diaspora Religions in Five Minutes
Edited by Emily D. Crews and Curtis J. Evans
Ancient Religion in Five Minutes
Edited by Andrew Durdin
Chinese Religions in Five Minutes
Edited by Ben Van Overmeire and James Miller
Christianity in Five Minutes
Edited by Robyn Faith Walsh
Islam in Five Minutes
Edited by Edith Szanto
Jainism in Five Minutes
Edited by Steven M. Vose
Judaism in Five Minutes
Edited by Sarah Imhoff
Mormonism in Five Minutes
Edited by Daniel O. McClellan
New Religious Movements in Five Minutes
Edited by Lukas K. Pokorny and Franz Winter

Yoga Studies in Five Minutes

Edited by
Theodora Wildcroft and Barbora Sojková

equinox

SHEFFIELD UK BRISTOL CT

Published by Equinox Publishing Ltd.

UK: Office 415, The Workstation, 15 Paternoster Row, Sheffield, South Yorkshire S1 2BX

USA: ISD, 70 Enterprise Drive, Bristol, CT 06010

www.equinoxpub.com

First published 2025

British Library Cataloguing-in-Publication Data

A catalogue record for this book is available from the British Library.

ISBN-13	978 1 80050 599 5	(hardback)
	978 1 80050 600 8	(paperback)
	978 1 80050 601 5	(ePDF)
	978 1 80050 622 0	(ePub)

Library of Congress Cataloging-in-Publication Data

Names: Wildcroft, Theodora, editor. | Sojková, Barbora, editor.
Title: Yoga studies in five minutes / edited by Theodora Wildcroft and Barbora Sojková.
Description: Sheffield, South Yorkshire ; Bristol, CT : Equinox Publishing Ltd., 2025. | Series: Religion in 5 minutes | Includes bibliographical references and index. | Summary: "Yoga Studies in Five Minutes provides an accessible guide to the diverse and growing field of research into yoga as a social, historical and cultural phenomenon. Leading scholars and innovative researchers offer brief responses to questions that offer insights into the study of yoga. The collection covers ancient history, modern developments, and contemporary issues, considers the diverse practices and philosophies of yoga in a range of contexts, and uses a range of approaches, from philology to anthropology to art history. This book is useful for established scholars looking to broaden their understanding of this rapidly developing field, as well as for those new to the subject. It is an ideal starting point for both independent study and the classroom"-- Provided by publisher.
Identifiers: LCCN 2024031167 (print) | LCCN 2024031168 (ebook) | ISBN 9781800505995 (hardback) | ISBN 9781800506008 (paperback) | ISBN 9781800506015 (epdf) | ISBN 9781800506220 (epub)
Subjects: LCSH: Yoga.
Classification: LCC B132.Y6 Y63 2025 (print) | LCC B132.Y6 (ebook) | DDC 181/.45--dc23/eng/20240912
LC record available at https://lccn.loc.gov/2024031167
LC ebook record available at https://lccn.loc.gov/2024031168

Typeset by Scribe Inc.

Contents

Introduction xi

What is yoga?

1. Is yoga a religion? 3
   Philip Deslippe
2. Is yoga a philosophy? 7
   Karen O'Brien-Kop
3. Is yoga a ritual? 12
   Brett W. Parris
4. Is there a role for faith in yoga? 16
   Jens U. Augspurger
5. Is yoga atheistic, nontheistic, or theistic? 20
   Corinna May Lhoir
6. Has yoga always been associated with Hinduism? 24
   Corinna May Lhoir
7. Is yoga Indian? 28
   C. Pierce Salguero
8. Are there sacred texts in yoga? 32
   Lubomír Ondračka
9. What is Sanskrit? 36
   Corinna May Lhoir
10. What is *OM*? 40
    Finnian M. M. Gerety

What is the point of yoga?

11. What are the goals of yoga? 47
    Barbora Sojková

12. Does yoga liberate or constrain? 51
Ruth Westoby

13. Do yogis want to transcend or transform the body? 55
Adrián Muñoz

14. Are ethics important in yoga? 59
Jens U. Augspurger

15. Are all yogis nonviolent? 63
Matylda Ciołkosz

16. What are the *yamas* and *niyamas*? 67
Graham Burns

17. Does a yogi need to renounce the world? 71
Daniela Bevilacqua

18. What is *samādhi*? 74
Brett W. Parris

19. Does yoga give you extraordinary powers? 77
Lubomír Ondračka

Is yoga healthy?

20. Is yoga safe? 83
Jens U. Augspurger

21. Is yoga good for your health? 87
Brett W. Parris

22. Why do yogis contort their bodies? 91
Daniela Bevilacqua

23. Are all yoga practitioners flexible? 95
Laura von Ostrowski

24. What is the role of diet in yoga? 99
Theodora Wildcroft and Barbora Sojková

25. What is the relationship between yoga and āyurveda? 104
Suzanne Newcombe

How do you practice yoga?

26. What life does the ideal yogi lead? 111
Barbora Sojková and Theodora Wildcroft

27. Has yoga always been a physical practice? 116
Laura von Ostrowski

28. What are *āsanas*? 120
Matylda Ciołkosz

29. What is *vinyasa*? 124
Marissa Clarke

30. What is *prāṇāyāma*? 128
Graham Burns

31. How do mantras relate to yoga? 132
Finnian M. M. Gerety

32. Why do yogis go upside down? 137
Matylda Ciołkosz

33. Why do yogis meditate? 141
Matylda Ciołkosz

34. What is *kuṇḍalinī*? 145
Ruth Westoby

35. What is a *yoginī*? 149
Ruth Westoby

How do you study yoga?

36. Do you need to practice yoga to understand it? 155
Laura von Ostrowski

37. How do academics study yoga? 158
Karen O'Brien-Kop

38. Is yoga only an individual endeavor? 162
Daniela Bevilacqua

39. Does a yogi need to be part of a lineage? 165
Theodora Wildcroft

40. What do the words *sampradāya* and *paramparā* mean? 169
Daniela Bevilacqua

41. What is the *Haṭhapradīpikā*? 173
Nils Jacob Liersch

42. Who are the *siddha yogis*? 177
Adrián Muñoz

How do you teach yoga?

43. What do we know about the teaching of yoga? 183
Theodora Wildcroft

44. Who was the first teacher of yoga? 187
Daniela Bevilacqua

45. Who was Patañjali? 191
Karen O'Brien-Kop

46. Who were Gorakṣanātha and Matsyendranātha? 194
Lubomír Ondračka

47. What is a guru? 198
Jens U. Augspurger

48. Are the teachers of yoga enlightened? 202
Amelia Wood

49. Does a yoga teacher need to be an advanced practitioner? 206
Theodora Wildcroft and Barbora Sojková

How did modern yoga develop?

50. What is the difference between *haṭhayoga* and Hatha Yoga? 213
James Mallinson

51. How has modern yoga developed around the world? 217
Firdose Moonda

52. Why did yoga start being practiced in the Western world? 221
Philip Deslippe

53. Where did all the women come from? 225
Suzanne Newcombe

54. Who was Swami Vivekananda? 229
Gwilym Beckerlegge

55. Who was Krishnamacharya? 233
Amelia Wood

What does yoga look like today?

56. How do modern practitioners relate to ancient texts? 239
Barbora Sojková

Introduction

Theodora Wildcroft and Barbora Sojková

Why is yoga important?

While there are many movement practices that have pop cultural appeal and many well-being practices that have mainstream interest, few of them have reached the global status of contemporary postural yoga. With an aspirational vision of slender flexibility and privileged calm, images of yoga dominate the marketing of a number of profitable industries. Most people's image of yoga is of bodies moving and sitting in a practice for health and well-being that academics most often call "modern postural yoga," after the groundbreaking work of Elizabeth Michelis in 2007, or sometimes "post-lineage yoga."

A quick online search reveals some staggering statistics for participation in this practice, but there are far fewer concrete sources for those statistics. The website MedAlertHelp.org reports that there are more than three hundred million yoga practitioners around the world, and the global yoga industry generated $37.46 billion in 2019. Zippia.com projects this figure to grow to $66.23 billion by 2027. Statista.com declares the US market to have generated $9.31 billion alone in 2020. Finder.com claims a UK revenue for "the pilates and yoga industry" of over £926 million in 2020, with up to 460,000 UK residents taking part in yoga classes every week. And most confidently of all, Comparecamp.com claims the current global yoga industry to be worth more than $84 billion. Yet the data supporting these claims is almost always unclear or ill-defined.

A peer-reviewed literature search for "yoga" will turn up a seemingly never-ending tide of small-scale pilot studies into the "effectiveness" of yoga for this or that condition, few of which trouble themselves to define the yogic practice that was prescribed. Alternately, we can discover through a YouTube search that the most popular yoga-tagged channel, Yoga with Adrienne, has 12.3 million subscribers as of December 2023, and we can be very clear about what form of practice is being proposed to viewers, although not how many of them actually follow her instructions.

More reputable demographic statistics are occasionally produced by polling organizations that have been commissioned by the yoga industry itself. A landmark 2016 study by Ipsos for Yoga Alliance, for example, found that yoga practitioners' *self-reported* spending on yoga classes and equipment, if it was multiplied on a national scale, would be the equivalent of over $16 million. A more recent study by the UK Yoga Teachers Union asked its members for their own estimations of how often they teach, how much they earn, and so on.

There is little truly reliable global or national data about how many people practice "yoga" or what they even mean when they use the term. Nonetheless, the very prevalence of yoga "statistics," media comment pieces, and exploratory medical studies means we can be sure that from health to tourism and business to education, "yoga" is of interest and importance to millions of people across the world.

What does "everyone know" about yoga?

The briefest attention paid to the history and contemporary practice of yoga reveals a vast river of philosophy, thought, and practice. Spanning three millennia and many lands and languages across South Asia, premodern yoga is as hard to define as its contemporary counterpart, if not more. While the oldest works of Indian literature, known as the Vedas, include forerunners of techniques later associated with yogic practices, there is very little evidence of a systematic yoga practice prior to circa 500 BCE. Around that time, we see the rise of a new worldview formulated by ascetic groups such as Buddhists and Jains. According to these groups, human existence was characterized by the seemingly endless cycle of rebirths (*saṃsāra*), driven by voluntary and involuntary actions. Since life was seen as ultimately filled with suffering, the goal of these groups became liberation (*mokṣa*) from or cessation (*nirvāṇa*) of the cycle of rebirths, which was attained by eradicating *karma* (the rebirth-generating power of individual past actions), facilitated by special knowledge or various bodily and mental practices. While these groups did not call their techniques "yoga" until much later, they are in essence our first evidence of what came to be known as a systematic yogic practice.

Subsequently, these ascetic teachings were adopted by the Brahmanical milieu. In the Brahmanical context, they were first formulated in the body of texts known as the Upaniṣads (ca. seventh to first century BCE). Their inclusion in the greatest Indian epic, the *Mahābhārata* (including the *Bhagavadgītā*), demonstrates how commonplace they later became. Their most famous expression is, however, the Sanskrit text colloquially known as the *Yogasūtra* (and more precisely as the *Pātañjalayogaśāstra*), written by an author called Patañjali between the fourth and fifth centuries CE. Building on ascetic teachings and practices from diverse sources, this philosophical text offers a practical method for liberation from the cycle of rebirths known as the "yoga of eight limbs" (*aṣṭāṅgayoga*). In contemporary yoga, the *Yogasūtra* is considered to be the founding text of yoga. Its influence on modern yoga is, however, more due to the fact that it was embraced by both the Theosophical Society and Swami Vivekananda and became a bestseller during the early development of modern yoga in the late nineteenth and early twentieth centuries.

From the sixth century CE, the Indian subcontinent became dominated by the doctrine of tantrism. One of Tantra's innovations was the understanding that the human body is composed of subtle channels (*nāḍī*) and energetic centers (*cakra*) through which flows the vital energy (*prāṇa*) of the body. Through yogic practices involving complex visualizations, meditations, and breath control, this vital energy can be manipulated, which in turn causes the tantric yogi to be liberated from the cycle of rebirth.

Later, toward the end of the first millennium CE, a new form of yoga known as *haṭhayoga* appeared in South Asia. It combined aspects of tantrism and Pātañjalayoga with newer physical practices, such as postures (*āsana*), cleansing techniques, complex methods of breath control, and other ways of manipulating the vital energy (*mudrās*). These practices gift the yogi with a stable, supple body and the ability to hold one's breath, which, in turn, allows the yogi to attain *samādhi*, the stage of mental absorption in which the yogi escapes the cycle of rebirth. In the fifteenth century, the teachings of haṭhayoga were collected by Svātmārāma in a compendium known as the *Haṭhapradīpikā*.

While today yoga is understood to be a predominantly physical practice, up until the second half of the second millennium CE, these bodily exercises were only one aspect of yogic practices. In the sixteenth century, haṭhayoga schools began to gradually increase the number of physical postures (āsana) that were taught. Some aspects of these late medieval forms of haṭhayoga informed what is known today as modern postural yoga.

"Adaptation and mutation have always been features of yoga's history," write James Mallinson and Mark Singleton in 2017 in their important work *Roots of Yoga*, and this is especially true of yoga at the cusp of modernity. With calls for independence growing in India, yoga practitioners were confronted with Western conceptions of body and mind and a desire to transform and reclaim the physical practice of yoga. South Asian thinkers such as Swami Vivekananda began skillfully adapting the ideas of yoga to share them with Western audiences. There is a paradox, however: The yoga that came to the West was already westernized by its Indian teachers, and thus it not only appealed to Western audiences but later returned to dominate in South Asia and subsequently across the world.

Yoga is, in a contemporary sense, one of those things that "everyone knows" about. And yet what "everyone knows" is that yoga is ancient and modern, religious and secular. It makes you fit and aids relaxation. It is commercial and traditional. It is both Indian and transnational. As a researcher of contemporary yoga, one of the editors of this volume once cautiously defined contemporary yoga as a practice of self-conscious, ritualized movement and stillness that is focused on somatic experience, linked to diverse beliefs, and engaged in complex relationships with the religions and cultures of the Indian subcontinent.

Yet even this carefully precise description does not encompass everything that is called yoga today, and it falls far short of encompassing everything that has been called yoga in the past. Localizing and historically situating the diversity of yoga inevitably entangles us in debates about nationalism and appropriation, racism and colonialism, neoliberalism, self-surveillance, and eugenics. Yoga has shaped nations, cultures, and communities and been shaped by them in turn.

Despite the diversity of both premodern and contemporary yoga, modern yoga is nonetheless a product of encounters with very few premodern schools of thought. Even today, most yoga teachers will have an understanding of just a few premodern texts: the *Bhagavadgītā*, Patañjali's *Yogasūtra*, the *Haṭhapradīpikā*, and a few of the Upaniṣads. In contrast, the recent book *Roots of Yoga* by Mallinson and Singleton draws from over a hundred texts dating from about 1000 BCE to the nineteenth century, mostly in Sanskrit but also Tibetan, Arabic, Persian, Bengali, Tamil, Pali, and more.

Despite this, contemporary, transnational, postural yoga is a living practice that is highly diverse and individual in meaning, while its reflection in popular culture is highly uniform and superficial. Globally, yoga is generally perceived as a uniquely benevolent practice. But if we consider yoga teachers as a collective rather than the marketing material that is used to entice potential new practitioners, we find that claims to ownership and knowledge of the practice, its historical accuracy, its scientific relevance, and the most ethical ways to practice it are all hotly debated.

What is Yoga Studies?

The research field of yoga studies is, as a result, increasingly diverse, although perhaps surprisingly friendly. Patiently, painstakingly, scholars at every level from master's dissertations to major research projects such as the Hatha

Yoga Project and the AyurYog Project work to move beyond what "everyone knows" about yoga's past and present. The detail and complexity of the task are immense.

That research proceeds, in the main, in two directions: via the study of premodern yoga, which is largely but not entirely philological and Indological, and via the study of modern and contemporary yoga, which is largely but not entirely historical and anthropological. Bridging the gap between these two necessitates partnerships among diverse scholars in small departments scattered across the world. Yoga is considered by many funding administrations to be a subject of "niche" interest. However unsound or speculative, statistics on the number of practitioners worldwide, the benefits of practice, and the impact on national economies can help justify our research.

Perhaps most interestingly, the profession of yoga teaching benefits from an extremely close relationship to research into yoga as a practice. The Indian government oversees the training of yoga teachers in universities. Indian researchers seek to prove that yogic philosophies and practices are useful for everything from business to health. Internationally, an MA in yoga studies can function as an unofficial "advanced" qualification for yoga teachers and trainers. Yoga studies researchers provide content for independent educational platforms and drop in to guest teach in yoga teacher-training programs. This reflects the commercialization and increasing precariousness of the higher education sector but also the fact that, like dance studies and other somatic disciplines, yoga studies scholars, whether philologists or anthropologists, are often practitioners themselves.

The impact of research into yoga on yoga communities themselves can be profound. Mark Singleton's 2010 very accessible book on the origins of early modern yoga, *Yoga Body*, had a seismic impact on transnational yoga. More recently, in 2017, Singleton coauthored with Mallinson a second key historical text: *Roots of Yoga*. The public reception of these and numerous other books by yoga studies researchers is one reason why we are starting to see the persistent myth of "traditional yoga" as a single, ancient practice come to an end, but it is also why yoga studies as a field is deeply engaged with its audience and community of study.

Together, academic researchers and teacher-practitioners (and those who are both) are discovering that both the roots and the present reality of yoga practice are diverse, fragmented, and heavily blended, and the philosophies, ethics, intentions, practices, and experiences of practitioners have always been equally diverse.

Yoga studies as a field of research is much more fascinating than simple statistics suggest. International research collaborations are common.

Conferences, when they can happen, fizz with excitement and collegiate affection. The 2022 conference Yoga Darsana, Yoga Sadhana presented academic papers on such diverse topics as the origins of mantra repetition, early American yoga and the Indian independence movement, strategies of legitimization among yoga teachers, the purpose of enumeration in the *Tattvayogabindu*, the paradox of carceral yoga, the soteriology of straightness, and much, much more.

How is this book organized?

Following in the footsteps of Elizabeth J. Harris's excellent *Buddhism in Five Minutes*, this book has been organized as a series of questions that nonspecialists might ask about yoga or yoga studies. The book is aimed at readers who love yoga but are not academically trained in yoga studies, at researchers who need to understand some aspect of the practice that is outside of their specialisms, at teachers in need of accessible resources for sharing with students, and at anyone else who is fascinated by the practice of yoga.

We have chosen to name the volume *Yoga Studies in Five Minutes* because the often-blurred boundary between yoga *as a practice* and yoga *as a field of study* is one that we feel is vital we attempt to maintain. It speaks to the scope of this book. As academic scholars, we do not claim any authority over what might be right or wrong ways to practice.

Every entry has been written by a specialist in yoga studies. Given the diverse nature of the subject at hand, in many cases, they are writing about their own groundbreaking research. Each entry, which should take around five minutes to read, is a summary of years of work simplified to be as accessible as possible to nonspecialists. Nonetheless, depending on the reader's own preferences and experience, some entries will inevitably be more complicated to understand than others.

Although we, as the editors, include one premodern and one contemporary specialist, we have chosen not to divide the work by specialism or by historical period. Some questions are more time-specific than others. But we have found in our own collaborations that many of the most interesting and useful conversations in yoga studies are those that transcend these differences, bring together insights from philology and sociology, and span ancient and contemporary contexts. The book is therefore divided into the following sections:

- What is yoga?
- What is the point of yoga?
- Is yoga healthy?

- How do you practice yoga?
- How do you study yoga?
- How do you teach yoga?
- How did modern yoga develop?
- What does yoga look like today?

The first section includes attempts to define yoga, the second asks about intentions for the practice, and the third asks a simple question with multiple complex answers: Is yoga good for you? Subsequent sections discuss methods for the practice, study, and teaching of yoga in turn. The final two sections concern the development of yoga across its long history, asking how modern yoga developed and what yoga looks like today.

The book can be read from beginning to end, but after this introduction, each entry is designed to stand alone, and each one ends with recommendations for related entries elsewhere in the book. Each entry is numbered to make navigating the book easier. Just as in the practice of yoga, the reader is invited to take the most useful and interesting path for them, step by step and entry by entry. Sadly, no matter how long you wander in the pages, the editors cannot promise any reduction in karmic debt, although you will arguably emerge rich in *jñānayoga*, or the yoga of knowledge.

This book has often been a joy to edit, and our own understanding of the work of our colleagues and predecessors has been immensely enriched in the process. We would like to thank Equinox Publishing Ltd. for the invitation and every one of our contributors for their generosity and care and their gracious good humor when they realized just how difficult it is to summarize a life's work or an entire body of research in less than two thousand words.

How is Sanskrit pronounced?

The study of yoga involves at least a passing acquaintance with the ancient languages of South Asia, in particular Sanskrit. Sanskrit and other South Asian languages have more sounds than most Western languages and are therefore most accurately written with diacritical marks added to certain letters. There is no requirement for the reader to be able to read Sanskrit accurately, but as a helpful aid for those who wish it, we offer below a guide to Sanskrit pronunciation that allows for a lossless representation of the language in the Roman alphabet: Each sound is spelled in only one way, and each spelling represents only one sound. There are also two entries in the volume that answer further questions: "What is Sanskrit?" (9) and "How do modern practitioners relate to ancient texts?" (56).

Vowels

We list the full set of Sanskrit vowels here.

a, pronounced as in British English *but*
ā, as in *father*
i, as in *fit*
ī, as in *bee*
u, as in *put*
ū, as in *fool*
ṛ, as in American English *are*
ḷ, as in *table*
e, as in *where*
ai, as in *my*
o, as in *more*
au, as in *loud*

Consonants

We mention here only the consonants that are pronounced markedly different than in English or those with added diacritics.

kh, aspirated *k*, as in *key*
gh, aspirated *g*, as in *egghead*
ṅ, as in *sing*
c, as in *cappuccino*
ch, aspirated *c*, as in *ranch house*
j, as in *jam*
jh, aspirated *j*, as in *sponge holder*
ñ, as in Spanish *mañana*
ṭ/ṭh, t pronounced with the tip of the tongue against the teeth
ḍ/ḍh, d pronounced with the tip of the tongue against the teeth
th, as in *hotheaded*
ph, as in *uphold*
bh, as in *clubhouse*
ś/ṣ, both approximately as *sheet*

Theodora Wildcroft, Open University

Barbora Sojková, University of Oxford

What is yoga?

1 Is yoga a religion?

Philip Deslippe

The questions of whether yoga is religious in nature and if it belongs to the Hindu religious tradition are complicated and nuanced. Answers depend on the historical period, cultural context, practitioners of yoga themselves, and many definitions and understandings of both yoga and religion.

The word "yoga" made its first appearance within the *Ṛgveda* in approximately 1500 BCE as a term to denote yoking, as in a plow or chariot. Roughly a thousand years later, a more recognizable use of the word appeared in the *Kaṭha Upaniṣad*, in which yoga was elucidated as a path of meditation, self-knowledge, and liberation. Yoga as a philosophy and practice later appeared in texts such as the *Pātañjalayogaśāstra*, the *Bhagavadgītā*, and the medieval collection of texts known as the Yoga Upaniṣads. It is also a foundational aspect of various schools of Hindu philosophy and renunciant orders, including the Nāths.

But yoga was not strictly confined to the Hindu tradition. The term "yoga" in its many meanings appeared in other South Asian religious traditions, such as the Mahāyāna Buddhist philosophical system of Yogācāra and the use of "yoga" to denote mundane action in Jain texts. The first major work on *haṭhayoga*, the eleventh-century *Amṛtasiddhi*, was a tantric Buddhist text, and scholars have found a strong Buddhist influence on the *Pātañjalayogaśāstra*. Perhaps adding to the confusion, as postural forms of yoga have become popular, there have been recent claims to unearthed and rediscovered forms of yoga rooted in the Jain and Sikh traditions over the last half century—respectively, Preksha Dhyana and Kundalini Yoga as taught by Yogi Bhajan.

Yoga has also been understood to be outside the bounds of any particular religious tradition. The *Dattātreyayogaśāstra*, the first text to provide a system of haṭhayoga explicitly under the name *haṭha*, which appeared around the 1300s, described yoga as a practice that was open to all people regardless of their caste or religious affiliation. Some of the most important figures in the Indian haṭhayoga revival of the early twentieth century, which helped shape how yoga is practiced and understood today more than anything else, presented yoga as something that could be universally understood through anatomy, medical science, experimentation, and research. Two of the largest promoters of yoga outside of India during this time—the Vedanta Society, founded by Swami Vivekananda, and Yogananda's Self-Realization Fellowship—had their own monastic orders but also openly described their teachings as nondenominational and compatible with Christianity.

The question of whether the contemporary practice of yoga itself qualifies as a religion is similarly complicated. Recent surveys have found that the vast majority of practitioners in the United States do yoga for secular benefits, such as physical fitness or stress management, and mostly do it in health clubs or alone at home. Yoga teachers compose only a small fraction of a percent of all yoga practitioners, and few teachers would claim yoga as their primary religious identity. However, among the rising number of the religiously unaffiliated or "spiritual but not religious" who reject religious dogma and institutions, yoga is a relatively common method in their search for well-being and meaning.

As yoga has become a lucrative global industry and powerful cultural force over the last few decades, questions of who can claim yoga and whether yoga is religious in nature have become increasingly consequential. In 2008, an advocacy group known as the Hindu American Foundation launched a campaign called Take Back Yoga to fight against what it saw as a deliberate delinking of yoga from its roots in the Hindu tradition. Six years later, the United Nations passed a resolution introduced by India to declare June 21 the International Day of Yoga, which has been celebrated annually with large numbers of people practicing yoga around the world in large public displays. Many Indian officials have openly described the International Day of Yoga as an attempt to link the practice of yoga with Indian culture, and some critics have described it as an assertion of Indian soft power abroad and Hindu identity within India itself.

Ironically, some of those most strongly in agreement with the position that yoga is essentially religious in nature and cannot be separated from Hinduism have been non-Hindu opponents of yoga. Islamic clerics in Malaysia and Indonesia and an Eastern Catholic church in Kerala, India, each issued rulings that Muslims and Catholics, respectively, should not practice yoga. In 2013, the Supreme Court of India dismissed a petition to make yoga compulsory for schoolchildren in first through eighth grade across the country after objections from Christian and Muslim groups.

That same year, parents filed an action against a school district in Encinitas, California, and argued that its voluntary yoga program for students was a violation of their religious freedom. The Christian legal advocacy group that represented them, the National Center for Law and Policy, described yoga on its website as a worship of Hindu gods and connected yoga to demonic activity.

The judge in the Encinitas case ruled that yoga was permitted in local public schools, since the school program in question had removed cultural references and therefore did not "advance or inhibit religion." This kind of division, separating what is seen as religious about yoga from what is seen as nonreligious, is not unusual. Many Christians have created forms of "Christian yoga" by adding biblical verses and invocations to Jesus and removing references to Hindu deities and uses of Sanskrit terms while keeping the same postures and exercises. Conversely, many yoga studios and teachers have added or emphasized elements seen as Hindu and religious—such as chanting, textual study, and references to deities—over concerns about cultural appropriation and authenticity.

There is no clear consensus as to whether yoga is a religion. While some believe that the practice of yoga is decidedly religious and inextricably linked to the Hindu tradition, others see it as strictly a form of physical exercise, and still others see it as something that is spiritual and thus neither religious nor nonreligious. In much of the world, yoga is appropriate for a gym or health club, yet it is seen as more than just a physical practice. It can offer solace and meaning to many of its practitioners without conflicting with their preexisting religious affiliations. This flexible, if paradoxical, view of yoga has helped it spread throughout the world and facilitated its massive growth.

About the author

Philip Deslippe is a doctoral candidate in the Department of Religious Studies at the University of California, Santa Barbara, where his research focuses on Asian, metaphysical, and marginal religious traditions in the United States. He has published numerous articles for academic journals, including the *Journal of Yoga Studies* and *Japanese Religions*, and popular venues such as *Yoga Journal* and *Tricycle*.

Suggestions for further reading

In this book

See also chapters 4 (Is there a role for faith in yoga?), 5 (Is yoga atheistic, nontheistic, or theistic?), and 58 (What does yoga mean to Indians today?).

Elsewhere

Mallinson, James, and Mark Singleton. *Roots of Yoga*. Penguin Books, 2017.

White, David Gordon, ed. *Yoga in Practice*. Princeton University Press, 2012.

2

Is yoga a philosophy?

Karen O'Brien-Kop

Traditionally, yoga is considered a philosophy and is one of the six systems described in Indian scholarship as orthodox or adherent (*āstika*), indicating adherence to the authority of the Vedas. Yoga is also a fundamental part of the Hindu religion and is discussed to a lesser degree in the historical contexts of Buddhism and Jainism. We do not have to choose between the categories of philosophy and religion; yoga can simply belong to both. Specifically, yoga is found in the first systematized philosophy in South Asia, which was established between circa the second century BCE and second century CE through formal treatises called *śāstras* and their concise distillations, *sūtras*. Arguably, the most foundational work of yoga philosophy is the *Pātañjalayogaśāstra* (PYŚ), also known as the *Yogasūtra* of Patañjali, circa the fourth century CE.

The PYŚ is not the only early work of philosophy on yoga. We find philosophy in the "epic" yoga of the *Mahābhārata*, the protoformulations of the late Principal Upaniṣads, the popular yoga of the *Purāṇas*, the proto-Śaiva yoga of the *Pāśupatasūtra* and the *Śivadharma* corpus, the Vaiṣṇava yoga of the Pāñcarātrins, the Yogācāra of the Buddhist Mahāyānists, the proto-Tantra of Hinduism and Vajrayāna Buddhism, the Siddha Yoga of the early alchemists, the medical *āyurvedic* treatise *Carakasaṃhitā*, and the syncretic Jain yoga scheme of Haribhadra's *Yogadṛṣṭisamuccaya*—among other sources. But the PYŚ is nonetheless a landmark text and deserves to be studied for its character as a systematized philosophical work.

As a work of formal philosophy, the PYŚ engages a standard and compact formula to express the scope, principles, and depth of a tradition of inquiry. This inquiry is underpinned by both abstract and embodied rationality. The intellectual core of Patañjali's text addresses metaphysics, ontology, and ethics but also has much to impart on epistemology, logic, and philosophy of language—as conceptualized, argued, and practiced in the early Common Era. Indeed, the scope of philosophical topics is formidable given the brevity of the text. The fundamental questions and answers of Pātañjala philosophy are still relevant today and ensure a living, breathing context for this tradition globally.

Patañjali offers an account of the world that largely adheres to the metaphysics of the Sāṃkhya system. Unlike the dominant Indian worldviews of the period—across Brahmanism, Buddhism, and Jainism—Sāṃkhya metaphysics (as based on the *Sāṃkhyakārikā*) was dualist. Reality, then, is understood to be constituted by two aspects, materiality (*prakṛti*) and consciousness (*puruṣa*), which are each essential but noninteracting. Underpinning reality is a substantial and temporal substratum expressed through materiality, while pure consciousness itself is like a witnessing presence outside of space and time. In this scheme, reality is fundamentally eternal and permanent, and time moves in cycles. Early Indian philosophy commonly located the basic existential problem as an error in the perception of the self and hence also of the material world and, ultimately, of reality. By adopting the metaphysics of Sāṃkhya, a school that saturated the ancient philosophical disputes, Patañjali announced that yoga, although an archaic concept and contemplative practice, now had something innovative and distinct to contribute to this body of philosophical knowledge.

For most early Indian philosophies, the theoretical and practical quest is to know the self accurately in order to experience existential freedom. The PYŚ is no exception to this goal. Patañjali's ontology is oriented to an analysis of the human condition as associated with chronic existential dis-ease, categorized variously as "suffering" (*duḥkha*) or "pain/distress" (*tapas*). The text instructs on how to cultivate a lifestyle that is ethically based, oriented to asceticism, and focused on discipline in order to acquire stillness, clarity, and insight in the mental sphere (more or less within the confines of normative Brahmanical identity). Indeed, the end goal of the text promises knowledge of the self, such that there is a radical identification with consciousness over materiality to the degree that an ultimate state of isolated consciousness can be attained—a state labeled freedom.

In Sāṃkhya, the methods proposed are more abstract than yoga, in that they are focused on rational reflection—namely, deep contemplation of each constituent of reality (*tattva*) and how it sits in relation to other *tattvas*. Hence the contemplative method requires knowledge of twenty-five constituents and their causal relations. Scholarly opinion differs as to whether these constituents refer to subject-object relations or to mediated subjectivity and whether they are weighted toward the objective world.

In line with the broader concerns of Indian philosophy, the PYŚ grapples with the moral problem of action (*karma*), in that to act can result in harm to oneself or others. According to the pan-Indian theory of karma, actions not only are motivated by mental intentions but also, in turn, condition mental dispositions that produce future actions of a similar kind, thus creating a seemingly inescapable loop of conditioning. These moral failings are addressed through a standardized framework of ethical precepts divided into restraints and observances (*yamas* and *niyamas*).

The way in which Patañjali's text frames its values has a practical valence for our times, be it in how the ethics of nonharm informs environmental activism and veganism, in how care of the self is an instrument of ontological preservation in the political fight for social justice and equality, in discussions of whether consciousness can be preserved in artificial intelligence, in public health policies on how to achieve better mental health, in how a pared-back lifestyle can disrupt the machinery of consumer capitalism, or in the ways that cultural appropriation can constitute moral or epistemic violence. The PYŚ is still used as a lens through which to discuss these and other contemporary ethical issues.

In line with Sāṃkhya, the yoga tradition asserts that only three valid bases of knowledge (*pramāṇas*) lead to truth: perception, authority (or scripture), and inference. Indeed, Patañjali asserts that epistemology is a means to attain "the highest yoga" (*yoga uttamam*; PYŚ 1.48).

Meditative practice is correlated to the pramāṇa of perception. Authority (or scripture) is at work in practices such as reciting or studying the Vedas (*svādhyāya*), and inference underpins the formal reasoning of the PYŚ, discussed below. By aligning the methods of "yoga" to the three valid bases of knowledge, Patañjali not only situates his text among the recognized schools of philosophy but demonstrates that his yoga methods are valid means to reach true conclusions.

We should pay close attention to the internal logic and dynamic reasoning of Patañjali's systematized worldview. Logic is a key means in Indian philosophy, used to correct wrong views and to know reality as it is—and hence to become liberated. The very format of the text as a sūtra indicates that its conventional philosophical purpose has some measure of logic. Not only are sūtras condensed doctrines or discourses with mnemonic value, but they are also, as the word *sūtra* (thread) itself indicates, beads of thought that are "threaded" in a specific pattern underpinned by logic. A sūtra text was designed in order to be digested systematically. Hence the text opens like many other philosophy treatises by stating its subject (*viṣaya*), its scope or context (*saṃbandha*), and the goal (*prayojana*).

In the PYŚ, inference is the process of reasoning that pervades the rational reflection called concentration (*samādhi*). Patañjali's yoga is not an affective method that entails "bliss" or "rapture"; rather, it proposes steady, regulated, and reasoned reflection on the nature of reality. Hence, inference is the unraveling of subtle causal effects as made visible through the constituents of reality. The inferential process leads one back to the "source" of the material world (*mūlaprakṛti*), a ground of dissolution that we might call primordial materiality. Taken from Sāṃkhya ontological contemplation, these inferential processes are designed to lead one to a true apprehension of reality and form the basis of concentrative meditation in the *Yogasūtra*.

There are several contexts in which language is discussed reflexively by Patañjali. Some of the more obvious include the well-known acceptance of the authority of the Vedic language, the effects of scriptural utterance (recitation), and cosmogonic understandings of a primordial syllable (*akṣara*; *oṃ*) that gives rise to the world. However, language is also analyzed in the more technical contexts of grammar and epistemology. What are the rules of a system of linguistic utterance such that meaning can be grasped? How does language direct us to the truth or obscure it? What is the relationship between a word and the object it refers to? As a learned treatise of philosophy, addressing such questions was an expected feature of an *āstika* text. For Patañjali, the relation between word-concept, word-sound, and word-referent was subject to confusion, and he advocates that the three categories be strictly separated for a clear and correct perception of reality to take place.

To conclude, not only is the PYŚ a work of philosophy that instructs us about its specific method for reaching consciousness-as-liberation; it is also a tapestry of philosophical methods, ideas, principles, and frameworks from the age of the sūtras and śāstras.

About the author

Karen O'Brien-Kop is a lecturer in Asian religions at King's College London and acquired her PhD from SOAS University of London. She researches philosophy of mind, asceticism, and Sanskrit texts in Buddhist and Hindu traditions. Her books include *Rethinking "Classical Yoga" and Buddhism: Meditation, Metaphors and Materiality* (Bloomsbury, 2022), *The Philosophy of the Yogasutra* (Bloomsbury, 2023), and the coedited volume *The Routledge Handbook of Yoga and Meditation Studies* (Routledge, 2021).

Suggestions for further reading

In this book

See also chapters 14 (Are ethics important in yoga?) and 45 (Who was Patañjali?).

Elsewhere

Burley, M. *Classical Sāṃkhya and Yoga: An Indian Metaphysics of Experience.* Routledge, 2007.

O'Brien-Kop, K. *The Philosophy of the Yogasutra: An Introduction.* Bloomsbury Introduction to World Philosophies. Bloomsbury Academic, 2023.

Larson, G., and R. S. Bhattacharya, eds. *Yoga: India's Philosophy of Meditation.* Vol. 12 of *Encyclopedia of Indian Philosophies.* Motilal Banarsidass, 2008.

Perrett, R. "Sāṃkhya-Yoga Ethics." In *Indian Ethics: Classical Traditions and Contemporary Challenges*, edited by P. Bilimoria, J. Prabhu, and S. Sharma. Vol. 1. Routledge, 2007.

3

Is yoga a ritual?

Brett W. Parris

The practice of yoga can be a form of ritual but does not have to be. As is so often the case, it depends on what we mean by "yoga" here and on what constitutes a "ritual."

The concept of ritual is notoriously difficult to define, with no consensus among scholars. For the purposes of this entry, we may consider a ritual to include not only those formal spiritual rites established by traditional lineages but also any action, or set of actions, that we infuse with an intention and meaning beyond the everyday appearance of the action. So, for example, an elaborate religious ceremony with chanting, liturgy, and symbolic acts is obviously a ritual—but so too could be casting a flower into a stream as a way of silently saying goodbye to a loved one and wishing them well on their journey. A ritual may be a set of actions that is repeated at regular intervals, or it may be a symbolic act that is performed only once.

There is an important synergy between yoga and ritual that may pass unnoticed, in that both are *embodied* actions. Whatever else yoga and ritual may be, they are practices and acts that we perform with our bodies. Neither is merely an intellectual exercise. The field of "embodied cognition" explores the role of our bodies in how we know things—not just the use of our senses or knowing *how* to do things, like a concert pianist's hands dancing across a keyboard, but in various ways, how our bodies may store memories, emotions, and trauma. One word for these embodied emotional memories in yogic traditions is *saṃskāras*—latent impressions created by previous actions or events. The *Pātañjalayogaśāstra* (PYŚ) mentions saṃskāras in several places (PYŚ 1.18, 1.50, 2.15, 3.9, 3.18, and 4.9). For yoga practitioners, embodied ritual and yoga practice can be powerful ways of working with these saṃskāras, helping to move the embodied energy holding the memory, and perhaps providing some release. Interestingly, one of the alternative meanings of the word *saṃskāra* given in Monier-Williams's Sanskrit dictionary is "a sacred or sanctifying ceremony." This conjunction of meanings suggests a deep understanding of how rituals can be important ways of working through latent embodied impressions. The fact that most yoga classes and many rituals are also experiences that are shared with others provides yet another dimension of synergy—there is something powerful in the shared energy of a group of people enacting the same movements.

In premodern India, various forms of yoga were practiced in different traditions, ranging from Buddhist lineages to more theistic forms of what today would be called "Hinduism," though the term was not used when the practices were developed. In traditions focused on meditation, physical *āsana* practice was used primarily as either a preparation for meditation, as in the PYŚ, or a form of austerity (*tapas*). Yoga as a means or goal of practice was often integrated into highly ritualized traditions, including initiation (*dīkṣā*) rituals, daily (*nitya*) or special (*naimittika*) rituals, worship (*pūjā*) rituals, devotion (*bhakti*) rituals, and ultimately funeral rituals. The extensive preparatory cleansing practices—described, for example, in yogic texts such as the fifteenth-century *Haṭhapradīpikā* or the eighteenth-century *Gheraṇḍasaṃhitā*—could also be viewed as forms of ritual that were once considered necessary for the practice of yoga.

Modern yoga classes that do not self-identify as being a part of any particular yogic lineage can nevertheless become ritualized. A class may be bracketed with a Sanskrit greeting, such as *namaste*, and an invitation to "set an intention" (*saṃkalpaḥ/saṅkalpaḥ*). In Buddhist-influenced classes, there may be an invitation to dedicate the merit gained by the practice to others or to all sentient beings. Sometimes classes are ended with the threefold *OṂ, OṂ, OṂ, śāntiḥ, śāntiḥ, śāntiḥ* (*OṂ*, peace). The use of Sanskrit terminology for the poses and a mini-sermon on a particular theme by the teacher, building throughout the class, can add to the practitioner's experience of the yoga practice as a form of spiritual ritual, not just another exercise class.

Some of these modern forms of ritualization can be problematic if they involve unthinking cultural appropriation—such as decorating studios with Indian motifs and paraphernalia in a haphazard and unthinking manner in order to create an Eastern "vibe" rather than authentically arising from a specific tradition. This issue can be a minefield though, since it can be argued that, in the right circumstances and with the right intentions, the same items may reflect a genuine desire to honor and respect the sources of the lineages that have contributed to the evolution of the particular form of yoga that is being taught in the studio. It is important to bear in mind, in these sometimes fraught debates, that yoga has always been diverse. It was never only "Hindu" or even "Indian," if by "Indian" we mean the modern nation-state of India. Yoga was a highly diverse pan-Indian-subcontinental phenomenon emerging from a range of traditions, including ancient *śramaṇa* practices as well as Buddhist, Jaina, and various forms of "Hindu" traditions, such as Vaiṣṇava and Śaiva. There was never a "pure" form of yoga, and the desire for clear demarcations between traditions can sometimes reflect not the often eclectic and fluid traditions that were found traditionally but rather either a Western preoccupation with tight definitions or an ethnonationalist desire to "claim" yoga for a particular group.

Today, yoga can also form an important part of any student's "ritual" practice—in the sense of being integrated into whatever form of psychospiritual well-being routine works best for them. One of the most important texts of the *haṭhayoga* tradition, the *Haṭhapradīpikā* mentioned above, stripped out most of the sectarian content, leaving a text focused on yogic techniques. In the same way, yogic techniques of physical āsana, breath practices (*prāṇāyāma*), meditation (*dhyāna*, *bhāvanā*), mantra recitation (*japa*), and communal chanting (*kīrtana*) can all be used to enhance the psychospiritual health of students from any spiritual tradition. In ancient and premodern India, there were Buddhist yogis, yogis from various Hindu streams, Jain yogis, and later, Sufi Muslim yogis. Judaism and Christianity were also present in India, interacting with local practices, the latter possibly since the first century CE and no later than the second century. Buddhist monks later took yogic techniques from India deep into Tibet, China, and Japan. Yogic techniques and rituals can be adapted and integrated into any spiritual tradition—and it is important to emphasize that this is not in itself a misappropriation and betrayal of traditional yoga but is rather entirely in keeping with yoga's evolution across and beyond sectarian boundaries in premodern India.

About the author

Brett W. Parris is a DPhil candidate in the Faculty of Theology and Religion at the University of Oxford. He has an MPhil in Classical Indian Religion from Oxford, as well as a PhD in development economics from Monash University in Melbourne. He worked for NGOs focused on poverty, human rights, and climate change for many years. His current research focuses on the ethical dimensions of yogic philosophy and practice and broader interreligious dialogue. He has taught yoga in both Australia and the UK.

Suggestions for further reading

In this book

See also chapters 22 (Why do yogis contort their bodies?) and 31 (How do mantras relate to yoga?).

Elsewhere

Grimes, Ronald L. "Ritual." In *Guide to the Study of Religion*, edited by Willi Braun and Russell T. McCutcheon. Cassell, 2000.

Mallinson, James, and Mark Singleton. "Preliminaries." In *Roots of Yoga*, edited by James Mallinson and Mark Singleton. Penguin Books, 2017.

Sanderson, Alexis. "Ritual for Oneself and Ritual for Others." In *Ritual Dynamics and the Science of Ritual*. Vol. 2, *Body, Performance, Agency, and Experience*, edited by Angelos Chaniotis. Harrassowitz Verlag, 2010.

4

Is there a role for faith in yoga?

Jens U. Augspurger

Whether there is a role for belief or faith in yoga, and of which nature, is both a subjective and a normative question. My goal is to primarily understand the role that practitioners themselves assign to faith and belief.

We should begin by examining the meanings of faith and belief in yoga, focusing on religious meanings, and then discussing references to yoga philosophy. That will enable us to consider how these findings compare with theoretical and empirical arguments and address limitations of the "religion" framework, such as the problem the "spiritual but not religious" phenomenon poses to the hegemonic dominance of the term "religion." The reader should also refer to entries in this volume that discuss yoga's connection with Hinduism, as well as its Indian heritage. While these discussions also matter for the question at hand, I attempt not to reproduce them here.

First, let us examine the meanings of faith and belief in yoga. I stated this question is subjective. By that, I mean it may depend on the individual's personal circumstances, preferences, socialization, and current needs. Belief and faith do not have to be tied to religion, and many yoga practitioners may have faith in the practice for its ability to improve well-being or physical health or for other personal purposes. Faith, in the sense of deep trust, can also be associated with improving well-being or increasing the efficacy of a health-care intervention or preventive medicine. At the same time, faith or belief can have religious or spiritual dimensions. In the case of yoga, a religious or spiritual faith might involve seeking for liberation (*samādhi*), enlightenment (*mokṣa*), or union with the divine.

Bhaktiyoga, the yoga of devotion, offers a distinct perspective on the religious role of faith and belief. Bhaktiyoga is one of several paths of yoga, including *karmayoga* (the yoga of action), *jñānayoga* (the yoga of knowledge), and *rājayoga* (the "royal" yoga). Bhaktiyoga is prominently described in the *Bhagavadgītā*, a sacred text of the *bhakti* Hindu tradition that is also widely respected and popularly used in contemporary yoga practices. The

Bhagavadgītā is part of the Sanskrit epic *Mahābhārata* and is believed to have been authored by the sage Vyāsa, an important figure in Indian mythology.

In the *Bhagavadgītā*, devotion as a path of yoga is especially recommended for those who are inclined toward emotion and want to practice self-surrender. The aim of this devotion is often described as the union of the ego with the divine through the purification of the heart, which requires trust, or in other words, faith in the methods outlined in the *Gītā*. The narrative of the *Bhagavadgītā* revolves around Arjuna, its princely protagonist, who finds himself on a battlefield when Lord Kṛṣṇa, an *avatāra* (incarnation) of Viṣṇu, appears. During this extraordinary situation, Kṛṣṇa engages in a dialogue with Arjuna, who does not know whether to fight. Kṛṣṇa's treatise outlines the three yoga paths, describing bhakti as a steadfast connection with the divine (here, Kṛṣṇa) through surrender and trust. In this dialogue, Kṛṣṇa commands Arjuna to fight against the opposing army, even though Arjuna recognizes family and friends among them. Arjuna's reluctance to do what seems counterintuitive ultimately becomes a matter of faith in God.

The practice of bhakti is an essential part of many modern yoga styles that incorporate religious elements. Expressions of bhakti include rituals or ceremonies such as *ārati* (light waving), *pūjā* (offering rituals), chanting of *mantras* (the names of God), *kīrtana* (communal devotional chanting), or *bhajana* (religious songs). These practices of modern yoga have sometimes been criticized as problematic cultural appropriations, especially when dislocated from their cultural context or embodied experience and placed into commodified contexts. There are also yoga groups that almost entirely focus on the practice of bhakti, such as the neo-Hindu movement International Society for Krishna Consciousness, also known as the Hare Krishna movement. On the other hand, bhakti plays little or no role in secular or entirely postural yoga styles.

For scholars of yoga or religion, discussing the religious dimensions of belief in yoga presents two problems. The first problem is that faith and belief as related to religion are often viewed from a Judeo-Christian perspective, which has ultimately shaped the concept of "religion" as a whole. Applying this lens can be limiting, fail to provide a thorough analysis, or even be potentially harmful when considering traditions outside of the "world religions" paradigm. One casualty of this forced framework is the colonial construction of "Hinduism," which is now commonly understood as a single monolithic religion. Many scholars have demonstrated that the emergence of the "Hindu religion" was a product of colonial efforts to subsume many diverse practices and traditions south of the Indus River into a form that suited and could be controlled by colonizers.

The second problem is that the notion of religion is often based on an etic understanding. Many practitioners in the modern yoga field reject the idea that their practice is "religion." While some forms of modern transnational yoga may be classified as "new religious movements," practitioners often prefer, for a variety of reasons, the term "spirituality" to describe their practice. They argue, for example, that they find religion too rigid, profane, difficult to access, overly dogmatic, and patriarchal or that they simply do not connect with it, while they consider spirituality more open, universal, based on experience rather than scriptures, and therefore more inviting. Some also distinguish between religion as a means of control and spirituality as a means of personal liberation. This phenomenon is commonly found among a much broader demographic of New Age religion and new religious movements and increasingly also in alternative health markets and has been termed SBNR, or "spiritual but not religious," by scholars.

The distinction made between religion and spirituality is primarily an emic description. Scholars of religion may not agree with this distinction, but from an ethnographic perspective, the choices of practitioners matter and need to be put in conversation with scholarly understandings. Many practitioners of contemporary yoga styles who identify as "spiritual but not religious" previously had personal experiences with established religions, predominantly strains of Christianity, which they adhered to with different grades of participation. As a result, many actively reject the idea of being religious in favor of being spiritual. Some describe having had an epiphany that led them to universalist religious movements (considered "spirituality") that allow for the inclusion of elements from other practices. Véronique Altglas, a sociologist of religion, has used the anthropological term "bricolage" to describe this form of religious eclecticism in which practitioners "build" a framework from various practices that otherwise seem disconnected. This phenomenon relates to Sheila-ism, a term coined by an interlocutor named Sheila, in conversation with American sociologist Robert N. Bellah, to describe her own form of religious practice in lieu of naming it after any preexisting one. The strong focus on self-development in many esoteric teachings of the New Age and post–New Age movement has also led British sociologist Paul Heelas to refer to these as "self-religions."

In conclusion, we can say that practitioners of contemporary yoga might or might not believe in God, multiple deities, a higher power, or cosmic energy. This discussion is often not relevant in exclusively postural forms of yoga that either ignore or do not incorporate the philosophical and theological presuppositions of yoga into their practice. However, for many practitioners of other forms of yoga, the role of faith and belief does matter.

About the author

Jens U. Augspurger is a PhD candidate in the Department of Religions and Philosophies at SOAS University of London. His research and teaching focus on modern transnational yoga and spiritual movements, as well as their respective intersections with politics. He is also a recovering yoga teacher and the cofounder of Project SATYA, a community movement that supports survivors of sexualized violence and advocates for accountability and truth in the yoga industry. Considering spiritual tourism as a journey for self-discovery, his ethnographic dissertation project explores yoga tourism in India and the complex relationships the yoga tourist builds while journeying (toward) the destination.

Suggestions for further reading

In this book

See also chapters 5 (Is yoga atheistic, nontheistic, or theistic?) and 12 (Does yoga liberate or constrain?).

Elsewhere

Altglas, Véronique. *From Yoga to Kabbalah: Religious Exoticism and the Logics of Bricolage*. Oxford University Press, 2014.

Heelas, Paul. "Western Europe: Self-Religions." In *The World's Religions: The Study of Religion, Traditional and New Religion*, edited by Peter Clarke. Routledge, 1991.

5

Is yoga atheistic, nontheistic, or theistic?

Corinna May Lhoir

Yoga today is practiced by people around the globe, of diverse backgrounds, and of different beliefs. The interpretation and practice of yoga have become highly individualized, and practitioners have adapted their practice according to their personal values and beliefs. But how have the aims of yoga in the course of its history been related to the question of the existence of a being higher than oneself? Is there a belief or a disbelief in a God?

Early Vedic beliefs included a variety of deities, usually connected to natural phenomena such as the sun, wind, or fire. The gods, each for themselves admired in various hymns in the *Ṛgveda*, formed a monotheism of this very moment in their devotees: one God, almighty in the moment of the performance of the hymn or the sacrifice, conducted by a mediator between the heavens and the earth, the almost almighty Brahman.

With the rise in *śramaṇa* ascetic movements around 800 BCE, new questions demanded new answers and new practices. Life on earth was regarded as full of suffering, and their practices were aimed at finding liberation from the cycle of birth and rebirth (*saṃsāra*). To reach liberation, recognition of the true self (*ātman*) was to be achieved by the practice of some sort of mental training. This training process, in the form of meditation for self-realization, was then called "yoga." It was assumed that union with the ātman (individual self) could be realized by focusing on one's internal reality and by eliminating *karma* (action and its consequences) through meditation, ascetic practice and austerities, and nonactivity. These practices may be regarded as atheistic, as they did not involve the adoration of a personal god. However, consistent with the belief in *brahman* (absolute reality), they contained an impersonal concept of the divine that involves no creator and no controller but rather an absolute being that is without beginning and without end. Ultimately, the individual self (ātman) and the absolute reality (brahman) constitute one undivided consciousness, and the goal of all spiritual practice is to realize this non-dual nature of reality, which is beyond name and form.

Yoga was later included in the six orthodox *darśanas*, the classical philosophical traditions of India in the twelfth century CE, and within these darśanas, it forms a philosophical pair together with the atheistic philosophy of Sāṃkhya. Before this, around 400 CE, the Indian philosopher Patañjali composed the *Pātañjalayogaśāstra*, "the work on the yoga of Patañjali," also known as the *Yogasūtra*. This work consists of 196 aphorisms outlining the philosophy and practice of yoga together with the oldest commentary (a descriptive text explaining the verses of the *Pātañjalayogaśāstra*) on these aphorisms. It became an important reference for many yoga traditions in the following centuries, and today, it is regarded as yoga's foundational text. Primarily *sāṃkhyan* in style, the *Pātañjalayogaśāstra* is a compilation of various sources and offers a framework for understanding the nature of reality and the path to spiritual realization through the practice of yoga. In its teaching, *samādhi* is the highest element of an eightfold path consisting of moral, physical, and mental instructions and the highest state of mental purification.

Sāṃkhya, the philosophical foundation for the *Pātañjalayogaśāstra*, is a dualist belief system that explains the universe with reference to two fundamental principles: *puruṣa*, pure consciousness, a plural immobile being that is unattached and eternal, and its antipode *prakṛti*, which is primal matter, the original substance of all things. The concept of puruṣa is not theistic in nature, but there have been interpretations of verses of the *Pātañjalayogaśāstra* as references to an ultimate higher power: Verses 1.23–1.28 of the text focus on a being called *īśvara*. The Sanskrit term *īśvara* usually indicates a personal god or master, and the verses introduce Īśvara as the object of contemplation, which promotes the attainment of samādhi. In subsequent verses, īśvara is characterized as a special puruṣa, eternal, not touched by impurities, a teacher, and not limited by time. Finally, the practitioner is instructed to mutter the syllable *om* and visualize īśvara, who represents it. These verses have been interpreted as possibly theistic, and one commentary in particular—the *Pātañjalayogaśāstravivaraṇa*, attributed to the famous Advaita philosopher Ādi Śaṅkara (who lived in the eighth and ninth centuries CE)—deals with this section in great detail.

Atheism is an absence of the belief in the existence of higher beings. Atheists explicitly believe that there is no god, while in nontheism, there is a range of both religious and nonreligious attitudes characterized by the absence of a belief in the existence of god or gods. Nontheists are not disbelievers in god; they merely do not believe in convincing evidence for a god. Theists are explicitly convinced that there is a God. Which of these ideas is most common in yoga?

Many gurus of modern yoga were descended from lineages of Advaita philosophers and teachers, as Advaita Vedānta was at that time the most popular philosophical tradition in modern India. Therefore, Advaita or non-dualist interpretations of the *Pātañjalayogaśāstra* in India have gained significant popularity in recent centuries.

Furthermore, today's interpretations of classical yoga philosophy are influenced by the popularity of idolization and devotion as a means to reach liberation, as it was practiced within the *bhakti* tradition, a powerful religious movement in medieval India that became important from the fifteenth century onward. Centering on different gods and goddesses, this movement developed regionally and was taught in the vernacular languages of the people, which made it easily conveyable and contributed to its increasing popularity. Scriptures of the bhakti movement include early orthodox Vedic literature such as the early Upaniṣads and the *Bhagavadgītā*, texts that also had already been commented on by the Advaita philosopher Śaṅkara.

In summary, yoga is a system of complex philosophies that offers differing perspectives on the question of the existence of a God and originates from contrasting philosophical traditions. The spiritual practices it includes can be understood in a variety of ways and are not necessarily tied to any specific deity or even to a defined belief system. In this way, the development of yoga epitomizes the historically diverse intellectual history of India.

This offers a broad range of possibilities for contemporary practitioners. While some people practice yoga within a theistic framework, devote themselves to a personal God or higher power, and incorporate elements of devotion into their practice, others may focus on the physical and mental benefits of yoga within a nontheistic and secular frame without reference to any higher power.

Today, the interpretation and practice of yoga have become personal choices, and the practice is constantly being adapted to fit the beliefs and values of each individual practitioner.

About the author

Corinna May Lhoir is a contract lecturer in Sanskrit and the history of yoga at Universität Hamburg. Her PhD research focuses on yoga and meditation in Jainism, and she is currently preparing a critical edition of a medieval Jain text on yoga called the *Yogapradīpa*.

Suggestions for further reading

In this book

See also chapters 1 (Is yoga a religion?) and 6 (Has yoga always been associated with Hinduism?).

Elsewhere

Frauwallner, Erich. *History of Indian Philosophy*. Motilal Banarsidass, 2008.

Maas, Philipp. "A Concise Historiography of Classical Yoga Philosophy." In *Historiography and Periodization of Indian Philosophy*, edited by Eli Franco. De Nobili Series, 2013.

6
Has yoga always been associated with Hinduism?

Corinna May Lhoir

Yoga in the West as well as in India is often associated with "Hinduism" and with Hindu spiritual practice. Western and Eastern yoga studios are adorned with little statuettes of traditional Hindu gods and goddesses such as Śiva, Kālī, or Gaṇeśa, and yoga practice, especially the spiritual variants, often contains Hindu mantras or other elements of Hindu origin, such as deity worship or other devotional practices. But when we follow the development of yoga back to its first traces and origins, Hinduism is not the first origin that pops up.

Yoga has a long history deeply rooted in early Indian meditation practice. The idea that yoga is already more than four thousand years old has been widely rejected; however, its origins can still be traced back to the first half of the first millennium BC in the region around the city of Magadha. Several non-Brahmanical ascetic religious strands developed in this area parallel to the prevailing Vedic religion and its Brahmanical priests. These ascetic practitioners, initially without belonging to a specific group, sought answers to questions about how to liberate themselves from *saṃsāra* (the cycle of life), defining (or denying) the concept of a soul, or the nature of *karma* (in these times: action) and how to get rid of it. The answers they came up with differed, but they were united in their refusal of the all-embracing authority claim of the Vedic Brahmans.

In the centuries to follow (with their heyday around the eighth to sixth century BCE), this so-called *śramaṇa* tradition became the cradle of many important nonorthodox religious and philosophical traditions, with Buddhism and Jainism as their most prominent representatives. *Śramaṇa* translates to "making effort or exertion" and denotes an ascetic practitioner who performs acts of mortification or austerity. The *śramaṇa* traditions, next to the Vedic Brahmanical tradition, developed new techniques to calm the mind and to gain new insights into one's innermost being. Their search for the answer to liberation, the question of the self, and the new relationship between the human and the divine required special approaches to enable this access: contemplation and meditation. These techniques had their roots in the practices of the Brahmans from the days of early Vedic ritual as well as in ascetic practices developed by mostly nondenominational forest dwellers, and they later evolved into the contemplative and meditative traditions that we now classify as part of the corpus of yogic practices and ideas. Further developments of these techniques also formed the nonorthodox traditions: Buddhists, not accepting the idea of a "self," developed a highly complex insight meditation practice, while Jain contemplative practice to this day is primarily associated with the idea of nonviolence, nonactivity, and the dissolution of karma.

"Hinduism" in itself is a complex construct. Going back in history, the term "Hindu" can be traced to the Persian word *hind* or Arabic *al-hind*. Derived from the Indo-Aryan *sindhu* ("ocean" or "river"), it denotes non-Muslims and was used by Persian authors from the eighth century when Muslims settled in the Indus Valley. Sanskrit sources show the use of the term from fifteenth-century Kashmir by Śaiva historian Śrīvara to distinguish between Muslims and non-Muslims. Much later, the British Empire adopted the term and started using it toward the end of the eighteenth century to refer to people from the area of northwest South Asia who were not Muslim, Sikh, Christian, or Jain. The "ism" was added to "Hindu" in the early nineteenth century. Before the nineteenth century, the term had been widely used by Muslims and non-Muslims to denote a distinction between Muslims living in India and non-Muslims who could not, due to their various religious practices, be described otherwise.

The term was also widely adopted by Indian social reformers during the nineteenth century in the context of establishing a national identity that would become opposed to colonialism and in the creation of a religion that could match Christianity and meet it on an equal basis. One important representative of these social reformers is Vivekananda, who popularized the term in two public speeches before the Parliament of the World's Religions in Chicago with the aim of demonstrating equality between the "Hindu" tradition and Western religious traditions.

Having clearly had a social connotation before the establishment of an Indian "national identity," as defining a group of persons *not* belonging to the Muslim community, the term "Hindu" was redefined as "Hinduism," was given the connotation of a "religion," and became broadly accepted first under British colonialism and then by the independence movement.

The term "Hinduism" today comprises and denotes numerous religious currents and developments within the Indian subcontinent, united by their acceptance of the Vedic text corpus as holy and as the supreme source of knowledge. Their followers, however, are multifaceted in their beliefs, practices, and rituals. Among them, we find devotees of Śiva (Śaivas) as well as disciples of Viṣṇu (Vaiṣṇavas), devotees of Kṛṣṇa, supporters of various forms of nature worship, admirers of female goddesses, practitioners of tantric traditions, and ascetic communities in various manifestations. Members of these religious groups may be householders, monks, ascetics, or forest dwellers, and they may earn their living by begging for food or by profiting from the latest highs on the stock exchange.

Much has yet to be researched on the influence of other non-Vedic religious traditions on the development of yoga, especially in the centuries before British rule. However, the influence of Islam on Indian culture under Muslim reign and the continuous exchange between devotees of Muslim, Sufi, and Hindu-based *bhakti* religions especially in the first half of the second millennium CE is undisputed. The Indian contemplative tradition and its embodied yoga practice have influenced Muslim intellectual history whenever encounters were made. As early as the eleventh century CE, the Persian polymath Al-Biruni freely translated the *Pātañjalayogaśāstra* in his famous *Kitāb Pātanğal*, and the first illustrated textbook on *haṭhayoga*—the *Baḥr al-ḥayāt*, or *Ocean of Life*, composed in the middle of the sixteenth century—was also of Persian origin.

Yoga, over the course of its long history, has never been limited to a specific spiritual belief or to the devotees of a particular goddess or god. Members of all the groups mentioned above, whether the origins or their spiritual abodes be Vedic or non-Vedic, might choose some sort of practice of yoga or meditation. Such practices may be a set rite of their spiritual practice, or they may have simply integrated a few modern yoga exercises into their everyday lives, inspired by the yoga studio next door or yoga videos on YouTube.

Today, yoga is practiced by people around the globe—and from diverse cultural, social, and religious backgrounds. Practitioners can be Christians, Hindus, Muslims, Jews, Buddhists, or Jains or belong to any other religious environment. They may be agnostic or atheistic. The yoga of today comprises a wide range of spiritual, physical, and mental practices, and only a small part of these practices aims at reaching a state of liberation. For some practitioners, yoga is not more than a physical exercise, while for others, connecting with the inner self and finding inner peace are the main objectives. Therefore, no belief in a Hindu goddess or god is—or ever has been—a prerequisite.

About the author

Corinna May Lhoir is a contract lecturer in Sanskrit and the history of yoga at Universität Hamburg. Her PhD research focuses on yoga and meditation in Jainism, and she is currently preparing a critical edition of a medieval Jain text on yoga called the *Yogapradīpa*.

Suggestions for further reading

In this book

See also chapters 7 (Is yoga Indian?), 48 (Are the teachers of yoga enlightened?), and 58 (What does yoga mean to Indians today?).

Elsewhere

Flood, Gavin, ed. *The Blackwell Companion to Hinduism*. Blackwell, 2003.

Mallinson, James, and Mark Singleton. *Roots of Yoga*. Penguin Books, 2017.

7
Is yoga Indian?

C. Pierce Salguero

Among twenty-first-century practitioners, yoga is generally understood to have originated in India, specifically in Hindu contexts. As discussed in other entries in this book, political parties in India have highlighted the Hindu origins of yoga as a major source of ethnic pride and nationalism. Nevertheless, it is a fact that different forms of yoga historically developed outside of India, often in predominantly Buddhist contexts. These practices tend not to use the specific term "yoga" in describing themselves; however, they are closely related to Hindu forms of *āsana* and *prāṇāyāma* and thus can be thought of as forms of yoga in the generic sense of that word.

Numerous Buddhist texts around Asia discuss the subtle body, *prāṇa*, channels, and *cakras* and describe different forms of spiritual practice to influence these systems. Because the Silk Roads and maritime routes connected much of Asia as far back as the early first millennium CE, innovations in spiritual and therapeutic practice often were able to spread quickly from place to place. These are attested in historical texts from central Asia and China dating back to at least the fifth century CE and a few centuries later in India, Japan, and Tibet as well.

Were postural sequences also circulating among Buddhists at this time? It is difficult to say for sure, although there are a few tantalizing clues that they may have been. For example, a set of movement therapies identified as "Indian massage methods" or "Brahmanical techniques" appeared in China—possibly as early as the fourth century but certainly by the seventh. Including a number of self-massage and stretching techniques, these found their way into the writings of the prominent imperial physician Sun Simiao (581–682) and became part of the medical canon of classical Chinese medicine. It has also long been suggested that such Indian exercises may have influenced Chinese martial arts. The Shaolin Monastery, a Buddhist temple that played a major role in the historical development of martial arts, attributes some of its practices to Indian Buddhist monks who came to China in the medieval era.

Evidence for the circulation of postural yoga outside of India is more voluminous from the second millennium CE. For example, the encyclopedic eleventh-century Buddhist scripture *Kālacakratantra* describes various aspects of the subtle body and prescribes certain postures for therapeutic purposes (e.g., headstands for the alleviation of phlegm and the "vajra posture" for the elimination of backache). Another eleventh-century Buddhist composition, the *Amṛtasiddhi*, in fact represents the earliest extant source for certain key features of *haṭhayoga*. Given the patchy historical record, it is not always clear when these texts are repeating notions that derived from Śaiva practices versus when they are reporting Buddhist innovations. Nevertheless, both Indian compositions were translated into Tibetan and contributed to the development of unique forms of yoga in the Himalayan region.

In Tibet, therapeutic movements for the cultivation of the subtle body (Tib. *tsalung trulkhor*) historically were considered to be advanced practices suitable only for spiritually advanced individuals. As this knowledge was closely guarded and not written about openly, there are few historical sources that describe the practice in any detail. One major source, however, is a set of paintings on the walls of the Zongdag Lukhang, the secret temple of the fifth Dalai Lama (1617–1682). The murals show Buddhist adepts (Skt. *mahāsiddhas*) engaged in various physical *āsanas* as well as "inner fire" practice (Tib. *tummo*, analogous to Skt. *kuṇḍalinī*), alongside other advanced Buddhist subtle body cultivation techniques.

In modern times, these secretive practices have been taught more openly under the name "yantra yoga" or "Tibetan yoga." Beginning with the teachings and publications of Namkhai Norbu Rinpoche (1938–2018), these techniques have become more widely known in the West. Unlike those Indian forms of yoga that have turned into secularized forms of physical fitness, Tibetan yoga has thus far tended to maintain its association with Buddhist spirituality even while being popularized in mainstream magazines such as *Yoga Journal*. It is still normally taught in conjunction with Tibetan styles of meditation, particularly those associated with the Dzogchen school. Even so, Tibetan yoga has also recently become the object of scientific study, including the development of a seven-week program for lymphoma patients at the University of Texas M. D. Anderson Cancer Center in Houston in the 2000s.

Far away from the Himalayas and in a very different cultural sphere, other forms of Buddhist yoga emerged in Southeast Asia. Historical textual evidence for the circulation of yoga is even harder to come by in this part of the world, but we do have a set of statues and an accompanying manuscript from the kingdom of Siam in the 1830s. These artifacts were constructed during the renovation of the Wat Phra Chetuphon temple in Bangkok and were part of an effort by a newly installed ruling dynasty to comprehensively catalog traditional medical knowledge from across the realm. The original statues, made of zinc and tin alloy, have long since deteriorated and been replaced by replicas. Nevertheless, drawings of the yoga postures and copies of the original inscriptions, which were published simultaneously in several manuscripts, are still extant.

The statues, numbering eighty in total, depict *ṛṣis* (Thai *ruesi*) and other adepts performing a variety of āsanas. In contrast with the Zongdag Lukhang's paintings of Tibetan adepts engaged in yoga as an advanced spiritual or religious practice, the Thai examples are strictly medical. The inscriptions give each ṛṣi a name, explain the posture they are engaged in, and detail the health benefits of each one. The āsanas treat conditions such as stiffness, pain, swellings, headaches, spirit-caused ailments, and other common afflictions. Several of the statues depict two ṛṣis, one assisting the other to get into the prescribed yoga posture in what we might think of as a premodern form of yoga therapy.

The individual practice of therapeutic postures continues today in Thailand under the name "ṛṣi self-stretching" (Thai *ruesi dat ton*, also sometimes translated as "hermit self-stretching"). The paired practice, on the other hand, came to be incorporated into "traditional Thai massage" (Thai *nuad phaen Thai* or *nuad phaen boran*), a form of therapeutic bodywork codified at Wat Phra Chetuphon in the 1960s. Like Tibetan yoga, both forms of Thai practice are widely taught today—particularly Thai massage, which has become a popular healing modality internationally. While at the time of this writing *ruesi dat ton* has yet to garner much attention among mainstream yoga enthusiasts around the world, short courses for tourists are offered in major cities throughout Thailand. On the grounds of Wat Phra Chetuphon itself, both traditional massage and *ruesi dat ton* are taught in Thai and English to a steady stream of curious visitors.

So is yoga Indian after all? It is true that the most popular and globally widespread forms of yoga have directly come from the Indian subcontinent. However, there are multiple forms of yoga that developed and were practiced historically outside of India. Although these practices ultimately can also trace their origins to India, they represent unique regional variations. Incubated for centuries in drastically different cultural and religious contexts, they evolved into distinct spiritual, therapeutic, or recreational practices that survive and thrive in modern times.

About the author

C. Pierce Salguero is a transdisciplinary scholar of health humanities who is fascinated by historical and contemporary intersections between Buddhism, medicine, and cross-cultural exchange. He has a PhD in the history of medicine from the Johns Hopkins School of Medicine (2010) and teaches Asian history, medicine, and religion at Penn State University's Abington College, located near Philadelphia. He also has been the editor in chief of the journal *Asian Medicine: Journal of the International Association for the Study of Traditional Asian Medicine* since 2016.

Suggestions for further reading

In this book

See also chapters 58 (What does yoga mean to Indians today?) and 59 (What is the relationship between race and yoga?).

Elsewhere

Mallinson, James. "Kālavañcana in the Konkan: How a Vajrayāna Haṭha-yoga Tradition Cheated Buddhism's Death in India." *Religions* 10 (2019): 273–306.

Salguero, C. Pierce. *Traditional Thai Medicine: Buddhism, Animism, Yoga, Ayurveda*. White Lotus, 2016.

Steavu, Dominic. "Is There Such a Thing as Chinese Yoga? Indian Postural Therapies in Mediaeval China." *Journal of Yoga Studies* 4 (2021): 375–412.

8
Are there sacred texts in yoga?

Lubomír Ondračka

The simple answer is yes, there are. The more complex answer depends on what we consider to be a yogic text, how we understand the category "sacred," and above all, the perspective of each individual person. A text may be highly sacred to someone but quite ordinary or even unacceptable to somebody else. Moreover, the status of a text can change over time. To make the simple answer more nuanced, perhaps we could say that there have always been yoga texts that were sacred to a certain group of people at a certain time. On the other hand, we can also say that there is no yogic text that has always been sacred to all.

The importance of the individual perspective can be well demonstrated by the example of the so-called Yoga Upaniṣads. From the Brahmanical perspective of scholarly, text-oriented Hinduism, the most sacred Hindu works form a canonical collection called *śruti* (what has been heard). This corpus of revealed texts includes not only the Vedas and other ancient Vedic works but also all the Upaniṣads. Some Upaniṣads are indeed old and important, but many are not. The Yoga Upaniṣads were produced in the early eighteenth century by a Sanskrit scholar belonging to the Advaita Vedānta tradition. It is a compilation of several older Upaniṣads and *haṭhayoga* texts embedded in Advaita Vedānta doctrine. The result is practically irrelevant to yoga practice and not very interesting for yoga history, but because the texts are formally Upaniṣads, from the standpoint of normative Hinduism, this collection paradoxically represents the most sacred of yoga texts.

A different perspective gives different results. From the standpoint of theistic traditions, the most sacred texts are those that are directly revealed by the supreme deity of a given religion. Such revealed texts are, for example, Śaiva, Vaiṣṇava, Śākta, and the Buddhist tantras. Although tantras are not usually considered to be strictly yogic works, they contain a large number of passages and often entire lengthy chapters describing tantric yoga. Some tantras, such as the Śaiva *Mālinīvijayottaratantra*, are almost entirely devoted to yogic practice. Therefore, for the tantric practitioner, these revelations represent the most sacred source of yogic teaching and practice.

The tantras, however, are not the only works relevant to yoga that, according to traditional belief, come directly from the gods and therefore have the highest sacred status. Several *haṭhayogic* texts also claim divine origin. Sometimes, this fact is evident from the title of the text itself. A good example is the work called *Śivasaṃhitā*, "The Collection [of Verses] of Śiva." In fact, Śiva is not the only divine actor in this text, as it is formally a dialogue between him and his partner Pārvatī. There are, however, other yogic works that have the same structure of a conversation between a divine couple, although their titles do not suggest it (e.g., *Khecarīvidyā*, *Yogabīja*, *Gorakṣayogaśāstra*, etc.). Sometimes the teaching is given by a god directly to a worthy human person, such as a yoga sage or disciple (e.g., in the *Amanaska* or *Candrāvalokana*). In any case, it is clear that such divine revelation constitutes a sacred text (at least for the followers of a given religious tradition).

Many yoga texts are attributed to various legendary or semilegendary Hindu sages, such as Gorakṣa, Matsyendra, Vasiṣṭha, Dattātreya, or Yājñavalkya. Compared to the works revealed by the gods, the sacred status of these scriptures is less clear, more complicated, and much more fluid. In theory, since these figures are human, it seems improper to classify their works as sacred. At the same time, these saints are highly respected and often have almost a semidivine status, so their texts are viewed as extraordinary and, to some extent, sacred. Perhaps we could say that these works are sacred but less than those revealed by gods—that is, that they constitute a category of sacred yogic texts of the second order.

A good example of the possible fluidity of the category of sacred text is provided by the works attributed to Gorakṣanātha. Originally, Gorakṣa appears as a yogi, though extraordinary, but still as a human being. Therefore, the works produced by him were certainly highly valued but hardly sacred in the strict sense of the word. In the course of time, Gorakṣa came to be regarded as the founder and supreme teacher of the Nāth tradition, by which he was eventually deified and declared to be a form of the god Śiva. As a result, the texts attributed to him are now considered revelations that come directly from Śiva's mouth and are therefore highly sacred.

Somewhat similar is the case of Patañjali, the author (or rather compiler) of one of the most famous yoga texts, the *Pātañjalayogaśāstra*. For many centuries, Patañjali was regarded in Indian tradition as the scholar who composed the doctrinal work explaining the Sāṃkhya philosophy. In the tenth century, however, one commentator, probably because of a misreading of a word in the *Pātañjalayogaśāstra*, connected Patañjali with the mythical divine serpent Ananta (also called Śeṣa), on whom the god Viṣṇu rests. Although Patañjali was first depicted as a devotee of Śiva, later tradition, both textual and visual, presents him as a Vaiṣṇava deity. Thus, the human author became a divine author, and consequently, the status of his text changed. This transformation is clearly visible in the modern yoga milieu, where verses in his praise are recited, his statues are worshipped, and his work is considered not only highly authoritative but at least semi-sacred, if not fully sacred.

Another extremely popular text in contemporary globalized yoga is the *Bhagavadgītā*. The level of its sacredness is not easy to determine. Being part of the *Mahābhārata*, a vast ancient Indian epic, it belongs to the category of scriptures that the Brahmanical Hindu tradition calls *smṛti*, "that which is remembered." According to the traditional view, these works have a human author, which means that they are not as sacred as the revealed śruti corpus. On the other hand, the *Bhagavadgītā* contains the direct discourse of Kṛṣṇa, who is the avatar of the god Viṣṇu, so it is possible to understand this teaching as a divine, sacred revelation. At the same time, it must be said that the *Bhagavadgītā* can hardly be considered a yogic text because it does not contain any substantial yogic teaching or description of yogic practice. Its extraordinary popularity in modern yoga is related to the prominence of this work in contemporary India, which has its roots in the formation of so-called neo-Hinduism in the late nineteenth century.

Finally, it should be stressed that the level of sacredness of a particular yoga text does not necessarily correspond to its importance. We have seen that from a certain point of view, the most sacred works are the Yoga Upaniṣads, yet their significance is quite limited. On the other hand, several texts composed by human authors who were never deified—so their writings cannot be considered sacred in any respect—are extremely important. The best example is probably the *Haṭhapradīpikā*, the most popular and influential text of haṭhayoga, written by a certain Svātmārāma, of whom we know absolutely nothing.

About the author

Lubomír Ondračka is a publisher, independent researcher, and occasional lecturer at the Department of Philosophy and Religious Studies, Faculty of Arts, Charles University in Prague. Currently, he is a research fellow at Balliol College, University of Oxford. His research is focused on the history of yoga, death, and dying in India and on the religions and culture of Bengal.

Suggestions for further reading

In this book

See also chapters 41 (What is the *Haṭhapradīpikā*?), 45 (Who was Patañjali?), and 56 (How do modern practitioners relate to ancient texts?).

Elsewhere

Bühnemann, Gudrun. "*Nāga*, *Siddha* and Sage: Visions of Patañjali as an Authority on Yoga." In *Yoga in Transformation: Historical and Contemporary Perspectives*, edited by Karl Baier, Philipp André Maas, and Karin Preisendanz. V&R unipress, 2018.

Larson, Gerald James, and Ram Shankar Bhattacharya, eds. *Yoga: India's Philosophy of Meditation*. Vol. 12 of *Encyclopedia of Indian Philosophies*. Motilal Banarsidass, 2008.

Ondračka, Lubomír. "Medieval Yoga Literature." In *The Oxford Handbook of Hindu Literature*, edited by Laxshmi Greaves and James Hegarty. Oxford University Press, forthcoming.

9

What is Sanskrit?

Corinna May Lhoir

Sanskrit has greatly shaped our understanding of modern yoga, although we might not always be aware of it. The use of Sanskrit greeting formulas and the chanting of mantras in yoga classes are ubiquitous. Sanskrit names for bodily postures are as omnipresent in our everyday language as some Sanskrit philosophical terms have become ("It's karma, baby!"). What is Sanskrit, and how has this language gained the importance in relation to yoga that it claims to this day even in the West?

Sanskrit has played an influential role in the practice and development of yoga throughout the ages. This is due to the fact that many yoga texts considered of significant importance have been composed in Sanskrit, such as the *Pātañjalayogaśāstra* (composed around the fourth century CE) or the *Haṭhapradīpikā* (composed around 1400 CE). Many of the terms and concepts used in yoga are taken from Sanskrit: *āsana* (body posture), *prāṇāyāma* (breath retention), or *mokṣa* (liberation).

Sanskrit (the term *saṃskṛta* can be translated as "well made," "highly elaborated," or "purified by grammar") is an ancient Indo-Aryan language. It has been in use on the Indian subcontinent from as early as the middle of the second millennium BCE and is still in use as a liturgical language in Hinduism and related philosophical strands in India. It is the oldest and most refined of the classical languages of India, and it has a rich literary and cultural history. Sanskrit is considered a language of scholarship and learning, and it is said that one needs at least twelve years of study to master this rich and complex language.

In most of India, particularly in the northern half, many languages are spoken that can be traced back to a single form of speech, a proto-Indo-Aryan language that was introduced into India by Indo-Aryan peoples coming from central Asia into the northern Indian subcontinent. These migrations took place in several waves and started around 1800 BCE. Theories that the Indo-Aryan languages first generated in India and evolved from India into the Western Hemisphere have been largely refuted by linguistic research; however, this "out-of-India" hypothesis is still hotly debated by some academics.

The Indo-Aryan languages are divided into three major groups: Old Indo-Aryan, Middle Indo-Aryan, and New Indo-Aryan. Several stages of Old Indo-Aryan are denoted by the term "Sanskrit," the earliest stage of which, used between 1800 and 1200 BCE, was the language of the *Ṛgveda*. This collection of hymns and mantras forms the earliest body of textual witnesses of the early Vedic text corpus and is accompanied by three other main collections of sacred texts, the *Sāmaveda*, *Yajurveda*, and *Atharvaveda*. These four collections form the so-called *śruti* (that which has been heard), holy scriptures that were said to have been directly received from the gods by *ṛṣis*, mythic seers. For centuries, these texts were transmitted entirely orally. Hence, correct pronunciation of the Sanskrit language came to be considered essential. Since Sanskrit was then predominantly used by the priestly class, the Brahmans, who held significant religious and social authority in ancient Indian society, access to Sanskrit education and practice was largely limited to this privileged group. In later centuries, however, Sanskrit began to transcend its exclusivity and spread beyond the Brahmanical circle. Sanskrit became the sacred language not only of Vedic Brahmanism or of classical Hindu philosophy but also of historical and sacred texts of Buddhism and Jainism, although the latter two, in their earlier stages, preferred to transmit their scriptural canon in vernacular Middle Indo-Aryan languages, the so-called Prakrits. *Prākṛta*, as opposed to *saṃskṛta*, may be translated as "naturally formed." The language of early Buddhism is called Pali, while the language of early Jainism is called Jain Prakrit.

During the classical era (from around the fourth century BCE to the twelfth century CE), Sanskrit education underwent a process of institutionalization, witnessing the emergence of specialized schools and centers of learning, the *gurukulas*. While in the beginning, these learning centers were predominantly attended by Brahman students, they gradually began to accept students from other social groups, including the *kṣatriyas* (warrior class) and *vaiśyas* (merchant class). This development, although with certain limitations, marked a slight expansion of access, enabling individuals from these upper castes to learn and engage with Sanskrit to varying extents. However, beyond the upper castes, Sanskrit education remained relatively inaccessible. The *śūdras*, belonging to the lower classes, faced considerable exclusion from opportunities to learn Sanskrit due to prevailing social and cultural barriers. This exclusion was reinforced by the *varṇa* system, a class-based division of labor that assigned specific roles and occupations to each social class. Consequently, the lower classes predominantly undertook menial tasks and were afforded limited access to education, including the study of Sanskrit.

Despite these social barriers, Sanskrit did influence regional languages, literature, and cultural practices across India. Many vernacular languages, such as Hindi, Bengali, and Marathi, developed and borrowed extensively from Sanskrit vocabulary and grammar. This integration allowed a broader spectrum of people to engage with Sanskrit-influenced works, even if they were not fluent in the classical language itself.

Sanskrit became standardized in the fourth century BCE, when the Indian grammarian Pāṇini composed the four thousand verses of the *Aṣṭādhyāyī*, a prescriptive and generative grammar with linguistic rules for every aspect of the Sanskrit language. His rules are still applied today, and from a grammatical perspective, no more changes have gone into the composition of the Sanskrit language, which is extremely unusual for a language in use for more than three thousand years. Today, we use the term "Vedic Sanskrit" for the Sanskrit composed before and "Classical Sanskrit" for the Sanskrit that came into being after Pāṇini.

Sanskrit's complex grammar is characterized by a declension system that includes eight cases, three numbers, and three genders and an elaborate system of verbal morphology. It also impresses with its complex usage of compounds, a feature that has been uniquely expanded in Sanskrit, both in terms of the number of elements making up a single compound and in the volume of compound usage in Sanskrit literature.

These complicated and convoluted grammatical features allow the composer of Sanskrit to present complex issues in a crisp and precise way. This led to various textbooks being written in the form of short aphorisms, so-called *sūtras*. These sūtras are almost impossible to decipher without further explanations, accompanying commentaries, or the help of a guru or teacher. However, due to their accuracy, sharpness, and verse format, they are easy to remember—an important asset in times when the oral transmission of knowledge dominated!

In its long history, the term "yoga," derived from Sanskrit, has received various definitions and typologies within various traditions and historical periods. The Indo-Aryan verbal root *√yuc-* denotes, among other meanings, "to unite" or "to connect," and in the long history of its use, it underwent tremendous changes of meaning. Yoga in one of the earliest Vedic sources, the *Ṛgveda*, was exclusively used to describe the yoking of a horse to a chariot. In the *Mahābhārata*, it is used inter alia for describing "tension of strength," "effort," "diligence," "zeal," or "attention." In other early texts—to mention, for example, the *Taittirīya Āraṇyaka* (a part of the *Yajurveda* of the Vedic tradition)—the meaning changed to "concentration of mental activity," "fixed direction of knowledge on one point," and "contemplation." As such, for many centuries, the term "yoga" was exclusively used for an activity of the mind, and the proliferation of body postures that are associated with yoga today is only found in texts from the thirteenth century CE onward. In Jainism, "yoga" primarily translates to "activity," while in Buddhism, it can also denote "bond" or "attachment."

Sanskrit, admired by many for its beauty and complexity, has always been considered a language of knowledge and spirituality, used with great emphasis on correctness in pronunciation and thus flawless oral transmission up to the present day. This is reflected in the importance attached to the correct use of Sanskrit throughout the centuries and in the continuous utilization of Sanskrit terms even in modern yoga practice today. Sanskrit is believed to help practitioners connect to the spiritual roots and traditions of their practice, which has recently led to a growing interest in its study. Sanskrit language lessons are not only included in many yoga teacher-training programs, but they are also on the rise in many higher education facilities. The study of Sanskrit in universities twenty years ago was mainly dominated by students interested in Buddhism. Today, a growing number of university students learning Sanskrit are primarily interested in yoga.

About the author

Corinna May Lhoir is a contract lecturer in Sanskrit and the history of yoga at Universität Hamburg. Her PhD research focuses on yoga and meditation in Jainism, and she is currently preparing a critical edition of a medieval Jain text on yoga called the *Yogapradīpa*.

Suggestions for further reading

In this book

See also chapters 8 (Are there sacred texts in yoga?) and 56 (How do modern practitioners relate to ancient texts?).

Elsewhere

Cardona, George. "Sanskrit." In *The Indo-Aryan Languages*, edited by George Cardona and Dhanesh Jain. Routledge, 2014.

Deshpande, Madhav. *Sanskrit & Prakrit: Sociolinguistic Issues*. Motilal Banarsidass, 1993.

Ruppel, Antonia. *The Cambridge Introduction to Sanskrit*. Cambridge University Press, 2017.

Scharfe, Helmut. *Education in Ancient India*. Brill, 2002.

10
What is *OM*?

Finnian M. M. Gerety

OM is the celebrated sacred syllable of chanting, yoga, and meditation. This syllable is generally regarded as the totality of knowledge, the cosmic vibration, and the sound of divinity and transcendence. Originating as a Sanskrit utterance and symbol some three thousand years ago in Vedic traditions, OM has long been known as the foremost mantra in Hinduism. Over the centuries, practitioners of other Asian religions—notably Buddhism, Jainism, Sufism, and Sikhism—have also claimed the syllable, incorporating it into their own mantra systems in Sanskrit and other Indic languages. With modernity, OM's fame has only increased: The syllable is now an icon of global spiritualities—nowhere more so than in transnational modern yoga, where it is central to the construction of yogic identities. Every day, millions of people worldwide chant the syllable, meditate on it, adorn bodies and spaces with it, and otherwise engage it in a range of materials, media, and wares. At the level of practice, many yogis audibly chant OM to start or finish a session; others mentally fixate on it for extended periods as a contemplative technique.

A traditional phonetic analysis divides the whole sound *om* into constituent parts, the phonemes *a*, *u*, and *m*—thus giving rise to the spelling *aum* in some texts and occasioning alternative pronunciations among modern yogis. While this *a-u-m* analysis dates back many centuries, *aum* does not convey the original Sanskrit pronunciation. Instead, the oldest and most consistently observed pronunciation of OM is akin to the first syllable of English words such as "*om*en" or "*om*it"—that is, a combination of a long, open-mouthed vowel (*o*) with a labial sound produced by closing the lips (*m*). Still, the intricacies of this basic pronunciation have varied historically according to several factors. As is common in Sanskrit words, when directly followed by a consonant, the final *-m* changes—usually to a nasal represented in transliteration by *ṃ*, *m̐*, or *ṅ* and pronounced like English "so*ng*." Because one of OM's primary functions is to introduce other mantras, as in the famous Hindu mantra *oṃ namo nārāyaṇāya*

(OM, homage to Nārāyaṇa!), this change frequently takes effect—so much so that many practitioners and traditions conceive the syllable as always ending with a nasal, regardless of actual pronunciation or particular phonetic context. Another variable factor is that in certain forms of Vedic recitation, the vowel may be lengthened to three or more beats (*mātrās*), visually represented by the numeral "3"—thus, *o3m*. This form is often used by contemporary Hindu traditions like the Arya Samaj as a sign of Vedic heritage. While the syllable has been written differently in different places and times—including tradition-specific renderings and regional variants in the many Indian scripts—it is most widely recognized these days by its dedicated character in the *devanāgarī* script (ॐ) or by Roman capital letters (OM, OṂ). None of these many variants is per se more "correct" than any other; convention and context usually offer the best guidance for pronouncing and writing the syllable. Here, we will use the spelling "OM" when referring to the syllable in general and *om* or *oṃ* when referring to specific examples and mantras.

OM is first attested in the Vedas, the canon of Sanskrit mantras and texts composed in ancient India by Hindu priests known as Brahmans. Of the thousands of mantras that make up this corpus, OM was singled out as the preeminent *akṣara*, a word that means both "syllable" and "imperishable"—thus aptly conveying OM's fusion of speech and transcendence. By the time of the Upaniṣads, Vedic OM was known as the essence of wisdom, the epitome of sacred speech, divinity made manifest, a tool for pursuing salvation, and the encapsulation of the cosmos as a whole. Although OM in some ritual utterances can mean "yes," its significance as a sacred syllable is not semantic but sonic and pragmatic: Brahman priests would add the syllable to other mantras in myriad ways to heighten the efficacy of recitation in sacrifice. For example, an ancient technique called the "humming" (*praṇava*) entails substituting *-om* for the final syllable of certain mantras, while the daily practice of "personal recitation" (*svādhyāya*) always begins with the intoning of OM. The ubiquity of OM in chanting—especially its penetration of the ritual soundscape—was taken as proof of the syllable's holism and supremacy. Somewhat later, Brahmanical *dharma* texts stipulate that OM must be chanted at the beginning and end of Vedic recitation so as to protect the sacred mantras. Permutations of this custom were widely adopted in tantric mantra systems—not only in Hinduism but also in Buddhism and Jainism, where it also became common practice to begin mantras with OM. Broadly, then, we might say that the major legacy of Vedic OM is that the syllable established itself as an integral, flexible, and authoritative component of Indian ritual culture—an outcome that, in turn, decisively influenced yoga in Asia and around the world.

A central paradigm of early yoga is what may be called OM's soteriology of sound—the idea that chanting and contemplating the syllable lead to liberation. Like mantra meditation generally, meditation on OM may consist of audible, murmured, or silent chanting. The *Kaṭha Upaniṣad*, which presents the oldest known systemization of yoga, regards the syllable as the best "support" (*ālambana*) for contemplative practice. Using the Vedic term *praṇava* in a broader sense, Patañjali recommends the murmured repetition (*japa*) of OM in contemplative worship of "the Lord" (*īśvara*) because the syllable is thought to be the verbal expression of this supreme divinity. This teaching has affinities with theistic currents in early Hinduism, where the highest mantras are those that name the highest deity. For instance, the god Kṛṣṇa in the *Bhagavadgītā*, having revealed himself as "the praṇava in all the Vedas," instructs his devotee Arjuna in a technique of uttering OM at the moment of death, by means of which he can ascend to heaven, leave his body, and merge with god. It is likely that such a technique is the origin of the idea of *utkrānti*, often glossed as yogic suicide—the soul's "ascension" precipitated by the intentional shedding of the body. A similar paradigm is evident in the Śaiva Tantric "ascending utterance" (*uccāra*), albeit without the necessity of leaving one's body behind. Instead, this version of spiritual ascent with OM serves the embodied goal of "liberation while living" (*jīvanmukti*). As the practitioner chants *oṃ* in the uccāra, he listens carefully to the sound's motion from the chest to the throat to the cranium, where it resonates and finally decays into silence. This trajectory marks the upward movement of OM's sonic energy in five stages, corresponding to the fivefold division of the syllable into audible parts (the phonemes *a*, *u*, and *m*) followed by subtle ones, "the drop" (*bindu*) and "resonance" (*nāda*), which herald the yogi's dissolution into divine consciousness.

Because Tantric traditions incorporate script and the writing of mantras, these divisions may also be mapped onto OM's written sign, linking the bindu to the *candrabindu*, the "half-moon and dot" sign representing the final nasal in *oṁ*. Parallel speculations on the division of OM are also attested in Brahmanical traditions: In addition to the threefold division already noted (*a*, *u*, *m*)—wherein the three syllables may represent the three Vedas or the three supreme gods—we encounter a fourfold segmentation of the syllable, with the three phonemes representing three states of consciousness and a fourth metaphysical part representing the supreme self (*ātman*). Phenomenologically, the yogi may experience this transcendent fourth (*turīya*) as a resonant feeling of ants crawling in the head.

As is the case with mantras in general, premodern constructions of OM from different traditions come together to shape the practice and interpretation of the sacred syllable in contemporary yoga. The above terms, approaches, and teachings crop up in many streams of yoga today and in countless variations and innovations. The term *praṇava*, for instance, is widely recognized as a name for OM. And it seems plausible that the custom in many postural yoga classes of beginning and ending the session with OM—thereby framing the *āsana* sequence with the syllable—is a distant echo of ancient recitational conventions meant to confer protection and auspiciousness. Moreover, immersive mantra meditation focused on the silent repetition of OM and aiming to elevate the practitioner's state of mind would seem to be adapted from the syllable's vaunted soteriology of sound. Alongside these ritualized and sonic dimensions, the prominence of OM as a visual sign has steadily increased in modernity, while its semiotic scope has expanded: Today, many people worldwide recognize the written OM not only as the sectarian marker of Hindu gods or enlightened Jain saints or the Sikh unity of the divine—but also as a symbol of the well-being and transformation sought by yogis through yoga.

About the author

Finnian M. M. Gerety is a historian of Indian religions focusing on sound and mantra. After earning a PhD in South Asian studies from Harvard University, he was a postdoctoral fellow at the Yale University Institute of Sacred Music; he currently teaches in the Department of Religious Studies at Brown University. Integrating the study of premodern texts with insights from fieldwork in contemporary India, his research explores how sound has shaped religious doctrines and practices on the subcontinent from the late Bronze Age up through today. His forthcoming book project for Oxford University Press, *This Whole World Is OM: A History of the Sacred Syllable in Early India*, is the first-ever academic monograph on OM, the preeminent mantra and ubiquitous sacred syllable of Indian religions.

Suggestions for further reading

In this book

See also chapters 31 (How do mantras relate to yoga?) and 33 (Why do yogis meditate?).

Elsewhere

Gerety, Finnian M. M. "Between Sound and Silence in Early Yoga: Meditation on 'Om' at Death." *History of Religions* 60, no. 3 (2021): 209–244.

Gough, Ellen. "When Sound Becomes an Image: Picturing Oṃ in Jainism." *Material Religion* 17, no. 4 (2021): 463–489.

Padoux, André. *Vāc: The Concept of the Word in Selected Hindu Tantras.* Translated by Jacques Gontier. State University of New York Press, 1990.

Ruff, Jeremy Clark. "Yoga in the Yoga Upaniṣads: Disciplines of the Mystical OṂ Sound." In *Yoga in Practice*, edited by David Gordon White. Princeton University Press, 2012.

What is the point of yoga?

11
What are the goals of yoga?

Barbora Sojková

In 2019, over three hundred million people worldwide were reported to have spent over $37 billion on activities and commodities connected to yoga. Judging from these statistics, yoga is clearly an important activity at present. Moreover, historical research shows that it has been so for at least two millennia, if not longer. Yet why are people engaging in this activity, and with what goals in mind? As is the case in all entries in this volume, the answer to this question will differ widely depending on the context of the "yoga" in question. Broadly speaking, however, the goals of yoga can be distinguished according to the time period: Contemporary and modern forms of yoga generally promise different outcomes than the premodern ones.

The majority of people who are interested in yoga today understand it to be a *practice*: a systematic, regular, and intentional activity. Although yoga practice can take on multiple forms—postural, meditative, or centered on breath control, to name a few examples—its goal is generally thought to be physical health and, stemming from it, mental well-being. There are a number of modern and contemporary yoga movements and schools whose goals could be described as spiritual. Nevertheless, the majority of contemporary practitioners list health as one of the primary motivations. The idea that yoga is an activity promoting physical and mental health is increasingly supported by a growing body of research. Yoga is endorsed by biomedical professionals as well as public figures. The British National Health Service, for example, recommends yoga to patients who experience high blood pressure, heart disease, various aches and pains, depression, and anxiety, to name just a few. In short, people practice yoga today because they believe it makes them healthy and calm.

The idea that health is the goal of yoga practice is, however, relatively recent. Although some historic forms of yoga demonstrated an interest in maintaining a practitioner's health and curing specific diseases, and some considered a healthy body to be a necessary condition for yoga practice, health was not their primary goal. On the contrary, some premodern texts, such as the *Gorakṣaśataka*, warn that yoga can make a practitioner sick. The strong association between yoga and health has only existed since the early twentieth century when—influenced by globalized ideas of biomedicine, physical discipline, and spirituality—foundational figures of the modern yoga movement started using the practice as a therapeutic intervention and an antidote to modern life.

Before we start discussing the kinds of goals associated with premodern yoga in more detail, it is worth noting that even the understanding of yoga as a *practice* is relatively modern. In the majority of premodern texts, the word "yoga" indicates a *state*. That is, yoga itself is understood to be synonymous with the primary goal of the practice that is achieved through the manifold practices associated with the tradition. The nature of this goal, however, varies from text to text. For certain traditions, especially those influenced by tantrism or non-dualism (*advaita*), yoga was understood as a state of union: union of the adept with the highest deity (Śiva, Śakti), union of an individual and supreme self, or union with an element of reality (*tattva*). Traditions related to the metaphysical system of Sāṃkhya, such as the *Pātañjalayogaśāstra*, defined yoga as the separation (*kaivalya*) of the categories of *puruṣa* (the spiritual principle) and *prakṛti* (the material nature). The *Bhagavadgītā* defines yoga as equanimity and skill in action; the *Liṅgapurāṇa* considers it to be *nirvāṇa*, the condition of Śiva; and so on. Though disparate, these definitions have in common the understanding of yoga as the final *state* of the practice.

To achieve the state of yoga, the adept has to attain a certain state of meditative absorption, generally known as *samādhi*. While for most schools, samādhi is understood to be the most elevated state of consciousness, there is little consensus on what constitutes its nature. For some traditions, like the *Pātañjalayogaśāstra*, samādhi is the highest state of meditation, where all the fluctuations of the mind disappear. In the medieval *haṭhayoga* texts, samādhi is synonymous with a deathlike trance in which the yogi is insensible to any stimuli. The *Haṭhatattvakaumudī*, for example, remarks that in the final state, the adept resembles a block of wood. Although most premodern yoga traditions value samādhi as the necessary precursor of liberation, there are exceptions: Some texts associated with tantrism consider it to be simply a preliminary technique that does not contribute to the aim of tantric yoga—that is, union with the deity.

Although samādhi is the highest meditative state, for the majority of premodern yoga traditions, it is not the goal itself. It is, however, a necessary and sufficient cause for the real aim of the practice: liberation (*mokṣa*, *mukti*, etc.) from the chain of rebirths (*saṃsāra*). Liberation is an axiom of premodern Indian yogic thought that has taken on a multitude of various forms over the centuries. As the twelfth-century yoga text *Amaraughaprabodha* states, it is really "impossible to describe." Among the various schools, there is no consensus on what causes it or even what or who is to be liberated.

What is clear, however, is that in the majority of cases, a yogi will never be born again upon attaining liberation. This can be experienced either at the moment of death (*videhamukti*) or in life (*jīvanmukti*). The first option, liberation at the time of death, is the default position of most of the traditions predating the haṭhayoga texts, both Brahmanical and extra-Vedic. There are many examples we could quote, including the *Bhagavadgītā*, according to which one attains liberation at the time of death, provided one practices yoga of the mind, body, and breath; recites *oṃ*; and thinks of the god Kṛṣṇa. The second option—that is, when the yogi remains alive after liberation (jīvanmukti)—started gaining traction at the end of the first millennium CE. This concept manifests itself in the texts in two forms. For some traditions, the yogi is mentally and physically inactive and essentially transcends the world. Other traditions emphasize a yogi's power to act in the world at will, with access to certain supernatural powers (*siddhis*).

In conclusion, although the concept of liberation is complex and nuanced, it is generally the primary motivation for the actions of premodern yogis. Most modern and contemporary practitioners of yoga, on the other hand, engage in a health-forward practice that has very little to do with metaphysics.

About the author

Barbora Sojková holds a DPhil in Asian and Middle Eastern studies (Sanskrit) from the University of Oxford, where her research focused on human-animal relationships in Vedic Sanskrit literature. She works as an academic librarian at the All Souls College, Oxford, and as a Sanskrit cataloger at the Bodleian Library, Oxford. She is a certified yoga teacher and trainer focusing on the history and philosophy of yoga.

Suggestions for further reading

In this book

See also chapters 12 (Does yoga liberate or constrain?), 18 (What is *samādhi*?), and 21 (Is yoga good for your health?).

Elsewhere

Birch, Jason. "The Quest for Liberation-in-Life: A Survey of Early Works on Haṭha- and Rājayoga." In *The Oxford History of Hinduism: Hindu Practice*, edited by Gavin Flood. Oxford University Press, 2020.

Newcombe, Suzanne. "Yoga and Meditation as a Health Intervention." In *Routledge Handbook of Yoga and Meditation Studies*, edited by Suzanne Newcombe and Karen O'Brien-Kop. Routledge: 2020.

Schreiner, Peter. "How to Come Out of Samādhi?" In *Release from Life—Release in Life: Indian Perspectives on Individual Liberation*, edited by Andreas Bigger, Rita Krajnc, Annemarie Mertens, Markus Schüpbach, and Heinz Werner Wessler. Worlds of South and Inner Asia, vol. 1. Peter Lang, 2010.

12

Does yoga liberate or constrain?

Ruth Westoby

Obviously, yoga liberates. Or it is supposed to. But *liberate* from what? And what is this *yoga* that might liberate us? There are widely differing answers to these questions, and whether yoga liberates or constrains is itself a provocative one. This question could be seen to get to the heart of what yoga is supposed to do. The answers differ because yoga can be situated in the widely differing worldviews of the premodern as well as the modern periods, and the analysis can be applied to the techniques and to the outcome or objective.

What is yoga? In the premodern period, yoga is associated with techniques to achieve liberation, whether these are physical, meditative, ritual, or devotional. Yoga from the second millennium CE is associated with physical techniques, especially as formulated by *haṭhayoga*. *Haṭha*'s diverse physical practices include complex breathing techniques, postures, seals or locks, cleansing techniques, diet, ethics, and meditation. Yoga in the modern period is predominantly associated with physical postures while not entirely rejecting breathing and meditation techniques.

What is liberation? Liberation is freedom or release from a constraint. The nature of liberation and the nature of constraint depend on context. In the premodern period, yoga is freedom (*mokṣa*) from the causal doctrine of retributive reaction (*karma*), the round of repeated death and birth (*saṃsāra*) and suffering (*duḥkha*). Yoga undoes the laws of causality, thus relieving the suffering that characterizes repeated lives. Mokṣa is liberation precisely from the round of rebirth characterized by suffering. Mokṣa is conceived either as bodiless (*videhamukti*), coinciding with the death or abandonment of the body, or as embodied (*jīvanmukti*), where the usual constraints on the body are overcome. Conceptions of jīvanmukti include moving at will through the worlds; taking on any form, whether human or animal; and divine omnipotence. Thus, the body is no longer a constraining prison but a site of possibility.

It is less clear whether yoga liberates in the modern period because the premodern criteria against which liberation was judged have largely fallen away. As yoga has migrated from its Indian origins, it has, in many instances, become dissociated from the philosophical or theological presuppositions of its Indian heritage. Yoga has been recast in the health and well-being domains as alleviating poor physical and mental health and enhancing fitness, stress management, sleep, and even childbirth—and a multitude more benefits. In these contexts, yoga is presented and experienced as a release. Therefore, yoga can be seen to liberate in both premodern and modern contexts. Paradoxically, however, the opposite view is also valid: Becoming liberated may entail constraining behaviors and practices.

In the premodern period, the techniques of yoga can certainly be understood as constraint. These include rules of social and personal behavior, such as ethical or moral principles (the *yamas* and *niyamas* of Pātañjalayoga, for example), as well as techniques of practice that require time and effort. Another helpful framework through which to consider constraint is the comparison between liberation (*mukti*) and enjoyment (*bhukti*). Bhukti is often constrained in the interests of mukti. This is especially so in more arduous paths such as haṭhayoga or asceticism (*tapas*). Paths of royal (*rāja*) yoga appear to allow more possibility for enjoyment, or at least less effort, as one is instructed to allow the mind to follow the objects of sense before becoming still, as an elephant having been free to follow its inclinations will then settle. This characterization of *rājayoga* stands in contrast to the forceful subjugation of the mind and breath where the same metaphor is used in descriptions of haṭhayoga, but this time, a goad is used to control the elephant of the mind. However, there are occasional textual instances when the rules are relaxed once one is established in yoga: where freedom is attained even though pleasure has been enjoyed.

Can modern yoga be understood as constraint? In relation to modern yoga, there is a persuasive critique of yoga in the neoliberal domain such that yoga becomes a method of disciplining the self and body in ways that may not also be liberative. The modern neoliberal context reframes liberation and constraint. The focus is no longer on ultimate liberation from the round of rebirth, or at least this objective has been significantly displaced to the periphery of occult practice. Instead, when yoga is defined as posture, yoga is often evaluated in terms of bodily perfection. The criterion of bodily perfection is seen to be externally verifiable, such as on the basis of flexibility and body image. Whether or not practitioners themselves make such assessments, the marketing forces of the neoliberal economy do so in their harnessing of yoga and meditation to sell products. Seen in terms of external verification, yoga might "liberate" those who possess or can cultivate such characteristics while doing little to alleviate internal health and well-being. Some scholars have argued that the self-help practices of yoga and meditation function to enable people to cope with the unlivable demands of the neoliberal economy. While this might appear as liberation, the constraints of cultivating "perfect" bodies in terms of leisure time and expenditure on diet and broader cultural accouterments such as leisure wear are restricted only to the few. Nevertheless, this analysis does not preclude that people may experience yoga as liberative even within neoliberal contexts. Furthermore, the neoliberal critique itself is flattening: It captures the dynamics of the market but not the diverse experiences of practitioners.

I have suggested that the body is a criterion against which the values of neoliberalism are assessed. There is also evidence in the historical textual record where the body is the site to be evaluated to assess the progress of the student.

The question of whether yoga liberates or constrains really becomes interesting when we put it in conversation with liberation theologies and critical theoretical approaches that broadly seek to enhance liberation or freedom in a number of ways. Such approaches frame liberation as economic, political, and psychological freedoms. Psychological freedoms could be construed as the alleviation of restrictive habitual thought processes or patterns, such as habitual negativity or the normalization of the institutional privilege of patriarchy. Critically evaluating personal perspectives and the institutions of society can be seen to contribute to liberation as people become aware of and potentially free from limiting thoughts and behaviors.

How does this relate to yoga? In a neoliberal worldview, the individual, not society, is the unit of inquiry. According to the neoliberal critique, yoga has become the cultivation of the individual—the cultivation of the "perfect" industrial or postindustrial worker. Seen in a systems or social approach, yoga maintains the oppressive structures of capitalism rather than challenging the system that contributes to social, economic, and political inequality.

Yet yoga can also be a tool for critical inquiry at the individual and systemic level. Even so, this analysis is all rather external. What of the inner experience of spiritual liberation? Do yoga practitioners feel more free? This is very difficult to assess on the basis of empirical criteria, especially as the goals of modern yoga are internally divergent and diverge from the premodern. These perspectives are more susceptible to capture by, for example, ethnographic approaches.

The question of whether yoga liberates or constrains has been approached here using a broad and therefore not particularly precise division into premodern and modern and by considering constraint in terms of both techniques and objectives. The answer depends on the perspective of the practitioner and the context or worldview within which the yoga practice is structured in terms of both techniques and objectives. On these indices, yoga can liberate, but its techniques also imply constraints. Some schools of yoga include analysis or inquiry (*tarka*) as an aspect of yoga technique. On that view, analyses such as this on whether yoga liberates or constrains could themselves contribute to liberation.

About the author

Ruth Westoby is a doctoral candidate at SOAS University of London, and she teaches for SOAS Yoga Studies Online. Her thesis is a historical textual study of the yoga body in Sanskrit sources on early *haṭhayoga* identifying the functional paradigms of the body that explain how yoga works. As a practitioner, she has collaborated on the reconstruction of historical textual sequences of postures, contributing to the development of a new methodology: embodied philology. Her 2021 article, "Raising *Rajas* in *Haṭha* Yoga and Beyond," appears in *Religions of South Asia*, also published by Equinox Publishing Ltd. Her research interests include yoga, the body, gender, textual history, and critical theory.

Suggestions for further reading

In this book

See also chapters 19 (Does yoga give you extraordinary powers?) and 48 (Are the teachers of yoga enlightened?).

Elsewhere

Black, Shameem. "Decolonising Yoga." In *Routledge Handbook of Yoga and Meditation Studies*, edited by Suzanne Newcombe and Karen O'Brien-Kop. Routledge, 2020.

Mallinson, James, and Mark Singleton. *Roots of Yoga*. Penguin Books, 2017.

13

Do yogis want to transcend or transform the body?

Adrián Muñoz

In many ways, the key to this question lies in where we answer from. Since there is no one form of yoga but several forms, the answer can take on different hues. Still, in a general sense, it can be agreed that yoga seeks to achieve some ultimate, deep experience. This experience may or may not be body oriented, but it tends to be transformative and usually takes the material realm into account. The first thing to consider is that there are many yoga schools with distinctive philosophical stances: the early Upaniṣads, the *Pātañjalayogaśāstra*, the Yogācāra school, the *Yoga Vāsiṣṭha*, *haṭhayoga*, *bhaktiyoga*, *karmayoga*, and so on. This translates into different soteriological strategies and goals. If one were to select written sources from three or four different yogic schools, the means and ends of the specific school would differ greatly.

One underlying aspect of most yogic currents is that the mind must be controlled. Most of the meditation or breathing techniques are meant to effect a profound operation on the mind. In his *Yogaśāstra*, Patañjali comments on the transformations of both the mind and the actions of the yogi, which impinge on the individual thoughts that spring from the ego or the personality (*asmitā*). Yet Patañjali does not care much about what happens to the body, since the aim of his method is to separate matter (*prakṛti*) from consciousness (*puruṣa*). In a similar vein, the circa twelfth-century *Amanaska* elaborates on the transformations of the yogi's mind more than his body.

It is in different yogic trends that we can find a more palpable concern with either transformation or transcendence of the body—most notably in the trend known as haṭhayoga. There are explicit discussions on not just the mental but also the physical benefits that emerge from practice. The benefits are generally seen as profound transformations that generate extraordinary faculties (*siddhis*). Whereas Patañjali usually dismisses these powers, *haṭhayogic* sources recommend their acquisition and harnessing. Indeed, the work with the body is a crucial component of *haṭha* practice, and as with other forms of asceticism and meditation from Asia, the public in the West considers this aspect as fundamental to transcendental and millenary wisdom.

The haṭhayogic transformation of the body implies a total perfection of the physical dimension of the yogi. At its core, it is an alchemical operation: The gross and imperfect shall become perfect and pure. In this sense, the perfected body becomes immune to the natural decay of matter, which strikes imperfect bodies. An undecaying body becomes divine (*divya-deha*). Thus, one recurrent image in some tantric and yogic texts is that of the diamond. *Vajra* (a Sanskrit word) means both thunder and jewel or diamond; it is included in the name of the strand of Tantric Buddhism, or Vajrayāna. In the yogic context, the body is by nature polluted and imperfect; it is weak and is subjected to the forces of nature, as well as the passing of time. Therefore, it invariably will fall prey to sickness and death.

Even though eminently a physical practice, haṭhayoga does not deny the relevance of a particular knowledge that supports this practice. Moreover, what this practice considers fundamental is the acquisition of immortality and the development of supernatural capacities. Most of haṭhayoga's techniques are explicitly directed at controlling different energetic currents and liquids, such as thoughts, sexual fluids, and the inner serpentine energy known as *kuṇḍalinī*. This control is believed to ignite the alchemical transformation of the yogic body.

In this sense, the fourteenth-century *Yogabīja* speaks of a transformative process brought about by the "fire of yoga" (*yogāgni*). People are divided into two groups: uncooked (*apakva*) and cooked (*paripakva*). This imagery suggests that the body can be metaphorically cooked and prepared by the fire of yogic practice. The "uncooked" ones are subject to decay, whereas the bodies that have undergone the mystical cooking through yogāgni become immutable and immortal. As a flame of sorts, the yogāgni is kindled by some techniques of breath control (*prāṇāyāma*), in the same way that wind is used to start a bonfire and increase or maintain the flames. This inner heat "cooks" the body not only in a metaphorical sense; in a literal sense, ascetic practice, or *tapas*, generates bodily heat, here understood as a "yogic temperature," as it were, that transforms the body into a much better equipped vessel to tread on the higher steps in the path of yoga *sādhanā*.

Thus, sources such as the *Amaraughaprabodha* and the *Śivasaṃhitā* classify *sādhakas*, or practitioners, into four groups, depending on their skills and their training: *mṛdu* (soft), *madhya* (intermediate), *adhimātra* (outstanding), and *adhimātratara* (excellent). A specific yogic method is accorded to each of these sādhakas, respectively: *mantrayoga*, *layayoga*, *haṭhayoga*, and *amaraugha/rājayoga*. In the end, the goal is to end suffering due to bodily afflictions. According to texts such as the *Yogabīja*, ordinary people (the "uncooked") are constantly defeated by both the sensory and the physical realms. The true yogis (the "well cooked"), on the other hand, can defeat the body by overcoming its natural limitations. Their body becomes a "yogic body" (*yogadeha*), which is like an incorruptible diamond full of perfections (siddhis). In this sense, a yogi's body becomes *śaktimān*, "endowed with power or energy."

Perhaps in the light of modern postural practice, it is worth considering that haṭhayoga has probably been one of the most successful yogic trends in the last five hundred years, gaining a very strong renaissance in the first decades of the twentieth century. In part, some issues that were important in the classic treatises of haṭhayoga are still of primary concern for modern practices, despite some important differences in both worldview and expectations, as well as innovations. Unlike other yogic schools, haṭhayoga has always emphasized bodily functioning and a progressive perfectioning of its potentialities.

One final consideration should be made. Since yogis (and sometimes also other sorts of ascetics) have overcome human limitations, especially those of sickness and death, their bodies are not cremated after their demise. Indeed, it is understood that there is no actual demise; in other words, whereas the physical body expires, the yogic body (the true self) does not and cannot die. In consequence, instead of cremating the body, as is standard Hindu practice, the yogis' bodies are buried. This is ideally done in *padmāsana*, or lotus posture, indicating that the yogis are not literally dead but immersed in deep meditation, a temporary, however long, trance. As a matter of fact, yogis' burial mounds are usually known as *samādhis*, indicating their achievement of the highest level in the yogic path. To be in continuous samādhi would mean to be installed in total and eternal enlightenment, a state where all physical limitations have been transcended.

About the author

Adrián Muñoz is faculty member at the Centre for Asian and African Studies, El Colegio de México. His main areas of research are premodern religious movements and yogic hagiography and literature. He is currently leading a collective project on the history and practice of yoga in Latin America. Among other titles, he has coauthored *Historia mínima del yoga* (El Colegio de México, 2019) and coedited *Yogi Heroes and Poets: Histories* *and Legends of the Nāths* (State University of New York Press, 2011). He has also contributed to *The Routledge Handbook of Yoga and Meditation Studies* (Routledge, 2021) and *The Routledge Handbook of South Asian Religions* (Routledge, 2021).

Suggestions for further reading

In this book

See also chapters 20 (Is yoga safe?) and 22 (Why do yogis contort their bodies?).

Elsewhere

Bevilacqua, Daniela, and Eloisa Stuparich, eds. *The Power of the Nāth Yogīs: Yogic Charisma, Political Influence and Social Authority*. Amsterdam University Press, 2022.

Jacobsen, Knut A., ed. *Yoga Powers: Extraordinary Capacities Attained Through Meditation and Concentration*. Brill's Indological Library, vol. 37. Brill, 2012.

White, David Gordon. *The Alchemical Body: Siddha Traditions in Medieval India*. University of Chicago Press, 1996.

14
Are ethics important in yoga?

Jens U. Augspurger

Understanding the role of ethics in yoga necessitates examining the codified ethical principles in teachings and scriptures, as well as the actual enactment of ethics. As my own research is profoundly rooted in ethnographic approaches to the field, I gather my insights through observations made in interviews and field visits with practitioners of contemporary yoga. I do not work with a philological approach, and my access to scripture is through what my interlocutors encounter, prioritize, understand, and then report back. It should, therefore, be noted that other methodological approaches will likely produce different insights.

For the first part of this question, I consider scriptural references to ethics in yoga that are important to practitioners of modern transnational yoga. The reference most frequently drawn on is the *Pātañjalayogaśāstra*. This consists of nearly two hundred aphorisms (*sūtras*) on yoga, the eightfold path to liberation (also called *aṣṭāṅga*). Scholars and yoga communities hold diverse opinions on the date when these sūtras were compiled, ranging from the second century BCE to the fourth century CE. More recent and critical editions lean toward a later date. Philipp Maas, who has conducted a critical edition of the first chapter, argues that the earliest eligible date is in the fourth century BCE, but definitive proof would be difficult to produce. There is also little known about the historical figure of Patañjali, said to be the author of these sūtras; indeed, some scholars are uncertain whether he actually existed or is a mythical placeholder for one or more actual authors.

The sūtras describe eight limbs that lead to liberation: *yama* (restraint), *niyama* (observances), *āsana* (postures), *prāṇāyāma* (control of breath), *pratyāhāra* (restraint of senses), *dhāraṇā* (concentration), *dhyāna* (meditation), and *samādhi* (liberation). The first two limbs, yama and niyama, are often referred to as the ethical tenets of yoga philosophy. Meanwhile, āsana and prāṇāyāma are the most popular practices in contemporary styles of yoga and are the roots of the body-oriented practice of Hatha Yoga.

There are five yamas that prescribe patterns of behavior toward others: *ahiṃsā* (nonviolence), *satya* (truthfulness), *asteya* (not stealing), *brahmacarya* (celibacy, chastity, or sexual continence), and *aparigraha* (nonpossessiveness). The five niyamas are commands and consist of *śauca* (purity or cleanliness, usually referring to body, mind, and speech), *saṃtoṣa* (contentment), *tapas* (austerities and self-discipline), *svādhyāya* (self-reflection and introspection), and *īśvarapraṇidhāna* (contemplation of the divine).

The *Pātañjalayogaśāstra* outlines an approach to yoga that goes beyond the purely physical. The eight limbs it presents are considered an essential part of yoga philosophy and ethics in many modern yoga traditions. As the eight limbs are often understood to be practiced step by step, the first two limbs, yama and niyama, are sometimes referred to as an ethical foundation and prerequisite for (successful) yoga practice. The sūtras are also often included as a philosophy unit in many yoga teacher-training programs and are suggested under the two-hundred-hour standard by Yoga Alliance. These Yoga Alliance two-hundred-hour credentials are widely considered an industry-standard framework for entry-level yoga teacher-training courses. Many prominent yoga teaching organizations also base their professional codes of conduct on Patañjali's yamas and niyamas.

The strong focus many yoga schools place on the *Pātañjalayogaśāstra*'s understanding of ethics does present some issues. Firstly, the text is presented as an eternal authority on yoga philosophy, but its importance might be a relatively recent development. David Gordon White argues that the text experienced a resurgence in popularity when it was used by Swami Vivekananda and the Theosophical Society during the late nineteenth and early twentieth centuries, after receiving little attention throughout the earlier history of yoga. If the sūtras were indeed rather unimportant in the past, this would call into question the dominant narrative in modern yoga that they describe a centuries-old and proven practice passed down by great yogis, a narrative that has also earned Patañjali the reputation as being a "father of yoga."

If the historical relevance of the ethical principles in the sūtras remains unclear, additionally, their practicability in modern and/or secular approaches to yoga is also uncertain. The sūtras are not only difficult to interpret, but their *do's* and *don'ts* also carry religious and cultural connotations and were written for a very different context. Many yoga schools, for instance, promote vegetarianism or veganism based on ahiṃsā (nonviolence), but this is an interpretation likely adopted from South Asian religious traditions, both historical, such as Buddhism, and contemporary, such as Jainism or certain strands of Hinduism. In some contexts of modern yoga, Patañjali's suggestions are interpreted in a more universal way. *Īśvarapraṇidhāna*, essentially devotion to the divine, may be adjusted to suggest surrender to one's higher self or simply being conscious that there is a higher cause or power. Another yama that also sparks much debate in contemporary yoga is brahmacarya, which is traditionally understood to constitute celibacy. While this is prescribed in monastic or religious yoga traditions, it often conflicts with the lives of modern practitioners, who are, in the majority, householders, not renunciates. Newer reinterpretations of brahmacarya might transform this to mean the avoidance of sexual misconduct or the responsible and self-restrained use of sexual energy.

While the yamas and niyamas do provide some starting points for a modernized and relevant discussion of ethics in yoga, they also raise the question of whether a discussion based on the sūtras is sufficient to produce a code of conduct that is fit for modern life, does not reproduce religious conservatism, and is in line with social and legal standards. In some cases, an overemphasis on yoga's own philosophy has hindered outside accountability in addressing instances of abuse. During modern yoga's shocking abuse history, requirements like celibacy have often been blamed for abusive actions by renunciate gurus, rather than addressing the complex and violent power dynamics and patriarchal structures that have enabled and condoned abuse over decades.

The major challenge for ethical conduct in modern yoga is, therefore, structural. There are currently few to no mechanisms in place for enforcing ethical principles among teachers, let alone students, of modern yoga. Yoga teaching organizations that have set up guidelines for ethical principles have little power to enforce them or to investigate and discipline any violations. Those that are membership associations such as Yoga Alliance can expel members or withdraw their credentials, but they are limited in their ability to effectively prevent harm, halt an individual's teaching, or hold individuals and organizations accountable in what remains a highly unregulated and unorganized industry. Often, victims of abuse are members of marginalized and underserved populations or are foreigners in the place where the abuse took place (often at training or retreat centers abroad). This leaves them at an even greater disadvantage in accessing proper recourse and exacerbates the impact of the abuse on their lives.

The lack of enforceable ethical standards in the yoga teaching profession poses an ongoing risk that can potentially harm the integrity of the entire industry and practice, put individuals into dangerous situations, and erode trust between teachers and students more generally. Establishing ethical principles that are enforceable and applicable to all would be crucial in addressing these risks. This may require the establishment of reliable governing bodies or at the very least general agreement on best practices to regulate teacher-student relationships, which are highly vulnerable to all kinds of physical, emotional, and psychological transgressions.

About the author

Jens U. Augspurger is a PhD candidate in the Department of Religions and Philosophies at SOAS University of London. His research and teaching focus on modern transnational yoga and spiritual movements, as well as their respective intersections with politics. He is also a recovering yoga teacher and the cofounder of Project SATYA, a community movement that supports survivors of sexualized violence and advocates for accountability and truth in the yoga industry. Considering spiritual tourism as a journey for self-discovery, his ethnographic dissertation project explores yoga tourism in India and the complex relationships the yoga tourist builds while journeying (toward) the destination.

Suggestions for further reading

In this book

See also chapters 16 (What are the *yamas* and *niyamas*?) and 45 (Who was Patañjali?).

Elsewhere

Maas, Phillip André. *Samādhipāda: Das erste Kapitel des Pātañjalayogaśāstra zum ersten Mal kritisch ediert*. Shaker, 2006.

Remski, Matthew. *Practice and All Is Coming: Abuse, Cult Dynamics, and Healing in Yoga and Beyond*. Embodied Wisdom, 2019.

White, David Gordon. *The Yoga Sutra of Patanjali: A Biography*. Princeton University Press, 2019.

15
Are all yogis nonviolent?

Matylda Ciołkosz

It is nowadays common to associate yoga practice with nonviolence. This association is a result of the popularity among modern yoga practitioners of the yoga teachings of Patañjali, together with their system of social ethics. This system encompasses five *yamas* (social observances), with *ahiṃsā* (nonviolence) followed by *satya* (truthfulness), *asteya* (nonstealing), *brahmacarya* (continence), and *aparigraha* (renouncing possession). Ahiṃsā receives substantial treatment in Patañjali's work, the *Pātañjalayogaśāstra*. In modernity, it was brought to light as a fundamental yogic virtue by Mohandas Gandhi, who expressed the notion of nonviolence in his peaceful, passive approach to public protests. However, as different examples show, nonviolence has not always been inherent in the understanding and application of yoga.

The five ethical principles listed as yamas by Patañjali are also known as the five great vows in Jainism. In fact, they seem more fundamental for Jainism than for Brahmanism, within which Patañjali's yoga system was developed. In other Brahmanical texts that take up the concept of yoga, the virtue of nonviolence is not always relevant. In the *Mahābhārata*—the Sanskrit epic weaving the discussion of social ethics into a tale of a great battle between two kindred clans—different understandings of yoga are used to support the ideal of a skilled and righteous warrior. In the twelfth book of the epic, yogic powers are construed in terms of strength that allows for such feats as entering into the bodies of others, withstanding the power of angry gods, or even multiplying oneself. These feats can make one a better warrior—not through nonviolence but through making violence more efficient.

The *Bhagavadgītā*—a part of the sixth book of the *Mahābhārata*—goes a step further by introducing a definition of "yoga" that makes killing and maiming ethical under some circumstances. According to the rules of *karmayoga*—the yoga of action—an ethical attitude is the performance of the duties determined by one's social position in a disciplined, detached way, without desiring their fruits. A warrior applying himself to karmayoga does not refrain from violence but performs necessary violent acts with dedication, detachment, and resolve. While yoga as a nonviolent renunciate practice is also discussed in the *Mahābhārata*, the concept of karmayoga was a way to legitimize the Brahmanical social order, in which priests were expected to perform rituals, warriors to fight and conquer, peasants to work the soil, and servants to serve others.

Although the *Mahābhārata* presented a mythologized social ideal, yogic warriors indeed emerged in India over a millennium after the epic's completion. They did so, however, in a renunciate milieu. Sometime between the sixteenth and the seventeenth centuries, in response to various political factors, orders of fighting ascetics started to emerge. Ascetic discipline, group organization, and stamina acquired through practices of mental and bodily control made it easy to turn groups of renouncers into military units. The *nāgas*—yogic mercenaries—were employed by local North Indian regents to violently advance their political goals. At one point, they were also hired to fight the British. They were considered skilled and dangerous warriors, especially efficient in guerrilla operations. When ultimately banned at the end of the eighteenth century, some of them turned into wandering bandits.

Today, the image of yoga as an ancient technique for achieving peace, health, and equipoise prevails. However, this image sometimes belies forms of systemic violence. In India, the current authorities—nationalist, promoting Hindu supremacy, and implicated in acts of violence against religious minorities—use yoga as a soft power to advance an ideological agenda. In the milieus of yoga practitioners across the globe, violence is sometimes disguised as nurture and concern for human well-being.

In the wake of the #MeToo movement, a discussion about cases of sexual abuse was taken up within modern yoga milieus. Attention was drawn to forms of violence institutionalized within yoga practice. On the one hand, power relations within modern yoga lineages were brought to light, in which the authority of instructors or gurus and the vulnerability of practitioners could facilitate violent treatment of the latter by the former. On the other hand, the acceptance of physical proximity, often involving crossing the practitioners' intimate boundaries, was seen as a potential gateway to acts of violence.

In the case of modern postural yoga, potentially violent behavior was associated with the practice of manual adjustments. Across many systems of postural practice, it had been commonly accepted that an instructor may—or in fact should—correct the practitioners' *āsanas* by touching and moving their body parts. It had been assumed that practitioners consented to such treatment implicitly simply by joining a yoga class. Tales of instructors slapping, prodding, or forcefully pushing or pulling practitioners' body parts while vigorously shouting at them became a part of modern postural yoga folklore. They were also often interpreted as signs of the instructors' care and dedication to the practitioners' progress and well-being. B. K. S. Iyengar, one of the most influential figures of modern postural yoga, admits in his book *Light on the Yoga Sūtra of Patañjali* (p. 329) to being "intense, and . . . in the past even harsh" toward his students to keep them engaged in the practice or to give them "one and a half hours of present life in a lesson." In other words, acts of violence had been considered acts of "tough love" performed for the practitioners' good.

Interestingly, a gateway to thinking about yoga practice in terms of (self-inflicted) violence is present in the idea of ascetic renunciation that largely contributed to the development of yoga. The term *tapas* (Sanskrit term for ascetic practices) means "heat," as it is associated with the transformative (i.e., both destructive and creative) nature of fire. Austerities such as fasting, remaining in uncomfortable positions, or enduring extreme heat were seen as ways to burn away *karma*, thus allowing for liberation. The idea of hardship as part and parcel of transformative practice resounds in *haṭhayoga*, with the term *haṭha* meaning "force." Haṭha practices—including the control of breath and posture to induce extreme changes within the body—were meant to produce the desired effects in a forceful manner. This association of yoga and tapas with discomfort forced upon oneself was carried into some strands of modern yoga. The exhausting, pain-inducing practice of physically challenging āsanas—sometimes in very high ambient temperatures—became a trademark of some lineages of postural yoga.

Drawing attention to forms of violence in modern yoga led many to reconsider the principle of nonviolence. Asking for practitioners' consent to be touched has become normalized. Forms of gentle, noninvasive tactile adjustments have been proposed. Systems of post-lineage yoga practice have emerged that took as their principle an empathetic acceptance of practitioners' autonomy—including their physical and mental boundaries. Time will tell if ahiṃsā as part of yoga will remain a theoretical ideal or a lived and shared practice.

About the author

Matylda Ciołkosz is an assistant professor at the Institute of Religious Studies, Jagiellonian University in Kraków. She earned her PhD in culture and religion studies in 2019 for her research on the meaning-making role of kinesthetic experience in the practice of modern postural yoga. In her research, she draws from cognitive approaches to the study of religions to explore the influence of sensory, motor, and social contexts on the formation and application of religious concepts.

Suggestions for further reading

In this book

See also chapters 17 (Does a yogi need to renounce the world?) and 59 (What is the relationship between race and yoga?).

Elsewhere

Clark, Matthew. *Daśanāmī Saṃnyāsīs: The Integration of Ascetic Lineages into an Order*. Brill, 2006.

Khedar, Anusha. "Choreographing Tolerance: Narendra Modi, Hindu Nationalism, and International Yoga Day." *Race & Yoga* 5. no. 1 (2020): 42–59.

Lucia, Amanda. "Guru Sex: Charisma, Proxemic Desire, and the Haptic Logics of the Guru-Disciple Relationship." *Journal of the American Academy of Religion* 86, no. 4 (2018): 953–988.

Malinar, Angelika. "Yoga Practices in the *Bhagavadgītā*." In *Yoga in Practice*, edited by David G. White. Princeton University Press, 2012.

16
What are the *yamas* and *niyamas*?

Graham Burns

Put simply, *yamas* and *niyamas* are sets of ethical principles with which the yogi is expected to comply. The Sanskrit word *yama* is perhaps most accurately translated as "restraint" and, in general, indicates patterns of behavior toward others; *niyama*, perhaps best translated as "observance," signifies more personal behavioral requirements. Compliance with these principles is thought to help the yogi develop the single-pointed awareness and internal power needed to travel the yogic path.

Indian society has always placed a high premium on specific behavioral precepts—texts such as the *Dharmasūtras* and *Dharmaśāstras* in the late BCE / early CE contained detailed codes of conduct (and sanctions for breach) for all in the higher levels of society, with the specific requirements for the individual determined by their social status, stage of life, and gender. Religious traditions such as Buddhism and Jainism, both of which developed in India in the last few centuries BCE, also emphasized ethical behavior. The great epic the *Mahābhārata* specifically prescribes modes of behavior for yoga practitioners, some of which are said to remove the "five problems," or obstructions on the path of yoga—namely, lust, anger, greed, fear, and sleep.

The best-known yamas and niyamas are the sets of five of each contained in the *Pātañjalayogaśāstra* (the *Yogasūtra* and the so-called Vyāsa commentary, now widely considered to be a single composition from around the fourth century CE). Here, the yamas and niyamas are, respectively, the first two components of the *aṣṭāṅgayoga* path of eight "limbs," or "auxiliaries," which appears in *sūtras* 2.28 to 3.4. Lists of five are common in early Indian texts, probably for mnemonic purposes; in the *Pātañjalayogaśāstra*, the five yamas are *ahiṃsā* (nonharming), *satya* (truthfulness), *asteya* (not stealing), *brahmacarya* (variously translated as "celibacy" or "continence"), and *aparigraha* (not coveting, absence of greed). The five niyamas are *śauca* (cleanliness), *saṃtoṣa* (contentment), *tapas* (austerity), *svādhyāya* (self-study), and *īśvarapraṇidhāna* (devotion to "the Lord"). It is worth noting that the final three niyamas also form the three components of *kriyāyoga*, according to sūtra 2.1, sometimes considered an alternative path to the aṣṭāṅgayoga path.

Edwin Bryant has noted that "in traditional methods of scriptural interpretation, introductory . . . statements carry more weight," which he suggests indicates the importance of both the yamas and niyamas in the aṣṭāṅgayoga path and the preeminence of ahiṃsā among the yamas themselves (2009, 243). This is borne out, first, by sūtra 2.31, which describes the yamas as the *mahāvrata*, or "great vow," of universal application to all, irrespective of class, place, time, or circumstance, and, secondly, by the fact that, while Patañjali devotes minimal space to explanations of later elements of the aṣṭāṅgayoga path—such as *āsana* (posture) and *prāṇāyāma* (breath control)—each of the yamas and niyamas receives a sūtra to itself explaining the perceived results of the behavior in question.

While the yamas and niyamas may, at first glance, seem straightforward, the precise extent of their requirements has been the subject of much commentary and debate over many centuries. Obvious questions are, How absolute are they, and what happens if they conflict? Here, perhaps the most often quoted example is, What should the yogi do if speaking the truth (satya) causes harm and thereby contravenes ahiṃsā? The commentary to sūtra 2.30 helps us here by making clear that ahiṃsā does indeed trump everything—the yogi should "abstain from injuring any being, at any time and in any manner"; and while the yogi's speech should "correspond to fact," words should not be uttered "for inflicting harm" on others. This is, however, perhaps not a complete answer: Does it extend as far as enjoining the yogi to lie in certain circumstances?

Equally, even allowing for the primacy of ahiṃsā, can the requirement of nonharming realistically be as absolute as the commentary suggests? Can one ever truly act with complete ahiṃsā if one is operating in the world? Commentators have rightly noted that, even for an ascetic, it is nigh on impossible to avoid, for example, treading on insects in everyday life. Here, perhaps, motivation plays a part, for it is also clear (especially in the commentary's discussion of asteya and aparigraha) that the yamas apply at the mental level as well as the physical—it is just as much asteya to think about stealing something as it is actually to carry out the act of theft.

A similar question arises in respect to brahmacarya. Does this require the yogi to be completely celibate?—a somewhat unpalatable idea for many contemporary practitioners. The commentarial part of the *Pātañjalayogaśāstra* describes brahmacarya as "suppression of the urge of the sexual organs," as well as of all other organs that might increase sexual desire, and on a strict interpretation, it does seem that Patañjali is advocating full celibacy. However, adopting a more practical (and perhaps self-serving) view, several more recent commentators have suggested that brahmacarya does not extend to sexual activity within an established relationship, such as marriage, and only enjoins sexual control, rather than absolute chastity. However, as it is a common idea in yoga that the preservation of semen increases power and vitality (the stated result of brahmacarya), this interpretation—attractive though it may seem—may be questionable.

When we turn to the niyamas, it is notable that the first (and hence, perhaps, most important) of the five is śauca, cleanliness. While this may seem an obvious hygiene-related injunction (and, as a result, is often paid little attention), in *sūtras* 2.40 and 2.41, Patañjali explains that practicing śauca leads the yogi to an aversion not only to their own body, with all its imperfections and uncleanliness, but also to the bodies of others, in turn leading to the purification of the mind and subjugation of the senses and, implicitly, perhaps, removing any sexual desire.

The final two niyamas, svādhyāya (self-study) and īśvarapraṇidhāna (devotion to "the Lord"), also merit comment. For, while svādhyāya translates literally as "self-study," the commentary to sūtra 2.32 (where the five niyamas are listed) explains that svādhyāya specifically includes the study of scriptures relating to liberation (which focus on studying the nature of the self) and repetition of the syllable *OṂ*. This, in turn, enables the yogi to establish a connection with their chosen deity (sūtra 2.44) and, perhaps, move naturally into īśvarapraṇidhāna, a surrender to the divine that leads (apparently without bothering with the intervening components of the aṣṭāṅgayoga path) to the very final component, *samādhi*. This perhaps introduces a more devotional element to Patañjali's system than is often thought.

In yoga traditions later than Patañjali's, the number of yamas and niyamas expands, frequently to ten of each, as, for example, in the circa twelfth-century *Śāradātilaka* and some later recensions of the *Haṭhapradīpikā*. These generally incorporate the two sets of five from the *Pātañjalayogaśāstra* but add others, such as charity and moderation in diet. Additionally, in some traditions, notably those of tantric yoga, required codes of behavior were often separated from teachings on yoga, perhaps as part of the initiation process into the relevant lineage, but were nevertheless also expected of the yogi.

While the yamas and niyamas are often glossed over in contemporary yoga, with its frequent emphasis on the practicalities of āsana and prāṇāyāma, or presented as obvious and rather trite behavioral injunctions, it will be seen that they do in fact raise complex and often subtle questions about how the yogi should act in the world—both in their relationships with others and with themselves—if they are to progress along the path of yoga.

About the author

Graham Burns is an independent yoga teacher, teacher trainer, and scholar. As well as a law degree from Durham University, he holds an MA in religions and a PhD in ancient Indian philosophy from SOAS University of London. He is a former senior teaching fellow at SOAS, where he lectured on the MA in traditions of yoga and meditation and taught undergraduate Hinduism and philosophy. He is a member of the SOAS Centre of Yoga Studies.

Suggestions for further reading

In this book

See also chapters 14 (Are ethics important in yoga?) and 45 (Who was Patañjali?).

Elsewhere

Bryant, Edwin F. *The Yoga Sūtras of Patañjali*. North Point, 2009.

Hariharānanda Āraṇya, Swāmi. *Yoga Philosophy of Patañjali*. Translated by P. N. Mukerji. Rev. ed. State University of New York Press, 1983.

17

Does a yogi need to renounce the world?

Daniela Bevilacqua

If we consider yoga to be a method of ending the cycle of *saṃsāra* (wheel of life) and thus the process of reincarnation, the early practitioners of yoga must be contextualized within the framework of Upaniṣadic literature. It was in fact in the Upaniṣads that the relationship between the soul (*ātman*) and the ultimate reality (*brahman*) was questioned. New ideas of *karma*, rebirth, and transmigration were introduced, as well as a new life goal: the release from rebirth. The individual was imagined to be trapped in saṃsāra by the continuous alternance of birth and death, thus stuck in a continuous state of suffering. Since the cause of rebirth was recognized to be desire and ignorance, knowledge became the source of liberation (*mokṣa* or *nirvāṇa*). This knowledge was to be the result of the effective elimination of ignorance. But it was recognized that to eliminate ignorance, it was necessary to first remove desire, and this could be achieved by renouncing worldly gains. It was this need to detach oneself from the *saṃsāric* world in order to reach spiritual goals that led to the proliferation of ascetic groups, the choice of the ascetic life, and consequently the renunciation of the world. Some ascetics lived in forest hermitages, others were celibate, and among them, some lived in the wilderness, while others lived near towns and villages where they begged for food. The Upaniṣadic practitioner of yoga renounces the Brahmanical world—its rituals, *saṃskāras*, and so on—and renounces attachments, desires, and sensorial pleasure.

This framework should be our starting point for addressing the question of whether, therefore, a yogi should renounce the world. The answer is not as obvious as it seems because, over centuries, having been adopted in very different contexts, yoga has undergone many developments and adaptations.

Looking at the textual sources from the past that deal with yoga and then with *haṭhayoga*, it seems that the practitioner par excellence is still the renouncer, the ascetic who isolates himself in order to achieve his goal, to accomplish his practice. As Svātmārāma in the fifteenth century states in his *Haṭhapradīpikā* (4.11), "*Samādhi* appears automatically in the yogi whose *śakti* is awake and who has abandoned all actions." Similar methods of yoga for soteriological purposes, as well as for *siddhis* (extraordinary powers) and immortality, have been pursued by various groups of ascetics at different times in history. The idea of "renunciation" can, however, be understood in some traditions to be temporary: The yogi who has attained the ultimate reality can live in society without being affected by it. Therefore, it seems that a truly perfected yogi, who has overcome duality, instead of renouncing the world, can actually be in it because he is no longer affected by attachments, or bad and good karma. He is indeed a *jīvanmukta*, one who has freed himself while alive.

Since there were different yogic traditions and therefore different typologies of yogis and yogic goals, their relationship to renunciation was also different. In fact, not all yogic traditions were ascetic, although they still belonged to esoteric and initiatory contexts: Practitioners of some tantric paths who aimed at siddhis and immortality did not necessarily have to renounce the world. To give just one example, recent studies on the Śivadharma corpus—a collection of eight texts preserved in several Nepalese palm-leaf manuscripts from the eleventh and twelfth centuries—show evidence of a yoga based on meditative practices for laypeople, in contrast to initiatory Śaivism. The goals of this yoga were also supernatural powers or liberation.

In the last century, new forms of yoga have developed that have led to new representations and roles for the yogi. Since then, women's participation in the practice probably exceeds that of men, who were the main protagonists, authors, and recipients of yoga in premodern textual sources. The modern practitioner and thus the modern yogi and yogini fits into the path of a modern yoga that is taught and experienced in very different contexts, often collective settings, and for a variety of spiritual and secular purposes. The practice of modern yoga leads to modern aims as well. Modern yoga has added pragmatic goals—such as self-development, strength, flexibility, and stress reduction—that are perfectly understandable considering the needs of people today. These modern goals are also related to the spread and expansion of yoga beyond ascetic, religious, and initiatory contexts to embrace a more diverse range of practitioners.

We could therefore conclude by saying that, depending on the typology of yoga, the context in which it is practiced, and the goals of the particular practice, practitioners may or may not need to renounce the world.

About the author

Daniela Bevilacqua is an Indianist specialized in Hindu asceticism, investigated through an ethnographic and historical perspective. She received her PhD in civilizations of Africa and Asia from Sapienza University of Rome and in anthropology from the University of Paris Nanterre. She worked as a postdoc research fellow at SOAS for the ERC-funded Haṭha Yoga Project (2015–2020). She is currently a researcher at CRIA (ISCTE-IUL) in Lisbon. She has authored *Modern Hindu Traditionalism in Contemporary India* (Routledge, 2018) and *From Tapas to Modern Yoga: Sādhus' Understanding of Embodied Practices* (Equinox Publishing Ltd., 2024), edited volumes, and written several articles and book chapters on topics related to Hindu religious tradition, gender, and embodied practices.

Suggestions for further reading

In this book

See also chapters 11 (What are the goals of yoga?) and 26 (What life does the ideal yogi lead?).

Elsewhere

Burchett, Patton E. *A Genealogy of Devotion: Bhakti, Tantra, Yoga, and Sufism in North India.* Columbia University Press, 2019.

De Michelis, Elizabeth. *A History of Modern Yoga: Patañjali and Western Esotericism.* Continuum, 2004.

Olivelle, Patrick. *Ascetics and Brahmins: Studies in Ideologies and Institutions.* Anthem, 2011.

Singleton, Mark. *Yoga Body.* Oxford University Press, 2010.

18

What is *samādhi*?

Brett W. Parris

There is an old black-and-white photograph of the Hindu mystic Sri Ramakrishna Paramahamsa (1836–1886) standing with his arms outstretched, supported by a devotee, his eyes half closed as if in a trance, with an expression of contented bliss on his face. In some versions, the caption reads "Sri Ramakrishna in *samādhi*." Clearly, the state of *samādhi* was something desirable, perhaps only attained by the greatest mystics. But what exactly is it?

As with so much else in traditional yoga(s), there is no clear consensus as to what samādhi actually refers to, though it is generally described either as an advanced stage or state of meditative practice or as a summary of the yoga path as a whole in terms of its goal.

In the *Yogasūtra* (YS) of Patañjali, samādhi is the last of the eight limbs listed in sūtra 2.29 and is said to be a refinement of meditation to the point where the essential formless nature of an object shines forth, unobscured by random fluctuating thoughts (YS 3.3). The last three limbs, which also include fixation (*dhāraṇā*) and meditation (*dhyāna*), form a group of "inner limbs" (*antaraṅga*) known as *saṃyama*. The commentary by "Vyāsa," the *Vyāsabhāṣya* or *Yogabhāṣya*, on the first verse of the *sūtras* equates yoga itself with samādhi. Many scholars now believe "Vyāsa" was in fact "Patañjali," the author or compiler of the YS, and that the original combined text, the *Pātañjalayogaśāstra* was only separated into the *sūtras* and the commentary and attributed to different authors at a later date. If that is the case, this earliest auto-commentary on the YS should be given more weight in terms of the author's intentions than commentaries written in later centuries. On this view, we should see samādhi not merely as the last of the eight limbs, the final stage of yoga, but as the very meaning of yoga itself, which Patañjali defines in YS 1.2 as *yogaś cittavṛttinirodhaḥ*—"yoga is the restriction [or suppression] of the fluctuations of consciousness." The primary meaning of samādhi, then, would be this state of the restriction of the fluctuations of the mind.

Along with the restrictive (*nirodha*) goal of yoga, which Stuart Ray Sarbacker calls "cessative" in his book *Samādhi*, another important aspect of samādhi is *samāpatti* (coalescence, attainment), which appears in YS 1.41–42 and in some texts is also equated with samādhi. Sarbacker describes samāpatti as the "numinous," experiential aspect of samādhi that characterizes the clear insight necessary for the attainment of the ultimate goal of suppressing the fluctuations of the mind: "The numinous aspect of *samādhi* is tied to notions of attainment that are associated with the development of special powers of action and perception coexisting with cosmological conceptions of deity. The cessative aspect represents the drive toward detachment and release from the cosmological schema altogether" (2005, 128–129).

The YS later distinguishes two types of samādhi: samādhi with cognition (*saṃprajñāta samādhi*) in YS 1.17 and samādhi without cognition (*asaṃprajñāta samādhi*) in YS 1.18. Samādhi with cognition is still associated with mental activity and so continues to generate karmic traces—and is also described as being "with seed" (*sabīja*; YS 1.46). Samādhi without cognition, conversely, is not associated with ongoing mental fluctuations and so, because it no longer generates karmic traces, is described as being "without seed" (*nirbīja*; YS 1.51). This latter form of samādhi is the attainment of the goal of yoga described in YS 1.2, the restriction of the fluctuations of consciousness.

In their outstanding anthology of yogic texts, *Roots of Yoga*, James Mallinson and Mark Singleton note a number of other quite different understandings of samādhi. In texts influenced by Vedāntic thought, particularly Advaita (non-dual) Vedānta, samādhi is thought of more in terms of the state of the merger or recognition of one's identity with *brahman*, the ultimate reality, rather than the complete separation (*kaivalya*) between primordial spirit (*puruṣa*) and matter (*prakṛti*) that characterizes Patañjali's vision. In tantric Śaiva texts, samādhi tends to be viewed still as a preliminary state prior to ultimate liberation (*mukti*, *mokṣa*) where the most advanced practitioner might aspire to become a *jīvanmukta*—one liberated while still alive.

In later *haṭhayoga* texts, samādhi is sometimes described in terms of a trancelike state in which the yogi is completely impervious to external stimuli. This seems to be the meaning of samādhi implied by the caption to the photo of Sri Ramakrishna I mentioned above. There have been far more striking examples, however. Mallinson and Singleton quote Sir Claude Wade's eyewitness account of the yogi Hari Dās, who, in 1837, was locked in a sealed wooden box, under guard, in a garden in Lahore for forty days, before being slowly revived. After half an hour, in a barely audible voice, Dās asked, "Do you believe me now?" Wade recounts that they left "convinced there had been no fraud or collusion in the exhibition [they] had witnessed" (2017, 345).

Some haṭhayoga texts equate samādhi with dissolution (*laya*) and with "royal yoga" (*rājayoga*). Mallinson and Singleton quote the eighteenth-century *Gheraṇḍasaṃhitā* as listing six different kinds of samādhi, which it designates the "sixfold *rājayoga*." As expected, meditation (dhyāna) is one of the six, but the remaining five are surprisingly diverse, including "sound (*nāda*), bliss in taste (*rasānanda*), success in dissolution (*layasiddhi*), devotion (*bhakti*) and stupefaction of the mind (*manomūrcchā*)" (2017, 328).

Another use of samādhi found in some traditions is the use of the term *mahāsamādhi* (great or final samādhi) to mean death—particularly if undertaken consciously and intentionally, once the aged yogi feels it is time to give up their body. This intentional ejection of consciousness from the material body is a very advanced practice, also called *utkrānti*, or "yogic suicide" (e.g., YS 3.39), though that translation risks evoking misleading associations with depression and despair that are not intended.

We have seen that *samādhi* is a term that has a wide range of meanings and nuances in different traditions. The word *samādhi* may be used to describe a particularly advanced meditative stage, a trancelike state, a precursor to liberation, or perhaps even the sum and goal of the whole tradition.

About the author

Brett W. Parris is a DPhil candidate in the Faculty of Theology and Religion at the University of Oxford. He has an MPhil in Classical Indian Religion from Oxford, as well as a PhD in development economics from Monash University in Melbourne. He worked for NGOs focused on poverty, human rights, and climate change for many years. His current research focuses on the ethical dimensions of yogic philosophy and practice and broader interreligious dialogue. He has taught yoga in both Australia and the UK.

Suggestions for further reading

In this book

See also chapters 33 (Why do yogis meditate?) and 45 (Who was Patañjali?).

Elsewhere

Mallinson, James, and Mark Singleton. "*Samādhi*." In *Roots of Yoga*, edited by James Mallinson and Mark Singleton. Penguin Books, 2017.

Sarbacker, Stuart Ray. *Samādhi: The Numinous and Cessative in Indo-Tibetan Yoga*. State University of New York Press, 2005.

19

Does yoga give you extraordinary powers?

Lubomír Ondračka

Absolutely, and not only that, but extraordinary abilities are in fact one of the most important characteristics of premodern yoga. When we look at the different yogic traditions that have been present in South Asia at various times and in various regions and religious milieus, we predictably notice a tremendous diversity. This diversity is so great that it is often difficult to say what all these yoga lineages have in common and whether there is any shared characteristic at all. Extraordinary powers are the best candidate for such a common denominator because they are present, albeit to varying degrees, in the vast majority of yoga traditions.

On the other hand, extraordinary abilities are not a distinctive feature of yoga, as they are a widespread phenomenon in South Asia, present well outside the yoga environment. This means that yoga practice is not the only way to acquire these powers. For example, in tantric traditions, where extraordinary abilities are typically the main goal of practice, mantras are the primary means of achieving them. Various powers can also be granted by a deity as a reward for harsh asceticism. Further, they can be obtained through alchemy or herbs, or one may simply have them from birth due to auspicious karma. There are obviously many ways to acquire extraordinary powers, but yoga practice is one prominent way.

Unfortunately, yoga texts rarely explain the exact mechanism by which yoga practice can produce particular extraordinary abilities. Often implicit in the background is the teaching of Sāṃkhya philosophy in the form of a hierarchical system of planes of reality (*tattvas*) that can be gradually mastered. When a yogi conquers a certain plane, he acquires a specific power. In this way, he can progress from the lowest plane, which consists of the five (or four) gross elements of which the material world is made, to the highest level. In most cases, however, the precise process of receiving extraordinary abilities remains unexplained.

What are we actually supposed to imagine when we talk about extraordinary powers? Put simply, anything that is beyond the abilities of ordinary people. This naturally means that the repertoire of yoga skills is extremely broad and varied. Yogic texts make no attempt to categorize them; in fact, apart from a few Jaina works, we find no elaborate classification of extraordinary powers in Indian textual sources. Basically, we can divide these powers into two types, the first relating to the body (these form the majority) and the second affecting the surrounding world. The most spectacular are perhaps the physical bodily abilities: The yogi is not limited in his movement (he can fly, walk on water, or pass through rocks); he can transform his body (take any form, be of atomic or gigantic size, or even become invisible) or enter another body; he feels neither hunger nor thirst; he can make his body healthy, indestructible, and even immortal; and so on. Other groups of bodily powers are extraordinary sensory abilities (seeing and hearing at an extreme distance) and mental abilities (reading the minds of other people, knowing all one's own past reincarnations, or even omniscience—that is, knowledge of everything past, present, and future). With the second type of powers, a yogi can manipulate nature (cause an earthquake, burn a forest, or dry up a pond), conquer wild animals, transform iron into gold, and so on.

Just as the repertoire of extraordinary powers is diverse, so is their terminology. In Sanskrit sources, we find about twenty terms for these powers, of which around ten are quite common. Although it is possible to trace preferences for certain terms in particular types of texts (e.g., Buddhist, Jaina, and Tantric), in principle, they are all virtually synonymous. In yogic works, *siddhi* (perfection) is the most commonly used term. It already appears in the *sūtra* layer of the *Pātañjalayogaśāstra*, and later, it is common in the *haṭhayoga* texts.

Historically, the first textual evidence of the extraordinary powers produced by yoga is present in early Buddhist sources—namely, the Pali canon. Here, the powers are the result of a complex meditation practice when a yogi reaches its highest level (the fourth *jhāna*). Later on, the acquisition of extraordinary abilities through meditation is further elaborated in several Pali manuals, the most famous of which is Buddhaghosa's *Visuddhimagga* from the fifth century CE. The importance of these powers in early Buddhism is also evident in the stories of the Buddha and his disciples, in which they perform various marvelous deeds.

An extremely important insight into the history of yogic powers is provided by the *Mahābhārata*. In a chapter belonging to a later stratum of this epic (12.289), Yudhiṣṭhira asks the sage Bhīṣma about the relationship between yoga and Sāṃkhya. He learns that the two teachings are very close, but the followers of Sāṃkhya lack the power (*bala*) that only yogis possess. Thanks to this yogic power (*yogabala*), yogis can control anyone and anything in the world, and at the same time, no one can gain control over them, not even Yama, the god of death. The *Mahābhārata* thus illustrates the early association of power and yoga in the Hindu milieu.

This importance of power in yoga is well demonstrated in the first Hindu yoga text, the *Pātañjalayogaśāstra*, composed around 400 CE. A substantial part of this work (the entire third chapter) is devoted to the extraordinary abilities that result from the simultaneous application of the last three elements of the *aṣṭāṅga* system—namely, fixation (*dhāraṇā*), meditation (*dhyāna*), and absorption (*samādhi*). Although modern yoga practitioners tend to overlook the presence of these powers in Patañjali's work or try to dismiss their significance by explaining that they are merely a necessary side effect of yoga practice and actually an obstacle on the spiritual path, the reality is different: Extraordinary powers are undoubtedly an important and essential component of the *Pātañjalayogaśāstra*.

By far the richest sources of extraordinary powers are the tantric texts of all traditions (Śaiva, Kaula-Śākta, Vaiṣṇava, and Buddhist). This is not surprising, since the dominant goal of tantric practice is precisely the acquisition of extraordinary abilities (siddhis). Although tantric practitioners can obtain these powers through various means (especially through mantras), yoga is an important source of them. Needless to say, the tantric yoga system of the six auxiliaries (*ṣaḍaṅgayoga*) is, with the exception of *prāṇāyāma*, purely meditative, using primarily the technique of detailed visualization.

The first physical yoga tradition, haṭhayoga, inherited a number of tantric ideas and techniques, the concept of extraordinary powers being one of them. Haṭhayoga not only adopted the practices of attaining these powers from tantric sources but sometimes developed them further. Thus, for example, the mastery of the five gross elements (*bhūtajaya*), through which a yogi acquires a number of extraordinary skills related to the physical world, appears in a number of tantric texts, but it is not found in full form until the early works of haṭhayoga.

Although the concept of extraordinary powers may sound strange to a modern and Western-educated person, it must be stressed that it has been a commonplace part of South Asian culture for thousands of years. The natural connection between yoga and these powers is not only expressed in learned Sanskrit texts but also present in vernacular narratives, folk stories, and popular imagination to this day. A real yogi is simply a person who can do anything he wishes.

About the author

Lubomír Ondračka is a publisher, independent researcher, and occasional lecturer at the Department of Philosophy and Religious Studies, Faculty of Arts, Charles University in Prague. Currently, he is a research fellow at Balliol College, University of Oxford. His research is focused on the history of yoga, death, and dying in India and on the religions and culture of Bengal.

Suggestions for further reading

In this book

See also chapters 42 (Who are the *siddha yogis*?) and 49 (Does a yoga teacher need to be an advanced practitioner?).

Elsewhere

Jacobsen, Knut A., ed. *Yoga Powers: Extraordinary Capacities Attained Through Meditation and Concentration*. Brill's Indological Library, vol. 37. Brill, 2012.

Mallinson, James, and Mark Singleton. "Yogic Powers." In *Roots of Yoga*, edited by James Mallinson and Mark Singleton. Penguin Books, 2017.

White, David Gordon. *Sinister Yogis*. University of Chicago Press, 2009.

Is yoga healthy?

20
Is yoga safe?

Jens U. Augspurger

As yoga has gained increasing recognition as a means of promoting health and well-being, so too has the accumulation of evidence of its potential biomedical benefits. In response, yoga providers have produced strong claims to promote yoga in the health market—with considerable success. Today, yoga is widely endorsed by doctors, health professionals, and insurers as a practice that can support physical and mental health, as well as spiritual well-being.

But what about safety in yoga? Can practitioners rely on good standards, and does the yoga industry have practices in place to mitigate the potential risks of physical or psychological harm? It is important to consider the safety of yoga in relation to (a) health focus and the presumed "goodness" of yoga; (b) physical safety in an unregulated market; (c) somatic dominance, sexualized violence, and hands-on adjustments; and (d) yoga culture, endless meditation, and cultic dynamics.

With yoga's growing popularity in the health market, many stakeholders have endorsed it as a useful intervention for a variety of ailments, stress relief, or overall well-being. In some locations, health insurance companies or employers subsidize yoga classes or have partnered with online providers to offer on-demand streaming. Yoga has become a mainstream practice located at the intersection of the health, well-being, and spiritual markets. It is frequently recommended or "socially prescribed" as an antidote to many maladies by friend networks or by medical professionals and is marketed by fitness studios and wellness centers.

But the widespread perception of yoga as inherently beneficial also bears some risks. When seeking out yoga classes, individuals may have difficulty assessing the suitability of the various yoga brands, styles, and institutions they encounter. The lack of transparency in the market and nonexistence of (binding) coherent quality frameworks make it challenging to determine the qualifications of a teacher. As a result, depending on location, budget, and personal circumstances, it is challenging to discern whether a yoga class is offered by an experienced, well-trained teacher with integrity.

Physical safety in the yoga industry continues to receive insufficient attention even though a discussion on the harms could help create safer spaces. If individuals do have negative experiences while participating in yoga, they have historically been met with a level of disbelief that denies any experiences that seem to conflict with the perceived positive nature of the practice. This harmful response can cause individuals to internalize their negative experiences and does little to address underlying structural problems.

In actuality, a specific form of yoga may simply not be suitable for everyone, and sometimes it is clearly contraindicated. As an example, some medical professionals recommend that certain practices and postures should not be practiced during pregnancy or with specific preconditions. Yet the level of training yoga teachers receive on cautions and contraindications varies, and many may not be adequately trained to recognize or address specific needs, increasing the risk of injuries.

In a two-hundred-hour yoga teacher training, Yoga Alliance (one of the largest yoga teacher organizations in the world) today requires thirty hours of instruction spent on anatomy and physiology (an increase from twenty hours before 2020). But besides biomedical anatomy, this often also includes time spent on esoteric approaches to anatomy, such as the *nāḍīs* and *cakras*. While these are core teachings in yoga, they are less than helpful in addressing physical safety or special needs. Furthermore, Yoga Alliance's two-hundred-hour credentials are just one widely recognized but nonbinding standard in an otherwise largely unregulated market that lacks coherent standardization and quality assurance. Such credentials are also a suggested curriculum rather than a monitored quality assessment. Consequently, anyone can use the unprotected designation "yoga teacher," regardless of their level of training.

Student-teacher relationships are always potentially vulnerable to physical and psychological transgressions, and this may be particularly relevant in disciplines that involve somatic dominance, such as yoga. Somatic dominance is a concept suggested by investigative journalist Matthew Remski to describe the embodied power dynamics between teachers and students in many yoga classrooms. These dynamics may include teachers standing while the students are lying on their backs with their eyes closed, making unsolicited hands-on adjustments at any time, or prioritizing their own perception of how a posture should look over the students' physical responses or needs. Furthermore, the spiritual subtext of some yoga practices includes a belief in the importance of honoring teachers, which can contribute to the creation of a "guru effect" in which students may trust their teachers' guidance excessively. As a result, instances of physical abuse or sexualized violence within yoga communities have even happened in plain view of other participants, such as during a yoga class, but have still not been recognized as abusive. In one instance, video footage has documented sexualized and violent conduct by a well-known teacher of Ashtanga Vinyasa Yoga, Pattabhi Jois, toward his students, but his actions were not challenged by bystanders at the time. In return, victims of such abuse have accused yoga organizations or individual teachers of gaslighting, victim-offender reversal, and spiritual bypassing to silence victims rather than hold perpetrators accountable.

For many dedicated yoga practitioners, their practice extends beyond physical activity on the mat and encompasses a lifestyle that also determines their relationships, daily habits, and consumption choices. The yoga industry offers a wide range of products and services that suit this "yogic" lifestyle. While yoga evidently can have positive (health) effects when practiced in a healthy way, it is also important to consider the potential for unhealthy results from the practice. Many claims for modern yoga's efficacy remain scientifically unproven, and much of the life advice associated with yoga teachings is derived from religious content appropriate to the cultural settings of Hindu Brahmanical elites. Over the past century, yoga has also been at the core of several high-demand groups or cults that have used and developed these teachings to manipulative ends. These groups have participated considerably in the development of yoga teacher training, and their contribution to shaping modern yoga should not be underestimated. Scholars have yet to fully explore how belief, esoteric content, or even cultic dynamics have contributed to the modern evolution of yoga or created assumptions that are reflected in biomedical studies on the efficacy of yoga practice. One way in which this dynamic might matter is the overuse of meditation, which has been popularized as a tool for introspection and mindfulness but is also used for religious purposes or even coercive control. There are potentially adverse effects, such as unwanted dissociative states or other psychiatric conditions, which are understated and sometimes misinterpreted as spiritual experiences, only reinforcing the perceived success of the practice.

Overall, the widespread perception of modern yoga as a universally beneficial practice and the effective marketing strategies of providers attract many people to yoga in the hope of helping with a range of conditions and issues. This should prompt a serious concern over their physical well-being, the kinds of claims yoga providers should be allowed to make, and honest conversations about yoga's suitability and unsuitability for certain conditions and circumstances.

About the author

Jens U. Augspurger is a PhD candidate in the Department of Religions and Philosophies at SOAS University of London. His research and teaching focus on modern transnational yoga and spiritual movements, as well as their respective intersections with politics. He is also a recovering yoga teacher and the cofounder of Project SATYA, a community movement that supports survivors of sexualized violence and advocates for accountability and truth in the yoga industry. Considering spiritual tourism as a journey for self-discovery, his ethnographic dissertation project explores yoga tourism in India and the complex relationships the yoga tourist builds while journeying (toward) the destination.

Suggestions for further reading

In this book

See also chapters 21 (Is yoga good for your health?), 48 (Are the teachers of yoga enlightened?), and 60 (What is the relationship between yoga and capitalism?).

Elsewhere

Hauser, Beatrix. "The Health Imaginary of Postural Yoga." *Anthropology & Medicine* 28, no. 3 (2021): 297–319.

Remski, Matthew. *Practice and All Is Coming: Abuse, Cult Dynamics, and Healing in Yoga and Beyond*. Embodied Wisdom, 2019.

Van Dam, Nicholas T., et al. "Mind the Hype: A Critical Evaluation and Prescriptive Agenda for Research on Mindfulness and Meditation." *Perspectives on psychological science* 13, no. 1 (2018): 36–61.

21 Is yoga good for your health?

Brett W. Parris

Many people are attracted to modern yoga practice as a way to improve their overall health—and a regular yoga practice can indeed bring many health benefits, ranging from improvements in flexibility, strength, and balance to lower stress levels.

Health benefits were far from the primary goal in traditional forms of yoga, however. It is important to distinguish between modern usages of the word "yoga"—the kinds of physical classes that the average person on the street would think of when they hear the word "yoga"—and traditional usages of the term, which were much broader. The *Pātañjalayogaśāstra* discusses the eight limbs of yoga, of which *āsana* is only one. Its primary purpose is to provide a steady base for meditation, not a good workout.

The relationships between traditional forms of yoga practice and health are complex and varied. In many premodern yogic traditions—some of which still exist today—practices emerged that were decidedly *un*healthy for the body, such as extreme austerities (*tapas*) intended to subjugate and control the body. Examples include standing up for years on end or keeping one or both arms raised above the head until they were withered and atrophied. The *Pātañjalayogaśāstra* admonishes the yogi to cultivate "disgust" (*jugupsā*) for the body (YS 2.40) and promises that austerity (*tapas*) will destroy impurity and so bring the body and senses to perfection (2.43). A frequent refrain in many other traditional texts is that performing certain practices will cure disease. For example, the *Gheraṇḍasaṃhitā*, an eighteenth-century *haṭhayoga* text, includes techniques for lengthening the tongue, since a long tongue "can get rid of old age, death, disease and so forth" (1.28). Elsewhere it advises the yogi, as part of his regime of cleansing the body, to insert a stick down his throat into his stomach, stir it around, and then draw it out. By using this technique, the yogi is "sure to eliminate diseases of the gullet" (1.36–37). The *Śivasaṃhitā*, a fourteenth-century haṭhayoga text, promises that merely by practicing *mudrās* (techniques of controlling the breath and vital energies) "all diseases disappear" (4.1)

Few today would advocate extreme austerities or suggest that yoga could "cure all diseases," but even in modern times, there continue to be claims that certain poses have specific "detoxing" effects or other medical benefits that go well beyond what the evidence would support. B. K. S. Iyengar's immensely popular book *Light on Yoga*, for example, first published in 1966, contains an appendix listing poses that will supposedly help various diseases, including anemia, appendicitis, diabetes, dysentery, epilepsy, and so on. I well remember one teacher-training weekend where a fascinating and rigorous session on anatomy, using all the tools and insights of modern science, was followed by a class in which the teacher talked about certain twists being good for detoxing. Such unwarranted claims can be confusing and unhelpful for students—particularly since there is good evidence for more modest but nonetheless significant health benefits of yoga. Here I will focus on physical and mental health benefits.

Modern yoga classes range from slow and relaxed stretch-focused Yin Yoga classes to intense, high-energy Power Flow classes, with everything in between. By varying the intensity and working many different muscle groups, such classes can greatly improve students' overall strength, flexibility, cardiovascular health, and balance. Good teachers will respect the diversity of human anatomy and will help students grow into their practice, without being unnecessarily prescriptive about how a pose "should" look or holding an idealized version of a pose up as something that all students should strive toward. Certainly, an alignment that is dangerous for the student or is likely to cause injuries over time should be corrected, but students can also injure themselves trying to achieve an idealized version of a pose. For example, the classic meditation "lotus pose," or *padmāsana*, with each foot resting on the opposite thigh, can be impossible for many, since achieving it depends on the degree of external rotation of the thigh bone in the hip socket. Without that external rotation, students may try to achieve lotus by tugging on their lower legs and wrenching their knees sideways, which can be injurious. Similarly, the ability to achieve deep backbends depends greatly on a student's individual spinal anatomy, particularly the spacing of their spinous processes. Many students will never achieve the deep backbends of more extreme yoga postures. Social media does not help matters, with a tendency to display images of more extreme poses, sometimes accompanied by explicit messaging saying that if only you practice enough, you too will be able to do this.

Closely related to the physical postures, *āsana*, is breath control, or *prāṇāyāma*. Again, in the past, some quite extreme practices were pursued, such as holding the breath for long periods of time. But in modern classes, various forms of prāṇāyāma may be used as a practice at the beginning or end of classes and as a preparation for meditation. In some classes, the close linking of the breath with movement may also be considered a form of prāṇāyāma. The ability to control the breath under stress has significant health benefits, since steady, deep breathing can activate the parasympathetic nervous system, helping us relax in stressful situations, when otherwise a surge of adrenaline can leave us breathing fast and shallow or even hyperventilating.

The physical health benefits of yoga, such as more exercise, greater strength, and better fitness, commonly transfer into mental health benefits, such as improved confidence, although much depends on the ethos of a student's studio and teachers. Teaching that is unwelcoming, exclusive, or elitist or that promotes a certain image of how a modern yoga practitioner "should" look can be quite damaging to students' mental health. On the other hand, teaching that is more welcoming and inclusive can provide mental health benefits for many students, as well as a sense of belonging and community.

About the author

Brett W. Parris is a DPhil candidate in the Faculty of Theology and Religion at the University of Oxford. He has an MPhil in Classical Indian Religion from Oxford, as well as a PhD in development economics from Monash University in Melbourne. He worked for NGOs focused on poverty, human rights, and climate change for many years. His current research focuses on the ethical dimensions of yogic philosophy and practice and broader interreligious dialogue. He has taught yoga in both Australia and the UK.

Suggestions for further reading

In this book

See also chapters 13 (Do yogis want to transcend or transform the body?), 23 (Are all yoga practitioners flexible?), and 25 (What is the relationship between yoga and āyurveda?).

Elsewhere

Emerson, David, and Hopper, Elizabeth. *Overcoming Trauma Through Yoga: Reclaiming Your Body*. North Atlantic Books, 2011.

McGonigle, Andrew, and Matthew Huy. *The Physiology of Yoga: An Evidence-Based Look at How Yoga Affects Health and Well-Being*. Human Kinetics, 2023.

van der Kolk, Bessel. *The Body Keeps the Score: Mind, Brain and Body in the Transformation of Trauma*. Penguin Books, 2014.

22

Why do yogis contort their bodies?

Daniela Bevilacqua

In his *Geography*, the Greek Strabo (64 BCE–ca. 24 CE) reports the encounter of members of Alexander the Great's entourage with "gymnosophists" in the fourth century BCE. From his words, we come to know that there were "fifteen men standing in different postures, sitting or lying down naked," who remained in these positions until the evening and then returned to the city. We cannot call them yogis because they are not mentioned as such in any source, and obviously we cannot call their postures *āsanas* because this term is not used, and moreover, at that time, the term *āsana* referred only to sitting postures. Nonetheless, we can interpret these postures and activities as expressions of *tapasyā*, or austerity. The practice of tapasyā, in fact, could be one of the reasons why (future) yogis contort their bodies. For this reason, we could also say that before yogis, *tapasvins* (practitioners of tapasyā) used to contort their bodies for various reasons: to obtain benefits from deities, to accumulate powers, or to achieve spiritual goals.

These two labels—*yogis* and *tapasvins*—have often been used as synonyms, especially in Sanskrit Epics, and indeed, *tapas* and *yoga* are closely related because various practices used to develop *tapas* (inner ascetic heat) have been adopted and adapted in yogic contexts.

However, yoga textual sources, such as the *Pātañjalayogaśāstra*, do not talk about uncomfortable postures; rather the opposite. In the context of the earliest *haṭhayoga* textual sources—such as, for example, the fifteenth-century *Haṭhapradīpikā*—practices that overexert the body are criticized, while āsanas are described as giving steadiness, health, and lightness to the body (1.15, 1.17).

The situation is different if we look at archaeological evidence: sites such as the Mahudi gate of Dabhoi (ca. twelfth century) or the pillars of the temples of Vijayanagara (fifteenth century) testify to the presence of ascetics in complex postures, postures that often find their way into textual sources from the eighteenth century onward. It should be noted, however, that since these are individual sculptures, it is difficult to clearly identify whether what is carved is actually an āsana or a form of tapasyā.

The presence of these sculpted ascetics must be contextualized in the temple landscape where several practitioners used to gather, especially during religious festivals. This could lead us to a second reason why yogis contort their bodies. It is here useful to consider the *Sāmrājyalakṣmīpīṭhikā* (ca. 1501–1539), a largely understudied tantric-based manuscript, and especially its chapter 107 on the celebration of *Navarātri*. This chapter not only testifies to the presence of various ascetics at court, but while describing the various entertainments the king is supposed to attend on the night of *Mahānavami*, it mentions magical and presumably yogic practices (*patalas* 101, 102), along with dance performances, wrestling fights, acrobatic shows, and so on.

A similar performative approach to āsanas can also be noted in the "shows" that Krishnamacharya used to present to the maharaja of Mysore for his amusement. In fact, Krishnamacharya regularly prepared dynamic performances to show the maharaja and other dignitaries in order to provide a challenge to similar displays of imported gymnastics and thus attract students.

The use of "yogic practices" to amuse an audience should not be surprising because it still happens: ascetics do on occasion perform difficult and contorted āsanas during religious gatherings to capture the attention of pilgrims or onlookers. Ascetics/yogis have admitted that āsanas that are not for meditative purposes can be performed as a *natak*, a theatrical act, or a *kalā*, a form of art. Thus āsanas, or particular positions or actions (such as putting one's head in the sand for days), are done to amuse a crowd, to give them *ānand* (delight).

Let us return to the link between āsanas and tapasyā already mentioned, as other interesting connections can be drawn. It is likely that complex āsanas come from a *tapasic* environment. Particularly useful evidence for this is given in the account of Jonathan Duncan (the later governor of Bombay, 1795–1811), who decided to transcribe the travels of the tapasvin Purn Purī, whom he interviewed in Benaras in May 1792. Purn Purī provides a unique list of eighteen possible tapasyās, among which the *caurāsī āsana tapasyā* is listed: the learning of eighty-four āsanas as a form of austerity, those āsanas being described as "difficult contortions to be held for hours on end" (Duncan 1810, 264).

Textual sources for haṭhayoga in the vernacular (such as the *Jog-pradīpakā*, which was probably written by the ascetic Jayatrāma in the eighteenth century) confirm that postures and activities that were considered tapasyā in earlier sources were introduced in later sources as āsanas. Such haṭhayoga texts provide us with a further explanation for the contortions of yogis: complex practices such as *mudrās* or *āsanas* may be aimed at awakening the *kuṇḍalinī*, curing diseases or old age, and also obtaining specific powers (*siddhis*).

Clearly, to answer the question we began with, we can claim that yogis contort their bodies—while doing tapasyā or āsana—as part of a (tapasic) *sādhanā* or as part of a performance for spiritual and pragmatic reasons. Considering more pragmatic reasons, we can mention the possibility of gaining powers, health benefits, and economic benefits by attracting devotees and supporters. Considering more spiritual reasons, with such "contorted" practices, yogis engage in a transformative process that, through body-mind efforts, prepares the individual to overcome the limits of the body and control the senses, bodily functions, and bodily needs, as well as to purify the mind and thought for higher achievements.

About the author

Daniela Bevilacqua is an Indianist specialized in Hindu asceticism, investigated through an ethnographic and historical perspective. She received her PhD in civilizations of Africa and Asia from Sapienza University of Rome and in anthropology from the University of Paris Nanterre. She worked as a postdoc research fellow at SOAS for the ERC-funded Haṭha Yoga Project (2015–2020). She is currently a researcher at CRIA (ISCTE-IUL) in Lisbon. She has authored *Modern Hindu Traditionalism in Contemporary India* (Routledge, 2018) and *From Tapas to Modern Yoga: Sādhus' Understanding of Embodied Practices* (Equinox Publishing Ltd., 2024), edited volumes, and written several articles and book chapters on topics related to Hindu religious tradition, gender, and embodied practices.

Suggestions for further reading

In this book

See also chapters 23 (Are all yoga practitioners flexible?), 28 (What are *āsanas*?), and 32 (Why do yogis go upside down?).

Elsewhere

Bevilacqua, Daniela. "Let the Sādhus Talk. Ascetic Understanding of Haṭha Yoga and Yogāsanas." *Religions of South Asia* 11, nos. 2–3 (2017): 182–206.

Birch, Jason. "Haṭhayoga's Floruit on the Eve of Colonialism." In *Śaivism and the Tantric Traditions: Essays in Honour of Alexis G. J. S. Sanderson*, edited by Dominic Goodall, Shaman Hatley, Harunaga Isaacson, and Srilata Raman. Brill, 2020.

Duncan, Jonathan. *The European Magazine and London Review, Containing Portraits, Views, Biography, Anecdotes, Literature, History, Politics, Arts, Manners, and Amusements of the Age*. Vol. 57. January–June 1810.

Powell, Seth. "Etched in Stone: Sixteenth-Century Visual and Material Evidence of Śaiva Ascetics and Yogis in Complex Non-Seated Āsanas at Vijayanagara." *Journal of Yoga Studies* 1 (2018): 45–106.

Suebsantiwongse, Saran. "Royal Amusements, Sports, Magic and Yogic Practices According to the Sāmrājyalakṣmīpīṭhikā." In *Yoga and the Traditional Physical Practices of South Asia, Entanglement and Confrontation*, edited by Daniela Bevilacqua and Mark Singleton. Special issue, *Journal of Yoga Studies* 4 (2023): 113–135.

23
Are all yoga practitioners flexible?

Laura von Ostrowski

When looking at common yoga hashtags on Instagram or other social media platforms, it might seem that the practice of yoga is about flexibility. Often, very intense postures are displayed, most of which require a great deal of muscular, fascial, or joint mobility, be it a seated lotus position, *padmāsana*, or more strenuous postures like *kūrmāsana*, "the turtle," which was already known to early *haṭhayoga* practitioners. Flexibility is in this context not only a somatic but also an aesthetic phenomenon that displays the body in positions that cannot be performed by every body and therefore attract attention through their very novelty and extreme nature.

Nevertheless, since *yoga* is a historically broad term that is by no means focused only on postures, clearly not all yoga practitioners are bendy. For example, the famous yoga text the *Bhagavadgītā* distinguishes four types of yoga: *karmayoga* (2.48–2.50), the path of activity; *jñānayoga* (4.33–4.42), the path of knowledge; *dhyānayoga* (chapter 6), the path of meditation; and *bhaktiyoga* (chapter 12), the path of devotion. Practitioners of such yoga forms might need some mobility to sit in a relaxed and still manner or to prostrate on the floor when a devotional ritual demands it. Even if yoga practice consists mainly of postures, as in many modern forms of yoga, the practitioner does not have to be flexible, as not all practices demand flexibility.

In the 2016 "Yoga in America" study, conducted on behalf of the industry's most well-known magazine, *Yoga Journal*, the most common reason that yoga practitioners gave for engaging in the practice was "flexibility": an answer that was given by 61 percent of respondents. The second reason was "stress relief," given by 56 percent of respondents. This leads us to ask where this strong connection between yoga and flexibility originates and how the quest for flexibility might be related to the second important motivation for a regular yoga practice—namely, stress reduction.

Historically, modern postural yoga has had a strong association with both flexibility and relaxation. Generally speaking, the reduction of nervous tension and stress was and still is a main concern in urban, industrialized societies.

In the history of Indian yoga, however, it was not stretching but a stable seated posture that helped in achieving a focused state of mind (*dhāraṇā*) and meditation (*dhyāna*). One of the most ancient postures is padmāsana, the crossed-legged and feet-bound lotus seat. It is already present in early Buddhist sources, in the commentary section (*bhāṣya*) of the fourth-to-fifth-century *Pātañjalayogaśāstra*, and in later haṭhayoga texts, such as the fifteenth-century *Haṭhapradīpikā*. Padmāsana became one of the strenuous postures of late haṭhayogas, described, for example, in the eighteenth-century Sanskrit text *Haṭhābhyāsapaddhati*. The lotus posture requires a high level of joint and muscular flexibility in and around the hips, or else it cannot be performed. Thus, being able to master this position might promise a strong gain in flexibility. Nevertheless, even with constant practice, it is not achievable for every body, as specific formations in the bones of the pelvis can completely prevent one from adopting such a strongly outwardly rotated sitting posture. However, as Pātañjalayoga does not describe physical flexibility among its goals, the *Pātañjalayogaśāstra* proposes other sitting postures as well, including a posture named *sthiraprasrabdhi*, "constant relaxation," which Philipp Maas describes as an "umbrella term that covers a number of postures with the common characteristic of leading the practitioner to relaxation." Maas goes on to write, "Śaṇkara leaves it to the individual practitioner to invent or find himself bodily configurations that serve this purpose best" (2018, 78). Thus, a certain flexibility might be a requirement or even an outcome of early *āsana* practices but not their focus. Psychophysical relaxation, on the other hand, was an important theme. In contrast, later haṭhayoga developments like the *Haṭhābhyāsapaddhati* were interested in cultivating strength and fitness through the practice of strenuous āsanas, not flexibility and relaxation. Strength is a common trope in different yoga systems and is mentioned in the *Mahābhārata*, where notions of yoga as strength are associated with the non-renunciate understanding of yoga as skillful action. Thus, in the premodern era, neither nonphysical yoga forms nor āsana practices were concerned with an increase in flexibility, even if some practices required it.

While classical or medieval yoga has little to say about the connection between tension versus flexibility and mental stress versus relaxation, it is an important theme in the discourses and practices of the late nineteenth- and early twentieth-century (largely female) physical culture movement. The relevant term here was "stretching," which, in the 1880s manuals of Annie Payson Call (1853–1940), an American author interested in mental health, was deeply associated with nerve relaxation and served as a preparation for calming the body down. In a similar manner, the stretching postures of modern postural yoga are commonly described as leading to an increase in mobility and muscular relaxation for those who desire it.

A more contemporary scientific view on stretching the body concerns itself with the difference between a passive and active range of bodily motion, and the term "mobility" is more commonly used instead of the term "stretching." Stretching is used to describe only a passive range of motion—that is, mobility created by prolonged holding and the influence of gravity or the help of a partner. Increasing the range of motion in joints through different work with muscles and fascia can also serve the purpose of an increase in active mobility, which is sought after by many contemporary yoga practitioners, as in other physical disciplines.

Associating or even equating yoga with flexibility can be further problematic in various ways. One problem lies in the fact that stretching does not play an explicit role in Indian yoga history. The other problem is related to the fact that striving for a highly flexible body and displaying it on social media reproduces idealized body images built on exclusivity. Lauding only healthy, bendy bodies is ableist, as it privileges people based on their physical abilities. How flexible a person's body is or can become is determined by genetics, gender, and habits, as much or more than by one's dedication to the practice of yoga. Many women have a different composition of connective tissue, muscle, fat, and water, depending on their hormonal profiles, and therefore have bodies that tend to be softer and more elastic than men. Many men, on the other hand, perform sports that tend to strengthen and thus shorten muscles and therefore might benefit from stretching exercises. Mobility might be better gained through other, non-yogic techniques like (self-)massage or strength and load training with weights.

We can conclude that despite the necessity of flexibility for the achievement of specific practices, yoga practitioners of diverse yoga paths do not necessarily need to be flexible to be proficient at their practice as a whole, even though relaxed muscles might facilitate a number of the breathing exercises and concentration and meditation techniques that have been associated with yoga for a very long time.

About the author

Laura von Ostrowski received her PhD in religious studies in 2021. The book to her PhD thesis was published open access under the title *A Text in Motion* in 2022. Her areas of research include modern and contemporary yoga, the reception of the *Yogasūtra*, the history of German yoga and the physical culture movement, contemporary religion, aesthetics, and embodiment. Since 2007, she has worked as a yoga teacher, including running her own yoga studio in the center of Munich since 2018 and teaching the history of modern yoga at the German online education portal Yogastudien.

Suggestions for further reading

In this book

See also chapters 27 (Has yoga always been a physical practice?) and 49 (Does a yoga teacher need to be an advanced practitioner?).

Elsewhere

Hariharānanda Āraṇya, Swāmi. *Yoga Philosophy of Patañjali*. Rev. ed. State University of New York Press, 1983.

Maas, Philipp A. "'*Sthirasukham Āsanam*': Posture and Performance in Classical Yoga and Beyond." In *Yoga in Transformation: Historical and Contemporary Perspectives*, edited by Karl Baier, Philipp A. Maas, and Karin Preisendanz. V&R unipress, 2018.

24

What is the role of diet in yoga?

Theodora Wildcroft and Barbora Sojková

In her influential 1966 book *Purity and Danger*, the British anthropologist Mary Douglas considers the set of Jewish dietary laws, also known as *kashrut*, found in the Old Testament. Why do the Jews eat only specific types of animals, such as cattle, but forbid others—namely, pork or shellfish? Douglas argues that these rules are not about hygiene, but they are meant to maintain a symbolic boundary between the Jewish community and its non-Jewish neighbors. Although Douglas's interpretation has been much discussed and revised in anthropology, its basic tenet—that people use food not only to nourish themselves but to distinguish themselves from others—still holds its value. Many religious and spiritual groups use dietary prescriptions and restrictions as a form of symbolic language, and premodern yoga texts are no exception.

Stereotypically, yoga practitioners are thought to be vegetarians. Many argue that vegetarianism has been associated with South Asian culture since the earliest historical period, documented in the Vedic literature. The Vedas provide us with a record of a pastoralist society that subsisted on dairy, beef, and various agricultural products. A vegetarian diet is briefly referenced in the later Vedic prose texts, such as the Brāhmaṇas, but it is unlikely that this was followed by the majority. The emphasis on vegetarianism instead evolved in the post-Vedic period, with the rise of the *śramaṇa* (mendicant) movements, such as Buddhism and Jainism, and it was subsequently adopted by many Hindus with reference to the later Vedas.

A vegetarian diet in this case is the logical conclusion of a worldview in which every being is caught in a never-ending cycle of rebirths (*saṃsāra*). This cycle, viewed as particularly negative, is perpetuated by action (*karma*): Any action, both positive and negative, leaves a trace that causes one to be reborn when each being dies. The goal of each being is to liberate (*mokṣa*, *mukti*) oneself from this unfavorable destiny and never be born again. In this worldview, the notion of *ahiṃsā*, nonviolence, gains particular prominence: If every action leaves a trace, negative, violent actions are particularly impactful, not only toward the creature that is harmed, but also for oneself. For many, vegetarianism became an extension and, in certain senses, a synonym for the precept of ahiṃsā itself. Due to its metaphysical connotations, vegetarianism also became associated with ritual purity, and thus vegetarianism gained the status of a widely adopted norm in South Asia, at least among certain social groups. Many South Asians still follow vegetarian diets today, although most are lacto-vegetarians. Others consume meat either as a part of a ritual or as a daily diet.

Turning to yoga specifically, in general, premodern texts recommend a restricted, measured diet that is preferably vegetarian. The *Haṭhapradīpikā*, for example, considers overeating as an obstacle to the goal of yoga. The *Bhagavadgītā* (6.16) argues that "yoga is not attained by he who eats too much or nothing at all." Other texts, such as the eighteenth-century *Gheraṇḍasaṃhitā*, are even more specific, detailing exactly which types of food the yogi can and cannot eat. Among those detrimental to yogic practice are foods that are pungent, sour, salty, bitter, tough, putrid, or off. Some specific ingredients are even prohibited, such as garlic, bitter melon, or asafetida.

While normative texts recommend a measured diet, stronger restrictions on diet are often associated with ascetic practices known as *tapas*. These acts of arduous self-discipline are believed to still the mind and annihilate past karma, which, in turn, leads to liberation. Among these austerities, fasting—that is, a complete restriction of food and often drink—is a common practice.

In summary, then, the premodern yogic attitude treats diet as of ritual, ethical, and practical importance, but although most practitioners would have been lacto-vegetarian in more recent times, this is not universal and is more recent than many might realize. And the stricter and more austere the practice, the stricter the diet or even the fast that is recommended. In modern times, it is interesting to note that the diet recommended to and by yoga practitioners has a similar range and diversity, but the reasoning for these dietary practices has changed somewhat.

The development of modern yoga was commonly associated with "natural" and holistic health movements that promoted organic, whole-food vegetarianism as both ethical and healthy but not ritually or religiously pure. It is this association that probably most influences the modern stereotype of yoga practitioners as having "clean," healthy diets, low in stimulants and animal products. In the late nineteenth and early twentieth centuries, for example, Eustace Miles was one of the first and most influential advocates of holistic health in Britain to advocate for the combination of yoga, vegetarianism, mental discipline, and fresh air in the development of healthy bodies and minds. Like many subsequent charismatic figures in modern yoga, Miles saw a direct connection between a moderate, simple diet and the self-discipline he saw as necessary for good health.

At the time, the broader idea that health is a product of personal discipline and thus both a moral issue and a social duty grew in prominence across the world. A similar worldview was the impetus for the modern yoga renaissance and its connection to the Indian independence movement, and it was the source for a wide diversity of standardized, professionalized movements, some long-lasting and globally influential, others more faddish and short-lived, from the nineteenth-century relaxationism to Pilates. Unfortunately, such worldviews have also been the justification for many more repressive, even eugenicist political ideas. But the idea that the most important influence on health is personal discipline as it is evidenced by everyday choices over diet and exercise has gained the status of a truism in most contemporary cultures.

It is thus unsurprising that contemporary yoga schools often recommend specific dietary regimes for reasons of health, morality, or ease in practice. Mostly, again, these consist of a lightly disciplined diet of primarily plant-based, organic foods in the hopes of building an equally light, flexible body unencumbered by excess toxicity or weight. Whether the archetypal modern yoga body is built by the practice or a priori attracted to it is a focus for ongoing debate. Beyond this, the details of a contemporary yogic diet are even more contested. Some, such as the founders of the transnational proprietary school of Jivamukti Yoga, teach an interpretation of ahiṃsā (see chapter 16 on the *yamas* and *niyamas*) that is strictly vegan. Other practitioners across South Asia and beyond adopt *āyurvedic* ideas about eating according to one's body type (*doṣa*) and as part of a wider balancing of internal energies with environmental influences. Yoga teachers will discuss eating cooling foods when menopausal, for example, alongside physical and meditational practices with similar effects.

Thus a yoga practitioner might be eating a specific diet for physical health or to balance their energies. But whatever the diet, it is usually part of a diffuse pattern of association between some food sources and purity (often low-processed or organic foods), between some food choices and personal morality (often more disciplined or controlled diets), and between some foodstuffs and interspecies ethics (often plant-based foods). Thus while modern and contemporary yoga diets might be less overtly ritualized, they are strongly inflected by religious ideas of purity and morality.

It is rare to find a committed yoga practitioner today who isn't making a conscious choice about the foods they consume. Unfortunately, on occasion, this disciplined attitude to diet means a commitment to a contemporary yogic lifestyle is also both attractive to and even a cover for more disordered eating practices. This has been enhanced by the ubiquity of social media, particularly image-heavy apps such as Instagram, in the marketing of contemporary yoga. As a result, recent years have also seen prominent articles in yoga-related media about yoga and eating disorders (such as the 2014 article in *Yoga Journal* by Chelsea Roff), activist campaigns about yoga and body image (such as those of the Yoga and Body Image Coalition), and academic research into yoga, food, and gender politics (by Melanie Klein, among others).

About the authors

Theodora Wildcroft, PhD, is a researcher investigating the democratization and evolution of physical practice as it moves beyond both traditional and early modern frameworks of relationship. Her PhD was a significant advance in the analysis of contemporary yoga pedagogies. Her research continues to consider the democratization of yoga post-lineage and meaning making in grassroots communities of practice. She is an associate lecturer at the Open University, UK; a former coordinator of the SOAS Centre of Yoga Studies; an editor of the *BASR Bulletin*; an honorary member of the British Wheel of Yoga; a member of the IAYT; and a continuing professional development trainer and consultant for Yoga Alliance (US). Her monograph *Post-Lineage Yoga: From Guru to #MeToo* is available from Equinox Publishing Ltd. (2020).

Barbora Sojková holds a DPhil in Asian and Middle Eastern studies (Sanskrit) from the University of Oxford, where her research focused on human-animal relationships in Vedic Sanskrit literature. She works as an academic librarian at the All Souls College, Oxford, and as a Sanskrit cataloger at the Bodleian Library, Oxford. She is a certified yoga teacher and trainer focusing on the history and philosophy of yoga.

Suggestions for further reading

In this book

See also chapters 14 (Are ethics important in yoga?), 15 (Are all yogis nonviolent?), and 25 (What is the relationship between yoga and āyurveda?).

Elsewhere

Berila, Beth, Melanie Klein, and Chelsea J. Roberts. *Yoga, the Body, and Embodied Social Change: An Intersectional Feminist Analysis*. Lexington Books, 2016.

Mallinson, James, and Mark Singleton. "Preliminaries." In *Roots of Yoga*, edited by James Mallinson and Mark Singleton. Penguin Books, 2017.

25
What is the relationship between yoga and āyurveda?

Suzanne Newcombe

During the twentieth century, yoga and āyurveda became closely linked as Indigenous systems of promoting health and healing, united in their contrast to colonial "Western" medicine. Their association became even more intimate from the 1970s onward as global countercultures championed both yoga and alternatives to Western medicine. From around this time, yoga and āyurveda became popularly associated as "sister sciences," and āyurveda became a subject of interest for Global North students of Indian yoga teachers. However, the historical association between the two traditions has been complex. Yoga and āyurveda might be best understood as two distinct traditions that draw on each other, overlapping in certain times and places but also offering distinct practices and goals.

Yoga and āyurveda share a prehistory. Evidence suggests that non-Brahmanical (*śramaṇa*) wandering ascetics' monastic centers were focuses of medical learning from at least 300 BCE. Prior to this point, Brahmanical (Vedic) tradition emphasized magical healing. Vedic society recognized healers (*bhiṣaj*) as skilled professionals within a highly stratified society; healers had a higher status than carpenters but were ritually impure and lower than priests (*brahmans*). Kenneth Zysk speculates that the structures of early Brahmanical society pushed those with an interest in direct observation as the basis of knowledge (which is the grounding for *āyurvedic* theory in contrast to the more magical Vedic rituals) into the heterodox ideological milieus—that is, those more closely associated with Buddhist, Jain, and other śramaṇa traditions. In later periods, the evidence is more characteristic of two entangled but largely distinct traditions.

The differences can be characterized by goals and identities. Those texts traditionally characterized as yoga focus on the attainment of liberation (*mokṣa* and *samādhi*), and techniques for promoting health are offered as eliminating obstacles that may prevent an aspirant from achieving their goals in this lifetime. The techniques in texts identified as yogic are self-administered and often focus on manipulating the movement of wind (*vāyu*) through the body. In contrast, āyurveda trains a practitioner (*vaidya*) to heal a patient and has as its goal the "knowledge for long life" (a literal translation of *āyurveda*).

Yet there are general overlaps, and a close reading of the *Pātañjalayogaśāstra* suggests that what is now understood as āyurvedic conceptions of the body were in the fourth century CE widespread in South Asia but also not completely systematized. There was a broad understanding of how the human body worked that was largely shared throughout premodern South Asia and common to physicians, yogis, and laypersons. The theoretical understanding of the human body offered by āyurveda is interesting and complex, being substantially different from an understanding based on anatomy. Disease is usually explained as being caused by an imbalance of the constituent elements of the body: *doṣa* (substances that circulate within the body), *dhātu* (substances whose quality and relationship to one another shape the physical body), and *mala* (substances that leave the body). Most contemporary popular presentations of āyurveda speak primarily of the three doṣa theory (*tridoṣa-upadeśaḥ*)—namely, *vāta*, *pitta*, and *kapha*, often glossed into English as "air," "fire," and "earth." A growing number of contemporary yoga texts use these categories to make recommendations for yoga-based well-being practices.

Two of the central canonical texts of āyurveda were systemized in their current forms before the composition of the *Pātañjalayogaśāstra* (i.e., the *Yogasūtra*), which is now dated to around the fourth century CE. In their systematized, written forms, the *Carakasaṃhitā* can be dated to about the first century CE and the *Suśrutasaṃhitā* to about the third century CE, although the healing practices were developing and being transmitted orally before this point. These two canonical texts were combined and further systematized in Vāgbhaṭa's *Aṣṭāṅgahṛdyasaṃhitā* ("the heart of medicine") in the seventh century; this later text quickly became the dominant medical manuscript found in both North and South India. These three texts are known as the "great three-some" of āyurveda, and all āyurvedic physicians refer to these canonical works for their practice as a defining feature. These classical texts do not discuss yoga as a healing technique or incorporate *āsana*, *prāṇāyāma*, or *ṣaṭkarma* into their recommendations.

In its chapter on the origin and structure of the human being, the āyurvedic text of the *Carakasaṃhitā* contains a section on yoga (verses 137–155). Predating Patañjali by several centuries, Caraka's text describes yoga as both spiritual liberation and the means of attaining it. Caraka includes descriptions of supernatural powers that might result from a specific practice of meditation. Central to Caraka's yoga is an eightfold (*aṣṭāṅga*) practice of meditation closely associated with *smṛti* (a word whose meaning spans both recollection and sudden insight) that clearly draws on a Buddhist ascetic tradition while dialoguing closely with Vaiśeṣika and, to a more limited extent, Sāṃkhya philosophical traditions. In the conclusion to this passage, yoga is presented as a means for the final cessation of all pains and their causes as the corporeal self becomes brahman.

Historically, yoga traditions focused on liberation but, from relatively early on, discussed the use of specific āsana and prāṇāyāma as remedies to ailments. This exploration has been documented as starting perhaps as early as the eighth century of the Common Era with the *Dharmaputrikā*, a Nepalese manuscript that contains a chapter on yoga therapy (*yogacikitsā*). However, the arguably more distinctive yogic techniques for promoting health with the *haṭhayoga* literature are the ṣaṭkarma, which are primarily aimed at yogis who are experiencing ill-health. These self-administered treatments include cleansing the stomach with cloth (*vastradhauti*), emesis (*gajakaraṇī*), a water enema (*jalabasti*), cleansing the sinuses with thread (*sūtraneti*), gazing at a fixed point (*trāṭaka*), churning the abdomen (*nauli*), and rapid breathing (*kapālabhāti*). These techniques are not found in the āyurvedic canon or in premodern descriptions of vaidya-led treatment. The seminal 1923 pan-Indian survey of āyurvedic vaidyas, the Usman Report, suggests that very few āyurvedic-trained practitioners incorporated any yogic techniques into their medical practices at that time.

The Usman Report also reveals a complicated relationship between yogis, āyurveda, and the Siddha medical traditions of southern India in the early twentieth century. Siddha and the āyurveda systems have common principles, but Siddha practices and texts are primarily transmitted in Tamil (as opposed to Sanskrit), their preparations have a stronger reliance on inorganic substances (i.e., salts, metals, and minerals), and their medical canon is characterized by mystico-religious works that combine yoga, medicine, and alchemy in a poetic language. The chronology of origin between āyurveda and Siddha is hotly contested, but the Siddha narrative emphasizes its origin in eighteen full-liberated Siddhas (yogis) who mastered immortality in the physical body and gave medicinal knowledge to alleviate the suffering and aid in the liberation of others.

Nevertheless, evidence of historical entanglements and associations between yogis and health-care providers can be found in premodern India. Mentions of ascetic "wandering physicians" are found in early Greek travelogues (ca. 0 CE), and similar figures can still be found in contemporary rural India. European travelogues also suggest that ascetics were sometimes present in the courts of princely states, offering medical advice. At least two premodern texts have been identified that suggest extended dialogue between āyurvedic *vaidyas* (physicians) and yogic *sādhakas* (practitioners/aspirants)—that is, the *Āyurvedasūtra* (sixteenth century) and the *Ṣaṭkarmasaṃgraha* (eighteenth century)—and it is likely more will be found in the future. In nineteenth-century Punjab, institutions of learning associated with ascetic orders, including those associated with the Dadupanthis, Nāth Yogī, Jain, Udasi, and Nirmala lineages, were known to teach Indigenous medical knowledge in their institutions.

There is also evidence that ascetic traditions kept some more ancient āyurvedic practices alive, with *haṭha* traditions sharing an interest in *rasāyana* preparations that aim to greatly extend the human lifespan. In contemporary India, one still finds wandering physicians, particularly in rural areas, offering a variety of herbal, spiritual, and magical cures that might be presented as either "yogic" or "āyurvedic." Āyurveda and other forms of traditional, Indigenous medicine continue to provide the majority of essential, accessible, and affordable health care for much of rural India. For those with more resources in Indian metropolises, āyurvedic vaidyas and yoga teachers operate as alternative and complementary medical options similarly as they are (largely) self-funded options for Global North populations.

Despite these overlaps, it is only in twenty-first-century India that Patañjali's formulation of yoga and specific āsana and prāṇāyāma have been incorporated into the syllabus for qualifying as a bachelor of āyurvedic medicine and surgery (BAMS) and only in 2003 that yoga and āyurveda were formally combined within the same department within India's Ministry of Health—that is, that of Ayurveda, Yoga and Naturopathy, Unani, Siddha, and Homeopathy (AYUSH). AYUSH was elevated to the level of an independent ministry by the government of India in 2014; the Bharatiya Janata Party has been enthusiastic in its promotion of yoga and āyurveda as paired. It is worth noting that in most contemporary contexts, the more invasive recommendations are avoided in favor of the less uncomfortable practices. Much more commonly, outside ascetic communities, therapeutic yoga involves āsana, prāṇāyāma, and some meditative practices. While yogic application of āyurveda may involve consultation with a trained vaidya, it is perhaps more likely to incorporate the principle of doṣa and the idea of energetic balancing into an experiential exploration of embodied āsana and prāṇāyāma practice.

About the author

Suzanne Newcombe is a senior lecturer in religious studies at the Open University and honorary director of the charity Inform, based in theology and religious studies at King's College London. From 2015 to 2020, she was part of the European Research Council–funded project "Ayuryog: Entangled Histories of Yoga, Ayurveda and Alchemy" in South Asia, which examined the histories of yoga, Ayurveda, and rasaśāstra (Indian alchemy and iatrochemistry) from the tenth century to the present, focusing on the disciplines' health, rejuvenation, and longevity practices. She is the coeditor of *The Routledge Handbook of Yoga and Meditation Studies* (Routledge, 2021) and the author of *Yoga in Britain: Stretching Spirituality and Educating Yogis* (Equinox Publishing Ltd., 2019).

Suggestions for further reading

In this book

See also chapters 37 (How do academics study yoga?) and 58 (What does yoga mean to Indians today?).

Elsewhere

Abraham, L. "Indian Systems of Medicine (ISM) and Public Health Care in India." In *Review of Health Care in India*, edited by L. Gangolli, R. Duggal, and A. Shukla. Centre for Enquiry into Health, 2005.

Birch, Jason E. "Premodern Yoga Traditions and Ayurveda: Preliminary Remarks on Shared Terminology, Theory and Praxis." *History of Science in South Asia* 6 (2018): 1–83. https://doi.org/10.18732/hssa.v6i0.25.

Sujatha, V. "The Universal and the Global: Contextualising European Ayurvedic Practices." *Society and Culture in South Asia* 6, no. 1 (2020): 52–73.

Wujastyk, D., and F. M. Smith, eds. *Modern and Global Ayurveda: Pluralism and Paradigms*. SUNY Press, 2008.

Wujastyk, Dagmar, Suzanne Newcombe, and Christèle Barois. "Transmutations: Rejuvenation, Longevity, and Immortality Practices in South and Inner Asia: Introduction." *History of Science in South Asia* 5, no. 2 (2017): i–xvii.

Zysk, Kenneth G. *Asceticism and Healing in Ancient India: Medicine in the Buddhist Monastery*. Montilal Banarsidass, 1991.

How do you practice yoga?

26

What life does the ideal yogi lead?

Barbora Sojková and Theodora Wildcroft

A large number of textual sources on yoga, both premodern and modern, consist of manuals that explain how an adept of yoga should live their life in order to achieve the desired goal of practice. These texts often imply that the ideal practitioner is someone who follows the guidance completely and without failure. Naturally, we cannot be sure that there has ever lived a yogi whose life would be unequivocally exemplary. The codes of conduct detailed in numerous yogic texts can serve, however, as a heuristic device, helping us understand the lifestyle and behavior of yogic practitioners of the past and present.

Our knowledge of what we could call the "premodern ideal yogi" comes largely from normative texts of the Sanskrit tradition. Perhaps the best-known and most influential ideal of yogic behavior and lifestyle (both in premodern yoga and today) was formulated in the famous *Pātañjalayogaśāstra*. According to Patañjali, the life of a practitioner is navigated by a number of strict behavioral precepts, the *yamas* (rules) and *niyamas* (observances). These rules influence everything a practitioner does, from their personal behavior, such as adhering to norms of cleanliness or sexual continence, to the ways in which they treat their community, such as striving for nonviolence, truthfulness, or nonstealing. From this, we can discern that for Patañjali, a practitioner of yoga was someone who lived a highly regulated life in order to achieve the goal of yoga, which is a final liberation from the cycle of rebirths.

Other premodern texts support this notion of a restrained life. For most, the ideal yogi is depicted as a man living a secluded, ascetic lifestyle. While there is some historical evidence that yoga has been accessible to female practitioners, the normative texts, in describing the ideal, speak almost exclusively of a male practitioner. Not every man, moreover, can be a practitioner: While some texts, such as the *Dattātreyayogaśāstra*, argue that a person of virtually any background can succeed in yoga provided they are diligent in their practice, for most sources, only men of higher castes initiated by a guru are able to obtain liberation.

In the premodern texts, yoga practice is said to be best carried out far away from the temptations of civilization. Some texts specifically state that a yogi should live in a hidden, quiet cave. This association of yogic practice with the wilderness has been common in ancient Indian literature since the Epics. However, other normative Sanskrit yogic texts, such as the *Gheraṇḍasaṃhitā*, recommend that a yogi should be more measured. There is no food or security in the wilderness and too much clamor and distraction in the city. Instead, a practitioner should live somewhere in between. In a similar manner, yogic texts list other similar precepts about the appropriate lifestyle for a practitioner, such as the need to follow a specific diet, a prohibition on associating with people, or forbidding the use of fire.

In comparison with rules governing lifestyle and behavior, only a few premodern texts detail a yogi's ideal appearance. Visual art, although usually of a much later date than textual sources, provides us with more detail. According to some visual records, yogis often wore their long hair matted; alternatively, they are elsewhere depicted as shaven headed. They were dressed in simple loincloths, sometimes supplemented with ocher robes or animal skins. Often, they carried staffs and begging bowls or dried gourds as their few possessions. In appearance, yoga practitioners resemble depictions of the god Śiva, who is considered to be the prototypical practitioner of yoga (*ādiyogi*) and its divine patron. In art, Śiva is often shown with the iconographic features of a yogi, sitting in a wilderness in a lotus pose, with his hands in a gesture of meditation, with matted hair, covered in ashes, and surrounded by wild animals.

Even today, there are practitioners, especially those associated with ascetic orders such as the Nāth or Daśanāmī *sampradāyas* (religious orders), who look and behave similarly to the ideal practitioner as delineated by premodern texts. Most contemporary yoga practitioners, however, follow yoga styles that are rooted in the modern renaissance of yoga, beginning in the late nineteenth century. With the modern transformations in yogic practice came changes in the socioeconomic situation and cultural background of the average practitioner, and the ideal practitioner's appearance and lifestyle have changed markedly.

In the late nineteenth and early twentieth centuries, written (and increasingly illustrated) manuals were a popular way of disseminating the practice of yoga both within and beyond the borders of India. In comparison with premodern texts whose authors are often not known to us, these modern instruction books were written by named authors, many of whom are considered now to be the founding gurus of modern yoga. In short order, these handbooks began to be illustrated with photographs, often of the guru modeling aspects of yoga practice. In this way, the ideal yogi is no longer to be implied or inferred—it is the exemplary practice of the yoga teacher, such as Shri Yogendra or Tirumalai Krishnamacharya, embodied in the image of the teacher themself, which should be followed as closely as possible.

The ideal yogi of early twentieth-century yoga is also a man, although no longer an ascetic but a married householder, reflecting their dual status as both a holy figure and secular businessman. Owing to the particular ways in which yoga evolved in the modern era, there are at least two further significant developments in the figure of the ideal yogi. Some teachers, such as Shri Yogendra, presented themselves as having a perfect, muscular, and healthy body, strengthened by physical yoga practice. This ideal aesthetic developed from the close connection in the development of modern yoga between gymnastics and bodybuilding. Other teachers, such as Krishnamacharya, Pattabhi Jois, or B. K. S. Iyengar, are often presented as traditionally educated pandits and don such characteristic features as traditional clothing, the *śikhā* hairstyle (shaven head with a lock of hair left at the crown), the *tilaka* (mark on the forehead denoting sectarian affiliation), or Brahmanical thread for their official photographic portraits. These attributes signify that the ideal (Indian) practitioner not only is healthy but also has a strong commitment to authenticity and tradition.

In descriptions and reports of their behavior and lifestyle, these early gurus of modern yoga were also often portrayed as archetypal yogis. The hagiographic life story of Tirumalai Krishnamacharya is an obvious example: He is said to have studied for seven years with a traditional guru in a cave in the Tibetan Himalayas before returning to South India. Such claims are still common for Indian gurus today, and even the most secular teachers of contemporary yoga will advertise themselves with a biography that includes hagiographic elements, such as dissatisfaction with a privileged social position, a long search for a teacher, and moments of serendipity. In the modern era, however, any perceived or actual gap between curated hagiography and actual behavior has become increasingly harder to conceal, and a number of these influential figures, such as Pattabhi Jois of Ashtanga Vinyasa Yoga, have been credibly accused or even convicted of significant interpersonal abuse of their followers and students.

Since the second half of the twentieth century, there has been a steady increase in women in positions of authority within yoga communities, consistent with the rise in the proportion of female practitioners of transnational yoga since the early twentieth century. Mirroring this growing gender imbalance, the ideal yoga practitioner has undergone a similarly striking evolution in contemporary yoga-related media and culture.

Many sociological researchers of yoga maintain that the contemporary ideal is exemplified by commercially oriented and visual representations of yoga, in particular on social media. From the majority of yoga-related social media posts, one could deduce that the contemporary ideal yoga practitioner is an upper-middle-class white Western woman of a specifically thin and mobile body type, wearing expensive exercise clothes and practicing a particularly acrobatic form of physical yoga in an environment of nature-inflected luxury.

Images of white women in high-end athleisure holding a perfect arm balance against the backdrop of a sunset beach in Bali and tagged with the hashtag #YogaEveryDamnDay are certainly common enough to be a cliché. There has been, however, a concerted effort within many contemporary yoga communities to promote and accommodate the reality that both experienced and beginner yoga practitioners come in every body shape, have varying levels of athleticism, and lead diverse lives in diverse contexts. Moreover, there has not been enough research focused on the demographic reality rather than the representation of contemporary yoga practitioners to enable us to distinguish between an ideal and a stereotype, between a norm, an average, and an exception. Such research would need to be part of a wider and ongoing attempt by researchers of contemporary yoga to map the diversity of devoted yoga communities and casual practitioners across the globe today.

If we consider the premodern ideal to be a practitioner who follows the precepts and attains liberation from the cycle of rebirths, it is possible to argue that an ideal yoga practitioner today is the one who similarly attains the goal of contemporary yoga, which for most, if not all, practitioners would be one of general health and well-being. But even such a generic goal could be challenged by those who believe the practice should primarily enable the practitioner to behave more ethically or devote themselves to a spiritual ideal. Perhaps it is enough to say that all yoga practitioners strive toward achieving an ideal self: Self-development after all could be considered to be the unifying principle that unites yoga as an extremely diverse set of practices and worldviews. But what an ideal yogic life would actually consist of is probably more contested than ever.

About the authors

Barbora Sojková holds a DPhil in Asian and Middle Eastern studies (Sanskrit) from the University of Oxford, where her research focused on human-animal relationships in Vedic Sanskrit literature. She works as an academic librarian at the All Souls College, Oxford, and as a Sanskrit cataloger at the Bodleian Library, Oxford. She is a certified yoga teacher and trainer focusing on the history and philosophy of yoga.

Theodora Wildcroft, PhD, is a researcher investigating the democratization and evolution of physical practice as it moves beyond both traditional and early modern frameworks of relationship. Her PhD was a significant advance in the analysis of contemporary yoga pedagogies. Her research continues to consider the democratization of yoga post-lineage and meaning making in grassroots communities of practice. She is an associate lecturer at the Open University, UK; a former coordinator of the SOAS Centre of Yoga Studies; an editor of the *BASR Bulletin*; an honorary member of the British Wheel of Yoga; a member of the IAYT; and a continuing professional development trainer and consultant for Yoga Alliance (US). Her monograph *Post-Lineage Yoga: From Guru to #MeToo* is available from Equinox Publishing Ltd. (2020).

Suggestions for further reading

In this book

See also chapters 3 (Is yoga a ritual?), 14 (Are ethics important in yoga?), and 36 (Do you need to practice yoga to understand it?).

Elsewhere

Birch, Jason, and Jacqueline Hargreaves. "Premodern Yogāsanas and Modern Postural Yoga Practice." In *Yoga and the Traditional Physical Practices of South Asia, Entanglement and Confrontation*, edited by Daniela Bevilacqua and Mark Singleton. Special issue, *Journal of Yoga Studies* 4 (2023): 31–82.

Singleton, Mark, and Ellen Goldberg. *Gurus of Modern Yoga*. Oxford University Press, 2014.

Wildcroft, Theodora. "Re-Telling the Self: The Lived Experience of Modern Yoga Practice." In *Routledge Companion to Performance Philosophy*, edited by Laura Cull Ó Maoilearca and Alice Lagaay. Routledge, 2020.

27

Has yoga always been a physical practice?

Laura von Ostrowski

To answer this question, two different understandings of yoga need to be taken into account: On the one hand, yoga can be understood as a practical method, and on the other hand and much more commonly, yoga is the goal, the state to which different methods lead. The earliest known definition of "yoga" as a goal is found in the *Kaṭha Upaniṣad* 6.10–6.11 (ca. third to second century BCE), which defines yoga as a state where the five sense perceptions as well as the mind are stilled.

Another famous example of a text that defines yoga as a goal is the fourth-to-fifth-century *Pātañjalayogaśāstra* (PYŚ), which in the commentary part (*bhāṣya*) of sūtra 1.1 equates yoga with *samādhi*, a psychophysical state of intense absorption.

When identifying yoga as a method, it must be based on some sort of practice. In the following, the term "physical practice" will be considered more closely in the context of Indian yoga history. Primarily, the term "physical" refers to the physique, or the body, but in the context of yoga practices, it is often employed as a counterpart to "mental" exercises. The conclusion of such an understanding is that yoga has not always been associated with physical practices because many premodern yogic practices focused on differing states of mental concentration or absorption, to be established in a motionless, seated position (*āsana*). In this way, the PYŚ defines the famous practice associated with yoga, āsana, as one of eight auxiliaries (*aṣṭāṅgas*) and as such as the precondition for the following five auxiliaries, thus for establishing *prāṇāyāma* (breath control), *pratyāhāra* (sense withdrawal), *dhāraṇā* (concentration), *dhyāna* (meditation), and *samādhi* (absorption), which leads to the state of *yoga*.

In contrast to such a body-mind dichotomy, the theory of embodiment broadens the view of what a physical practice is, as it highlights that indeed every practice a human performs is embodied in some way. That includes a motionless practice like lying, sitting, or standing; moving practices like walking; or even more complex and sophisticated movements, like dancing, riding a horse, or the performance of yogic āsanas. In every millisecond of human life, interoceptive processes like awareness of the breath, the heartbeat, or tiny movements in fascia, muscles, and joints are happening unconsciously and automatically and keep the body moving.

Based on this, *embodied cognition* is founded on the insight that sensorimotor and perceptual experiences as well as bodily interactions with physical and cultural environments are fundamental to our cognition. This leads to the conclusion that "mental" practices such as concentration exercises or meditation need not be accompanied by a moving physical exercise to be nonetheless embodied.

Based on this broader understanding of physicality and embodiment, since very early on in Indian history, techniques that have been associated with yoga traditions, such as earlier practices like seated *āsanas*, *prāṇāyāma* (breath control), and *tapas* (internal heat) or later ones like *bandha* or *mudrā*, make use of the body in some way. They can thus be defined as variations of physical practices, even though they may differentiate from today's globalized, āsana-based, but mostly moving set of physical yoga routines.

Nevertheless, when examining the history of prāṇāyāma, āsana, or tapas more closely, another aspect needs to be taken into account. In some early and medieval text sources, it becomes obvious that the intention behind such practices was to make use of the body for the sake of silencing bodily functions like the breath or the heartbeat and to even eventually discard the body. For example, prāṇāyāma has been identified with breath control for the longest part of its history in Indian thought. The techniques described in the PYŚ in *sūtras* 2.49–51 refer to different kinds of breath holding. The *bhāṣya* defines the external prāṇāyāma, called *bāhya*, when the breath becomes still after exhalation; the internal prāṇāyāma, *ābhyantara*, when there is no flow of breath after inhalation; and the restrained prāṇāyāma, *stambha-vṛtti*, the cessation of both. This changes in earlier *haṭhayoga* texts like the thirteenth-century *Dattātreyayogaśāstra*, even though breath retention, called *kevalakumbhaka*, is still described, and descriptions of *sahitakumbhakas* increase considerably. These are prāṇāyāma techniques that still include breath retention but are distinguished by their methods of inhalation and exhalation. They become more and more common in later haṭhayoga texts where prāṇāyāma becomes a practice with predominantly physical benefits, in contrast to earlier practices.

The term *tapas* refers to the heated effort of ascetic practice, as well as to the bodily, sweat-inducing, ritual heat, which is the effect produced by this practice. In Vedic texts as well as in extra-Vedic traditions such as Jainism, this heat is understood to burn the impurities of the ascetic. As tapas is an important concept in several Upaniṣads as well as in the *Bhagavadgītā* and the PYŚ (2.1, 2.32, 2.43), it can be defined as a yogic practice that uses the body to burn karma and eventually release the body entirely.

Finally, the physical postures popularly called *āsanas* today have ancient predecessors that have been transformed into more diverse, strenuous, and dynamic versions, becoming geared toward strength and fitness from the seventeenth century onward. In its commentary section, the PYŚ names twelve seated āsanas without describing any details. At the end, it adds "etc.," implying that there are more. In the context of Pātañjalayoga, a stable and comfortable posture is a prerequisite for breath control, concentration, and meditation but is itself, as sūtra 2.47 specifies, established through the slackening of effort or from merging meditatively into infinity. This example shows that in ancient Indian yoga texts, posture was also related to mental and affective states and vice versa.

Nonseated āsanas, even if not associated with "yoga" for much of its history, have in fact been used by some Indian ascetics for at least 2,500 years, as witnessed in the Buddhist Pali canon as well as in Greek travel reports from Alexander the Great's entourage. They involved standing on one leg for long periods of time or even hanging upside down from a tree, suspended by the feet (a posture known as the "bat penance," which is likely the precursor of today's inverted āsanas like the headstand). That Kṛṣṇa condemns such physical austerities in the *Bhagavadgītā* 17.5 because they are unauthorized by scriptures and weaken the body signals an ancient debate around the motivation for and the effect of physical practices. From a set of only a few āsanas that are held for long periods of time, the proliferation of āsana from the sixteenth century onward increasingly transformed the physical practice called yoga into one with a larger range of physical effects.

To summarize, the term "yoga" has not always been associated with physical practices but mainly with a state that arises as a result of certain practices. Yoga as a practical method has nevertheless always been using the body in one way or another but with different intentions, motivations, and effects.

About the author

Laura von Ostrowski received her PhD in religious studies in 2021. The book to her PhD thesis was published open access under the title *A Text in Motion* in 2022. Her areas of research include modern and contemporary yoga, the reception of the *Yogasūtra*, the history of German yoga and the physical culture movement, contemporary religion, aesthetics, and embodiment. Since 2007, she has worked as a yoga teacher, including running her own yoga studio in the center of Munich since 2018 and teaching the history of modern yoga at the German online education portal Yogastudien.

Suggestions for further reading

In this book

See also chapters 37 (How do academics study yoga?) and 46 (Who were Gorakṣanātha and Matsyendranātha?).

Elsewhere

Bouthillette, Karl-Stéphan. "Hermeneutic Praxis: The Yoga of Reason(ing)." *Studia Religiologica* 50, no. 2 (2017): 103–115.

Hariharānanda Āraṇya, Swāmi. *Yoga Philosophy of Patañjali*. Rev. ed. State University of New York Press, 1983.

28
What are *āsanas*?

Matylda Ciołkosz

The Sanskrit noun *āsana* means "a seat" or "a place," as well as an act of "sitting" or "dwelling." In the context of yoga, *āsana* means yogic posture. While nowadays hundreds of yogic postures are known—standing, seated, inverted, supine, or prone—originally *āsana* was a way of sitting adopted for the purpose of other practices, such as breath control or meditation.

According to Patañjali, an *āsana* is a steady and comfortable posture that results from the slackening of effort or from merging meditatively into infinity. Patañjali's text on yoga, the *Pātañjalayogaśāstra*, lists thirteen seated postures, some of them called *āsana*, others *niṣadana* (a noun also meaning "sitting down"). Among them are such now universally known poses as *padmāsana* (the lotus pose), *daṇḍāsana* (the staff pose), *bhadrāsana* (the auspicious pose), or *vīrāsana* (the hero pose).

A stand-alone practice of āsanas was gradually developed by the practitioners of *haṭhayoga* between the eleventh and the eighteenth centuries. While some texts on haṭhayoga claim the existence of as many as 8,400,000 postures and others state that there are as many poses as there are types of living creatures, the actual number of āsanas listed and described by these texts is relatively small. The earliest works on haṭhayoga name and describe as few as one or two āsanas, and it is not until the fifteenth century that the number of the described poses exceeds ten. The famous fifteenth-century *Haṭhapradīpikā*, authored by Svātmārāma, lists and describes fifteen postures, and in subsequent texts, this number increases to reach 112 in the late eighteenth-century *Haṭhābhyāsapaddhati*, written by Kapālakuruṇṭaka.

Texts on haṭhayoga are the first to postulate that different āsanas may produce therapeutic effects, such as helping digestion, cleaning the bodily channels, or simply destroying disease. Some āsanas are claimed to produce special powers—such as unparalleled knowledge—while others are believed to cause sudden liberation.

The haṭhayoga texts also introduce the first known nonseated postures. The first to be mentioned are *kukkuṭāsana* (the cock pose) and *mayūrāsana* (the peacock pose). In both of them, the practitioner lifts the body off the ground, balancing solely on the palms of their hands. It seems that such balancing was the first variation introduced to the formerly seated āsana practice. Postures involving standing, lying, or other ways to position the body known from contemporary yoga practice are not evidenced until the eighteenth century.

The majority of work on haṭhayoga treats āsanas as separate poses and provides no suggestions as to how to connect them into longer sequences. An exception in this regard is the aforementioned *Haṭhābhyāsapaddhati*—produced at the end of the eighteenth century—which describes six sequences of postures. In these sequences, many unique poses are found that are absent from earlier texts. Some of them are supine, prone, or stationary, and some involve the use of a rope or the support of a wall. Many of them involve movement—they are the first known dynamic āsanas to date.

While nowadays the practice of yogic postures is associated with nurturing and strengthening the body, āsanas have also had an ascetic aspect. Some of the poses may have been influenced by the postural austerities of Indian renunciates. Ascetics squatting, hanging upside down, or standing on one leg for a prolonged time are mentioned in the Buddhist Pali canon, as well as in the *Mahābhārata*. Such austerities were believed to destroy *karma* (the effects of one's actions accumulated throughout one's incarnations) and thus help achieve liberation from rebirth. Some of the postural austerities of Jain ascetics came to be known as āsanas and described in manuals such as the *Yogaśāstra*, an eleventh-century Jain text authored by Hemacandra.

Asceticism was not the only external influence on the development of āsanas. In early modern India, āsana practice started to intertwine with other forms of physical culture, both Indigenous and Western. Sections on āsana are found in Indian physical culture manuals, such as the *Mallapurāṇa*, a seventeenth-century compendium for wrestlers. By the early twentieth century, physical education at some notable facilities—including the Jaganmohan Palace in Mysore—included āsana practice among other exercises, such as bodybuilding or sun salutations (*sūryanamaskār*). By that time, various European systems of exercise made their way to colonial India, also influencing the way āsanas were practiced.

As a result, the curriculum of yogic postures practiced nowadays is vast. Some of them have ancient origins; others were added in modernity. Some are named after sages, animals, or other phenomena observed in the natural world; others have very technical names. Due to the contemporary interaction of postural yoga with other disciplines and movement practices, the number of āsanas practiced across the globe continues to grow.

In contemporary postural yoga, the majority of āsanas are known across different systems and lineages. However, they are often practiced in very different ways. They are performed in sequences, which may be unalterable (with poses always performed in the same order) or open to modification (with a different sequence performed during each practice session). They may be interspersed with special transitional sequences or simply performed one after another. They may be practiced dynamically (with continuous smooth transitions between one posture and another or with a single posture being repeated back and forth a few times) or statically (with a single posture lasting between a minute and several minutes). They may have variations (versions of the same posture that differ slightly in form) or be performed with props (such as belts, blocks, bolsters, wheels, or larger equipment) to accommodate the practitioners' capacities and needs. They may be practiced with as little physical effort involved as possible or forcefully, with an athletic attitude.

Contemporary yoga practitioners attribute a variety of effects to āsana practice. It is believed to develop strength and flexibility, help regulate physiological processes, relieve stress, promote mental equilibrium, and support the treatment of a variety of disorders and diseases. In some systems of postural yoga, sequences of āsanas are arranged that are believed to bring forth particular therapeutic effects, from relieving discomfort during menstruation or back pain to assisting the treatment of serious illnesses, such as depression or malignant tumors. However, the concept of āsana as a seated meditation pose is still a part of our shared imagination, and a silhouette seated in padmāsana (lotus pose) remains a universally understood symbol of yoga.

About the author

Matylda Ciołkosz is an assistant professor at the Institute of Religious Studies, Jagiellonian University in Kraków. She earned her PhD in culture and religion studies in 2019 for her research on the meaning-making role of kinesthetic experience in the practice of modern postural yoga. In her research, she draws from cognitive approaches to the study of religions to explore the influence of sensory, motor, and social contexts on the formation and application of religious concepts.

Suggestions for further reading

In this book

See also chapters 22 (Why do yogis contort their bodies?) and 32 (Why do yogis go upside down?).

Elsewhere

Alter, Joseph. "Yoga and Physical Education: Swami Kuvalayananda's Nationalist Project." *Asian Medicine* 3 (2007): 20–36.

Birch, Jason. "The Proliferation of Āsana-s in Late-Medieval Yoga Texts." In *Yoga in Transformation: Historical and Contemporary Perspectives*, edited by Karl Baier, Philipp A. Maas, and Karin Preisendanz. V&R unipress, 2018.

Birch, Jason, and Mark Singleton. "The Yoga of the *Haṭhābhyāsapaddhati*: Haṭhayoga on the Cusp of Modernity." *Journal of Yoga Studies* 2 (2019): 3–70.

Maas, Philipp A. "'*Sthirasukham Āsanam*': Posture and Performance in Classical Yoga and Beyond." In *Yoga in Transformation: Historical and Contemporary Perspectives*, edited by Karl Baier, Philipp A. Maas, and Karin Preisendanz. V&R unipress, 2018.

29
What is *vinyasa*?

Marissa Clarke

If you have ever been to a yoga studio or searched for a yoga class online, you have most likely encountered the term *vinyasa*. Perhaps it has been used colloquially in class to describe the transitions between āsanas where breath is supposedly performed in synchronization with movement. The class itself may have been called "Vinyasa Yoga" to signify that one will practice a dynamic sequence of linked movements in an aerobic fashion. Such understandings satisfy our partiality for naming movements or categorizing practices. Yet the deconstruction of vinyasa as a concept reveals its syncretic preliminaries and influences.

There are no records of vinyasa as we know it today appearing in premodern texts on yoga. Similar Sanskrit words, such as *nyāsa*, have been used in tantric texts to refer to the installation of mantras on the body. While some schools of yoga may claim that their vinyasa sequences, or *sūryanamaskār*, are cited in the Vedas, from a scholarly perspective, these accounts are historically and philologically unsound. Thus, the common understanding of vinyasa as a linking of breath with movement is a relatively modern phenomenon insofar as it has developed over the last century.

The contemporary idea of vinyasa can be traced back to Krishnamacharya (1888–1989) and his method of *vinyasa krama* (special sequence of steps) or *viniyoga* (appropriate application) that he developed during his days teaching at the Mysore Palace in the early 1930s to 1950s. Krishnamacharya reinterpreted the meaning of vinyasa to refer to his concept of linking movement with breath through a flowing progression of poses. In the early days, vinyasa involved transitional repetitions of "jump back" and "jump forward" movements. The conditioning nature of these exercises was influenced by both local and transnational physical culture movements such as Indigenous forms of wrestling, *mallakhamb*, military training techniques, and martial arts as well as European bodybuilding, calisthenics, and gymnastics. Physical culture reforms were significant in the early nineteenth century, particularly for males in the South Asian subcontinent, as strong and powerful masculine bodies represented cultural power, national pride, and resistance to colonial rule. The Mysore Palace was a hot spot for these reformations.

Textual sources such as the *Vyāyāmadīpike*, a Mysore gymnastics manual written by S. R. Bharadwaj in 1896, have enabled scholars on the Haṭha Yoga Project (2015–2020) to hypothesize that Krishnamacharya's concept of vinyasa may have been influenced by the dynamic movements understood as *jhoku* in this manual. The various movements of jhoku illustrate a transitional sequence starting from a standing or seated position whereby the weight of the body is transferred to the hands in between positions. The positions share various similarities with the movements in sūryanamaskār or an Ashtanga Yoga "vinyasa," including *ūrdhvamukhaśvānāsana* (upward-facing dog pose), *adhomukhaśvānāsana* (downward-facing dog pose), and *caturaṅga daṇḍāsana* (plank pose with bent elbows). The eighteenth-century text of the *Haṭhābhyāsapaddhati* by Kapāla Kurantaka is speculated to have influenced both Bharadwaj and Krishnamacharya, as this text gives further details on the sequencing of *āsanas* in *haṭhayoga* as well as vigorous *daṇḍ*, movements that look like jhoku and vinyasa. Nevertheless, it is likely that these dynamic movements were typical of a fusion of physical culture traditions that were continuously evolving and adapting to the various sociopolitical demands of the time.

Krishnamacharya's approach to vinyasa was always changing, which also reflects a core aspect of his teaching, that yoga should be adapted to suit the requirements of the individual, location, and period. It was his student Pattabhi Jois (1915–2009) who was influential in popularizing and systematizing the concept of vinyasa in the creation of Ashtanga Vinyasa Yoga. In Jois's system, vinyasa became known as a repetitive schema of taking either half or full sūryanamaskār between a set sequence of poses. It is worth noting that for Krishnamacharya, vinyasa was not limited to this understanding, as vinyasa for him also specified an appropriate sequence of steps (*krama*) for approaching a particular posture. Still, the concept of vinyasa as a linking sequence has radically influenced various offshoots of contemporary yoga styles such as "Power Yoga" or "Power Vinyasa" and "Vinyasa Flow" since the 1990s. Noteworthy examples of early Power Vinyasa pioneers include Beryl Bender Birch's "Power Yoga" and Larry Schultz's "Rocket Yoga," also known as "Progressive Ashtanga Yoga." These offshoots broke away from the rigidity of the Ashtanga Vinyasa Yoga series, allowing for more creativity and modifications in the practice. The Power Vinyasa craze prevails today, with most yoga studios and gyms offering styles reminiscent of rigorous, aerobic sequences.

Although vinyasa can be considered a novel outcome of various movement practices that were converging, Anya Foxen's scholarship has shown that the concept of linking breath with movement was not necessarily a new phenomenon in the West. The predecessor of vinyasa in Europe and North America was "harmonial gymnastics," a form of exercise that combined Western harmonial principles of spirituality with dance-like aesthetic gymnastics inspired by earlier modernizers of movement Pehr Henrik Ling (1776–1839) and François Delsarte (1811–1871). The harmonial wellness movement was popular with Euro-American women in the nineteenth century and was propelled by Genevieve Stebbins's (1857–1934) system of "psycho-physical culture," which aimed to synchronize breath with movement for contemplative ends. Exercises in this milieu were presented as ancient and universal but were later exoticized as "Oriental," which is evident in the context of dancers inspired by Delsarte and "psycho-physical culture" who performed in costumes evoking a Western gaze on the East. The practices were based on a harmonial worldview rather than yogic, but ultimately, the Western fetishism for the exotic facilitated the gradual rebranding of harmonial gymnastics as "yoga" and its contemporary colloquial cousin "vinyasa." Indian pioneers of yoga also supported this process by blending āsanas from the haṭhayoga corpus with Western physical culture practices in both their teachings and texts published in English for Western audiences. Foxen's scholarship has also shown that innovators such as Shri Yogendra (1897–1989) overtly quoted and integrated the techniques of Stebbins into his own publications, whereas figures such as Yogananda (1893–1952) would teach Swedish calisthenics advertised as "Yogoda" to American audiences while saving haṭha techniques for his inner circle of male initiates.

Vinyasa's syncretism and divergence from the stillness of āsana depicted in much of premodern haṭhayoga do not mean that it can be disregarded as nothing more than esoteric gymnastics or exoticized dance. Teachers and practitioners continue to ascribe their own soteriological aims and metaphysical meanings to vinyasa while turning to sources from the past to authenticate their practices. The concept of "flow," which is often associated with vinyasa, makes it a fascinating praxis to explore, especially for practitioners seeking to experience altered states of consciousness. Vinyasa can be considered a physical philosophy in its own right; hence it proposes an alternative for the "stable seat" of āsana by valorizing the transitions between postures as of equal importance, emphasizing the processual and reciprocal relationship of continuous fluid movement, leading to the potentiality for "flow" or transcendent experiences. The dynamic transitions of vinyasa and the stable postures of āsana consist of the same thing—the body. Interpretations of the experience, process, and technique of "vinyasa" will always be contextual and personal to the practitioner. There is much more to be discovered, experienced, and shared regarding the phenomenology of vinyasa in future scholarship.

About the author

Marissa Clarke is a PhD candidate at the University of Edinburgh (2021–2025) and visiting doctoral researcher at Universidade Federal do Rio Grande do Sul (2024). Her research explores the phenomenology of yoga, the body, and sound. She has an interdisciplinary background in marketing studies, religious studies, and health research. Her work is funded by the Scottish Graduate School for Arts & Humanities AHRC Doctoral Training Partnership.

Suggestions for further reading

In this book

See also chapters 50 (What is the difference between *haṭhayoga* and Hatha Yoga?) and 55 (Who was Krishnamacharya?).

Elsewhere

Birch, Jason, and Mark Singleton. "The Yoga of the *Haṭhābhyāsapaddhati*: Haṭhayoga on the Cusp of Modernity." *Journal of Yoga Studies* 2 (2019): 3–70.

Clark, Edward, and Laurie A. Greene. *Teaching Contemporary Yoga: Physical Philosophy and Critical Issues*. Routledge, 2022.

Foxen, Anya P. *Inhaling Spirit: Harmonialism, Orientalism, and the Western Roots of Modern Yoga*. Oxford University Press, 2020.

Singleton, Mark. *Yoga Body: The Origins of Modern Posture Practice*. Oxford University Press, 2010.

30
What is *prāṇāyāma*?

Graham Burns

Prāṇāyāma is the term used in yoga for a range of practices that involve the control, or manipulation, of breath. The word itself is a compound of the Sanskrit words *prāṇa*, as to which see further below, and *āyāma* (control).

It would not be unreasonable to say that prāṇāyāma has been a hallmark of yoga practice throughout its long existence. Since early times, Indian thinkers have acknowledged the importance of breath as the indicator of life—the *Atharvaveda*, around 1000–900 BCE, lauds breath (*prāṇa*) as the "lord" and support of the universe; prāṇa "clothes creatures," just as a parent provides clothes for their child; and prāṇa is exhorted not to depart, as that, of course, would signify the end of life. A couple of centuries later, early Upaniṣads contain stories about a competition between the senses to determine which of them is the most important. Each takes its turn to leave the body, but the body continues to live—even though blind, deaf, dumb, and so on. However, when prāṇa announces its intention to depart, the other senses implore it to stay, again realizing that without prāṇa, the body will die.

Neither of these sources mentions specific practices of controlling breath. One of the earliest known references to breath control comes in the *Jaiminīya Upaniṣad Brāhmaṇa*, from the early centuries of the first millennium BCE, which contains an instruction not to breathe during recitation of a particular chant, though without any explanation why. Breath control practices are also prescribed in the *Dharmasūtras* and *Dharmaśāstras* in the late BCE / early CE as penances for breaches of certain behavioral requirements, and also in the later centuries BCE, the Buddha is said to have practiced "nonbreathing meditation," though with somewhat negative results.

While prāṇa initially almost certainly denoted physical breath, the importance attached to it led to it receiving a somewhat extended meaning: not just the movement of air in the body, but a broader, generic "life force," or energy, flowing in the body in different ways. The *Śvetāśvatara*

Upaniṣad, dated to the last couple of centuries BCE or early CE, gives an early glimpse of breath control as part of yoga, where it advises that "compressing the breath . . . a person should exhale through one nostril, when their breath is exhausted." This helps the practitioner keep their mind "vigilantly under control," acknowledging something that the *Chāndogya Upaniṣad*, around 600–500 BCE, had already noted—namely, the link between state of breath and state of mind.

In the *Pātañjalayogaśāstra* (the *Yogasūtra* and the so-called Vyāsa commentary, now widely considered to be a single composition from around the fourth century CE), prāṇāyāma is the fourth component of the *aṣṭāṅgayoga* path of eight "limbs," or "auxiliaries," following *yama* and *niyama* (behavioral norms) and *āsana* (steady, comfortable posture). The yogi is said to be ready for prāṇāyāma when, through "perfection" of a steady, comfortable posture, they are no longer distracted by opposites, such as heat and cold. Here, prāṇāyāma is described as the regulation of the movements of inhalation and exhalation, which can be done by "place, time and number"—distance covered by the movement of air, duration of the respective phases of the breath, and number of cycles of breath—and can involve pausing after inhalation, exhalation, or both. As a result, breath becomes "long and subtle." Prāṇāyāma makes the yogi ready for the final stages of the aṣṭāṅgayoga path, the three-stage process of meditation. Practices involving measuring, regulating, or counting the different phases of the breath ("ratio breathing"), with or without retention, are commonly found in modern yoga classes.

Aside from these general instructions, the *Pātañjalayogaśāstra* does not teach any specific prāṇāyāma techniques. By the time, however, that we reach *haṭhayoga* around the eleventh to twelfth century CE, more detailed descriptions of specific and more sophisticated prāṇāyāma practices appear. While prāṇāyāma in the *Pātañjalayogaśāstra* is a step on the path toward meditation (again acknowledging the link between controlling breath and controlling mind), in haṭhayoga, the primary purpose of prāṇāyāma shifts. While it remains a step on the path toward deeper states of yoga, it becomes more closely associated with cleansing, or purifying, the subtle energetic channels of the body (*nāḍī*) and promoting the physical health that the practitioner will need for the deeper practices that follow.

While there are several descriptions of prāṇāyāma practices in haṭhayoga texts, the *Haṭhapradīpikā*, largely a compilation of earlier material put together in the fifteenth century, is broadly representative of the haṭhayoga approach to prāṇāyāma. Here, the practitioner is again required to master āsanas (now with a more extended meaning than simply a steady, comfortable posture) and to have a moderate diet before embarking on prāṇāyāma.

The first prāṇāyāma practice is one of breathing through alternate nostrils, with retention after inhalation, variations of which also frequently feature in modern yoga classes. Regular practice of alternate nostril breathing is said to purify the left and right energetic channels "in three months," making the body "lean and bright."

After a diversion to emphasize that prāṇāyāma should be approached slowly and with care and the introduction of six physical cleaning practices, the *Haṭhapradīpikā* introduces eight further prāṇāyāma practices—*sūryabhedana, ujjāyī, sitkārī, śītalī, bhastrikā, bhrāmarī, mūrcchā,* and *plāvinī.* These are stronger practices, often accompanied by *bandha* in order to retain and direct prāṇa within the body. Of these eight, versions of four are commonly encountered in contemporary yoga classes—*ujjāyī, śītalī, bhastrikā,* and *bhrāmarī.* In ujjāyī, the *Haṭhapradīpikā* instructs the practitioner to inhale slowly through both nostrils so that the breath "resonates," retain the breath, then exhale through the left nostril in order to cure diseases of the throat caused by phlegm and increase digestive fire. This differs somewhat from the ujjāyī breathing commonly taught in contemporary yoga, which normally calls for a subtle sound to be made in the throat while inhaling and exhaling through both nostrils. In contemporary yoga, too, ujjāyī is frequently employed during āsana practice rather than as a separate practice in its own right.

Śītalī prāṇāyāma occurs often in contemporary yoga as a cooling practice, though the *Haṭhapradīpikā* prescribes it for more specific quasi-therapeutic purposes. Here, the breath is drawn in through a rolled tongue, retained, and then exhaled through the nostrils. In bhastrikā, the breath is inhaled and exhaled quickly, like a bellows, with the option of breathing in only through the right nostril and out through the left (closing the nostrils with the fingers during retention) to alleviate fatigue. In bhrāmarī, inhalation is rapid, with the sound of a male bee; exhalation is very slow, with the (deeper) sound of a female bee. In contemporary yoga, the buzzing sound of the bee (of indeterminate gender) is often made only on exhalation, usually with the ears blocked.

Later texts introduce several variations on these techniques, sometimes incorporating mantra as well as bandha practices alongside them, but the purpose of prāṇāyāma remains broadly the same—to cleanse the energetic channels of the body and, as a therapeutic tool more broadly, to prepare for deeper practices that shift the flows of prāṇa and lead toward meditation. While these purposes are sometimes mentioned in contemporary yoga, prāṇāyāma is also frequently introduced after āsana as a precursor to meditation, reflecting the link of breath and mind and the role of prāṇāyāma in the *Pātañjalayogaśāstra.* In some contemporary traditions, any prāṇāyāma is considered "advanced" practice, reflecting the respect that yogis have always advised be paid to breath and to prāṇa more broadly.

About the author

Graham Burns is an independent yoga teacher, teacher trainer, and scholar. As well as a law degree from Durham University, he holds an MA in religions and a PhD in ancient Indian philosophy from SOAS University of London. He is a former senior teaching fellow at SOAS, where he lectured on the MA in traditions of yoga and meditation and taught undergraduate Hinduism and philosophy. He is a member of the SOAS Centre of Yoga Studies.

Suggestions for further reading

In this book

See also chapters 21 (Is yoga good for your health?), 40 (What do the words *sampradāya* and *paramparā* mean?), and 45 (Who was Patañjali?).

Elsewhere

Akers, Brian Dana. *The Hatha Yoga Pradipika*. YogaVidya, 2002.

Bryant, Edwin F. *The Yoga Sūtras of Patañjali*. North Point Press, 2009.

Olivelle, Patrick. *Upaniṣads*. Oxford University Press, 1996.

31
How do mantras relate to yoga?

Finnian M. M. Gerety

Mantras are utterances, formulas, verses, and syllables used in ritual, healing, magic, meditation—and yoga. While often spoken and sounded, mantras remain closely entwined with cognitive processes: The Sanskrit word *mantra* literally means an "instrument of thinking," and a venerable aphorism says that mantras protect the practitioner through constant contemplation. Variously akin to prayers, spells, chants, poems, eulogies, affirmations, meditation aids, and visualizations, mantras have been used for centuries across a wide range of yoga traditions in different ways and for different purposes. Mantras may be chanted audibly, repeated in a low tone, or contemplated in silence. Mantras circulate in diverse materials and media, from inscriptions to manuscripts, textiles to ritual diagrams (*maṇḍalas*, *yantras*), audio recordings to websites. Mantra as a category encompasses several kinds of sacred utterance in Asia, including *mantra*, *stotra*, *vidyā*, *dhāraṇī*, *paritta*, *shabad*, and so on. Historically composed in Sanskrit and Indic languages, mantras have been closely associated with Asian religious traditions. Yet in modern transnational yoga, mantras may be expressed in other languages and deployed in a variety of spiritual contexts.

Although yoga is best known today as a physical practice of postures and movements, it originated in early India as a system of meditation in which mantras sometimes played a key role. The oldest mantras, utterances in Sanskrit ascribed to sages and regarded as emanations of divine speech, were compiled some three thousand years ago in oral traditions called the Vedas (*veda*, "knowledge") and chanted in sacrificial ritual by Brahmans, members of the Hindu priesthood. The sacred syllable *om*, the quintessential yogic mantra, is originally a Vedic utterance used to introduce other mantras. The Hindu *gāyatrī* mantra has a similar pedigree and serves an analogous function. Other important Sanskrit mantras were compiled in medieval texts called tantras and āgamas—traditions known as the "path of mantras" (*mantramārga*), which blend antinomian practices with rites of worship in Hindu, Buddhist, and Jain traditions. Tantric traditions regard mantras as divine manifestations of sonic energy that find expression in verbal formulas and in the non-lexical monosyllables called "seeds" (*bījas*). Seed syllables may be used on their own—for example, in meditations on *klīṃ*, associated with the divine feminine, or *hrīṃ*, representing enlightened Jain teachers. They may be strung together in sequences, as in the death-defying Śaiva mantra *oṃ jūṃ sauḥ*, or combined with other words to form longer mantras, as in the famous Buddhist formula *oṃ maṇipadme hūṃ*. Alongside tantric mantras, another major current in the history of mantras is devotion (*bhakti*). Hindu devotional mantras of many kinds are collected in texts of "ancient lore" (*Purāṇas*). In these mantras, the names of deities and spiritual teachers are incorporated into formulas of praise (e.g., *oṃ namo vāsudevāya*, "OM, homage to Vāsudeva!") or else constitute mantras in themselves (e.g., *rām* or the *hare kṛṣṇa* mantra). Repetition of such formulas is a hallmark of devotional worship. All these streams—Vedic, Tantric, Puranic—overlap to varying degrees in shaping yogic approaches to mantra. *Namaste*, for example, is actually a mantra with Vedic origins that assimilated a bhakti sensibility on its way to becoming a pan-Indian greeting and global yogic catchphrase. Comparable syncretism is in play in the contemporary tradition of Siddha Yoga, which melds the Puranic formula *oṃ namaḥ śivāya* (*om*, homage to Śiva!) with tantric practices in a devotional mode. While mantras are widely acknowledged in yoga as potent tools that transform people physically and spiritually, not all yoga systems emphasize mantras to the same degree. Among Nāth Yogīs, for example, ascetics who engaged in the highly physical forms of practice associated with premodern *haṭhayoga*, mantras seem to have played a lesser role. Indeed, the classic taxonomy of yogas from this milieu places *mantrayoga* in the lowest position, subordinate to other types.

The practitioner's body, as a conduit between the self and the cosmos, is central to the ideology and practice of mantra. The *haṃsa* mantra, for example, is predicated on the notion of breathing as mantric sound: Natural exhalation makes the sound *ha*, inhalation makes the sound *sa*, and these together yield the word *haṃsa*, an esoteric name for the breath (*prāṇa*) as well as a bird associated with the flight of the soul. The repeated sounding of haṃsa can also be parsed as *so 'ham* (I am that), an Upaniṣadic statement linking the practitioner to the supreme soul. On the flesh-and-blood level of "gross" (*sthūla*) materiality, the efficacy of mantras depends on physiological processes: respiration, cognition, and vocalization. However, on the level of the so-called yogic body—the energetic anatomy of the body visualized and manipulated by the yogi—mantras are animated by "subtle" (*sūkṣma*) energy that moves in the breath and serves to connect the practitioner, spiritual beings, and various metaphysical states. Consider the raising of *kuṇḍalinī*, the activation of energy that ordinarily remains "coiled" at the base of the spine, which is a guiding aim of tantric yoga. (This term appears in a very different guise in the modern Kundalini Yoga taught by Yogi Bhajan in the American Sikh movement, where mantras such as *sat nam* are deployed with breath control and postures.) According to premodern tantric sources, the practitioner may use mantras to awaken kuṇḍalinī—apotheosized as the female deity of sacred speech—and thereby give impetus to her upward movement along the central channel of the yogic body. This trajectory is conceived as running through a series of energetic centers (*cakras*), each of which aligns with a certain bīja, culminating in a transcendent experiential state accessed through the crown of the head. This is the soteriological aim of the practice, conceived as "union" (*yoga*) with the supreme deity. Discourses of mantras and the yogic body often emphasize sonic levels beyond what the human ear can detect: notably, the "drop" (*bindu*), the nasal sound (*anusvāra, ṃ*) concluding a seed syllable, and "resonance" (*nāda*), the holistic vibration of the mantra as it fades into silence. Attunement to these subtle sound levels ultimately reveals their divine source, the "unstruck" (*anāhata*) sound, which is eternally resonating, free from material impetus, and identified with spiritual liberation. Alongside this tantric paradigm of the yogic body, mantras also blend with other cultural currents as they circulate worldwide in transnational yoga. In some Western societies, for example, yogis have cross-pollinated Asian mantra systems with European esoteric techniques of the voice and the body or with North American ideas of meditation as stress reduction, as in Transcendental Meditation.

In general, yogic approaches to mantra are predicated on the idea of regular practice. The daily routine of mantra chanting may be known as *svādhyāya*—an originally Vedic practice that was adapted as a yogic regimen by the time of the *Pātañjalayogaśāstra* and continues to be a widespread paradigm in modern yoga. Nowadays, svādhyāya is often understood as "self-study"—reflecting on mantras and canonical texts for the sake of edification and insight. Although the particulars of mantra practice vary considerably, several key features are widely shared across traditions, time periods, and regions. Many traditions require initiation (*dīkṣā*), including the ritualized teaching of a key mantra, in secret, by the lineage holder to the new practitioner; traditional initiation is frequently limited to high-caste men and boys.

Transnational modern yoga, however, generally eschews formal initiation as a prerequisite to mantra practice. Mantras may be chanted alone, with a teacher, or in a group. Reciting mantras at the start and finish of a yoga session often serves to enclose a central practice, which in turn may consist of rites, postures, silent meditation, or more mantras. Many yogis begin by assuming a seated lotus posture, fixing the eyes on the nose tip or closing them gently, regulating the breath (*prāṇāyāma*), holding the hands together at the chest (*añjali mudrā*), and intoning the introductory syllable *OM*. Then, a selection of mantras in praise of teachers, deities, or traditions opens the central practice, and an additional selection, conveying auspiciousness or completion, concludes it. Indeed, this is how mantras are often incorporated in postural yoga settings, as in the Mysore style taught by Krishnamacharya, Jois, and Iyengar, where mantras frame the main sequence of *āsanas*. Framed by opening and closing formulas in this way, recitation proper often consists of repeating a primary mantra or mantras some set number of times, a practice known as *japa* (muttering). The number of repetitions can extend into the thousands, with more repetitions understood to bring greater results. Prayer beads (*japamālā*) held in between the fingers can help the practitioner keep count. Japa may be performed in several vocal registers: "out loud" (*vācika*), "quietly" (*upāṃśu*), and "mentally" (*mānasa*). Of these three options, the quiet murmuring of mantras is deemed more efficacious than audible chanting, while mental chanting, in which the lips do not even move, is deemed the most efficacious of all—thus, the most potent form of yogic sound is silence! Whichever register of japa is deployed, the mantra serves as a support for meditation, helping the practitioner withdraw the senses and concentrate entirely on inward states. The goals of yogic mantra practice are diverse. In traditional religious contexts, mantras may be deployed to praise deities and enlightened beings, to facilitate visualizations, to acquire supernatural powers (*siddhi*), or to achieve release (*mokṣa*) from the cycle of rebirth. In transnational modern yoga, mantras are further credited with inducing gratitude and acceptance, providing affirmation, and helping practitioners cultivate well-being and equanimity.

About the author

Finnian M. M. Gerety is a historian of Indian religions focusing on sound and mantra. After earning a PhD in South Asian studies from Harvard University, he was a postdoctoral fellow at the Yale University Institute of Sacred Music; he currently teaches in the Department of Religious Studies at Brown University. Integrating the study of premodern texts with insights from fieldwork in contemporary India, his research explores how sound has shaped religious doctrines and practices on the subcontinent from the late Bronze Age up through today. His forthcoming book project for Oxford University Press, *This Whole World Is OM: A History of the Sacred Syllable in Early India*, is the first-ever academic monograph on OM, the preeminent mantra and ubiquitous sacred syllable of Indian religions.

Suggestions for further reading

In this book

See also chapters 9 (What is Sanskrit?), 10 (What is *OM*?), and 56 (How do modern practitioners relate to ancient texts?).

Elsewhere

Gerety, Finnian M. M. "Sound and Yoga." In *Routledge Handbook of Yoga and Meditation Studies*, edited by Suzanne Newcombe and Karen O'Brien-Kop. Routledge, 2021.

Hauser, Beatrix. "Following the Transcultural Circulation of Bodily Practices: Modern Yoga and the Corporeality of Mantras." In *Yoga in Transformation: Historical and Contemporary Perspectives*, edited by Karl Baier, Philipp A. Maas, and Karin Preisendanz. V&R unipress, 2018.

Padoux, André. *Tantric Mantras: Studies on Mantraśāstra*. Routledge Studies in Tantric Traditions. Routledge, 2011.

Rao, Mani. *Living Mantra: Mantra, Deity, and Visionary Experience Today*. Palgrave Macmillan, 2019.

32
Why do yogis go upside down?

Matylda Ciołkosz

Inverted *āsanas* are a staple feature of modern postural yoga practice. The headstand (*śīrṣāsana*, literally the head posture) and shoulder balance (*sarvāṅgāsana*, literally the all-limbs posture) are said by some to be the king and queen of yogic postures, and performing variations of these poses is a sure way to impress others with one's yogic prowess and grace.

Yoga practitioners commonly believe that inverting the body during āsana practice has numerous beneficial effects on the mind and body. In his famous āsana manual *Light on Yoga*, B. K. S. Iyengar assures the reader that "regular practice of *śīrṣāsana* makes healthy pure blood flow through the brain cells," rejuvenating them so that "thinking power increases and thoughts become clearer" (1979, 190). The posture is also claimed to relieve insomnia and constipation, prevent respiratory diseases and heart palpitations, and increase the amount of hemoglobin in the blood. Iyengar attributes beneficial effects to sarvāṅgāsana too. He explains that the posture supplies blood to the "thyroid and parathyroid glands"—a phenomenon facilitated by "the firm chinlock" (*jālandharabandha*)—while "healthy blood is allowed to circulate around the neck and chest" (213). Similar enthusiastic claims about the perks of turning upside down are widespread and are usually a matter of traditional beliefs rather than systematic empirical research. While some studies considering the (not always beneficial) influence of śīrṣāsana practice on human anatomy and physiology have been conducted, no comprehensive scientific discussion of this topic has been presented to date.

Inverted postures are a relatively new addition to the āsana curriculum. They are first found in eighteenth-century texts on *haṭhayoga*, such as the *Haṭhābhyāsapaddhati* or the *Jogpradīpakā*. However, the practice of turning the body upside down is ancient. Early Buddhist texts describe (and denounce) a form of austerity performed by ascetics called the "bat penance" (Pali, *vagguli vata*). It involved dangling upside down from a tree while suspended by the feet and—like other similar austerities—was meant to mortify the body and burn away *karma*, thus making liberation from the cycle of rebirths possible. Interestingly, the bat penance resurfaced as a yogic posture over a millennium later—included in the *Jogpradīpakā* as *tapkārāsana* (the ascetic's posture).

According to haṭhayoga texts, turning the body upside down has a very particular function—one related to a specific understanding of human anatomy. The human body is described as containing a vital substance called *bindu* (drop), stored at the base of the skull. The bindu—identified with semen—would be spent throughout one's lifetime, and with it a person's vitality. The precious substance would drip down from the head along the central axis of the body and be removed from the body (e.g., during ejaculation). A yogi's objective was to preserve the bindu, thus ensuring health and longevity. A variety of techniques were devised for that purpose, among them a *mudrā* called *viparītakaraṇī* (lit. "making an inversion"), tantamount to turning the body upside down. By bringing the entire body over the head, the practitioner could cause the bindu to reverse its flow and return to its reservoir in the head. Unsurprisingly, *viparītakaraṇī* was also reinterpreted as an āsana in the eighteenth century and included in the *Jogpradīpakā* as *viparītāsana*.

Clearly, the contemporary practice of inverted āsanas—with all the benefits attributed to it—has more affinity to haṭhayoga than to postural austerities. It seems that *vagguli vata* was simply meant as a form of discomfort, a means to subdue and emaciate the body, whereas *viparītakaraṇī* was expected to replenish bodily resources and improve its state. Notably, both haṭhayoga and its contemporary interpretations implicitly associate the alleged benefits of inverting the body with the working of gravity by assigning value to the vertical dimension (or, rather, to the position of different body parts on the vertical axis). In the haṭhayoga model, gravity brings the bindu back to the head. In B. K. S. Iyengar's interpretation, placing the head below the entire body forces more blood into the brain, which "rejuvenates" the brain cells. When the neck becomes the lowermost part of the body (as in sarvāṅgāsana), blood is to be supplied to the organ located there—the thyroid. The pressure applied through *jālandharabandha* is supposed to intensify this process. It is assumed that the supply of blood or bindu to the head or neck is beneficial, whereas their loss is detrimental. In an upright position, the beneficial substances are forced out of the head or neck by gravity, and turning the body upside down can reverse this process.

A similar explanation is implicit in Iyengar's association of śīrṣāsana practice with preventing respiratory diseases. One of the symptoms of many respiratory issues is the accumulation of mucus in the respiratory tract. If it is assumed that gravity is the main factor influencing human physiology, it may be concluded that inverting the body upside down will force the mucus out of the lungs and trachea so that it may be removed through the mouth. Notably, an analogous model is the rationale for a recommendation *not* to practice inverted āsanas under some circumstances. Iyengar Yoga instructors famously discourage turning upside down during menstruation, arguing—among others—that the downward flow of menstrual blood from the uterus must not be obstructed.

Naturally, not all rationales for the practice of bodily inversion can be explained by this model. For example, claims that headstands relieve constipation seem to go against this very logic. Yoga instructors often list among the benefits of inverted āsanas complex effects that cannot be easily explained. Some of these claims may be motivated by the instructors' personal experience (i.e., observation of their own subjective feelings produced by a given āsana) or by the testimonials of other practitioners. However, it seems that most of the benefits are attributed to inverted postures by convention. Practitioners learn about the effects of turning upside down from their instructors, they share this knowledge with others, and this shared knowledge becomes a commonly accepted truth. Until systematic, rigorously planned studies are conducted (specific, reliable, longitudinal, and involving control groups), the conviction about the perks of turning upside down remains a matter of traditional belief.

About the author

Matylda Ciołkosz is an assistant professor at the Institute of Religious Studies, Jagiellonian University in Kraków. She earned her PhD in culture and religion studies in 2019 for her research on the meaning-making role of kinesthetic experience in the practice of modern postural yoga. In her research, she draws from cognitive approaches to the study of religions to explore the influence of sensory, motor, and social contexts on the formation and application of religious concepts.

Suggestions for further reading

In this book

See also chapters 22 (Why do yogis contort their bodies?) and 42 (Who are the *siddha yogis*?).

Elsewhere

Birch, Jason. 2019. "Headstand on the Fingers: Yogis on Their Heads in the Early Modern Period." *Luminescent* 12 (February 2019). https://www.theluminescent.org/2019/02/headstand-on-fingers-Jason-Birch.html.

Iyengar, B. K. S. *Light on Yoga: Yoga Dipika*. Schocken, 1979.

Mallinson, James. "Haṭha Yoga." In *Brill's Encyclopedia of Hinduism*, vol. 3, edited by Knut A. Jacobsen et al. Brill, 2011.

33
Why do yogis meditate?

Matylda Ciołkosz

Contemporary Western yogis may meditate for various reasons. For some, it may be a way to reduce stress, to improve focus and productivity, or to better understand their own emotional and cognitive processes. Others may meditate because they simply assume it is the right thing to do. Some practitioners engage in seated meditation as part of their yoga practice; others supplement their postural yoga routine with other contemplative techniques (for example, with various forms of Buddhist meditation). Some claim that *āsana* practice itself is a form of meditation; others do not experience any meditative states at all. While the concepts of yoga and meditation have been interrelated for centuries, they are distinct to a considerable degree.

The term "meditation" has different meanings depending on the context. Contemporary researchers of contemplative techniques divide various forms of meditation into three basic categories. During *attentional meditation*, the practitioners' attention is focused on an object, such as the breath, a body part, or a mantra. This category also includes open-monitoring awareness of oneself and one's environment, without a single meditative focus. During *constructive meditation*, a practitioner construes and cultivates particular attitudes, such as compassion or loving-kindness. *Deconstructive meditation*, on the other hand, involves an analysis of the meditative experience, during which the underlying reality of one's own self and the world is to be exposed. In yogic forms of meditation described and prescribed across centuries, these three categories can be found.

According to the first known definition, yoga means "holding the senses steady" (*Kaṭha Upaniṣad*, ca. third century BCE). While not a form of meditation itself by contemporary understanding, this practice is more of a prerequisite to applying contemplative techniques. In Patañjali's eight-limbed (*aṣṭāṅga*) yoga, sense withdrawal (*pratyāhāra*) precedes the contemplative stages of *dhāraṇā*, *dhyāna*, and *samādhi*. The effect of controlling cognitive processes to prepare the practitioner for meditation has also been attributed to breath control practices. The earliest Upaniṣads realize the relation between harnessing the breath and stilling the mind; in the *Chāndogya Upaniṣad*, the mind is likened to a bird that can be held in one place by being tied by the thread of the breath. According to the *Pātañjalayogaśāstra*, the practice of breath retention (*prāṇāyāma*) gradually destroys the *karma* obscuring the light of liberating knowledge, thus preparing the yogi for the practice of dhāraṇā.

In Patañjali's model, dhāraṇā and dhyāna (the sixth and seventh limbs of *aṣṭāṅgayoga*) are clear cases of attentional meditation. The term *dhyāna* is commonly translated as "meditation," while *dhāraṇā* ("concentration" or "fixation") is understood as a prerequisite to it. However, according to the classification provided above, both dhāraṇā and dhyāna—as well as samādhi—can be understood as meditative practices. During the first of the three, consciousness (*citta*) is to be fixed to a chosen object; during the second, a passive flow of awareness between the practitioner and the object is to be established. Samādhi—the ultimate, eighth limb—is a deconstructive practice. During its subsequent substages, the object of meditative focus is analyzed into its ever subtler and more abstract aspects, until the practitioner arrives at the reality of the meditating subject. Exposing the true structure of reality is, according to Patañjali, the ultimate goal of yogic meditation. Through samādhi, a yogi discovers that citta, which they took for their consciousness before, is in fact unconscious, and the true conscious subject is the immutable and imperishable *puruṣa*.

Yoga as seated meditation (*dhyānayoga*) is also prescribed by the *Bhagavadgītā*. A meditating yogi is advised to control their senses and mind and to focus their attention on their imperishable self (*ātman*). If this effort is successful, the practitioner will not only realize the existence of ātman in all living beings but also realize that every being has been touched by *brahman*—the cosmic consciousness. The meditator is also advised to turn their heart toward Kṛṣṇa. According to the *Bhagavadgītā*, it is in fact Kṛṣṇa—the personal, omnipresent, and omnipotent god—who is present in all beings as ātman-brahman. It seems that this variety of meditation has not only an attentional but also a constructive aspect: As its result, one should be able to construe a conscious, imperishable, powerful, and loving being, Kṛṣṇa himself.

Descriptions of constructive practices can also be found in other sources. The *Pātañjalayogaśāstra* describes a constructive practice in the form of *pratipakṣabhāvana*. Meaning "producing the opposite," pratipakṣabhāvana is used to prevent oneself from performing harmful, unethical deeds and involves creating thoughts of positive intent. While not a meditative practice sensu stricto, it is worth considering as a contemplative technique in the contemporary understanding. Full-fledged forms of constructive meditation are best known from tantric yogic practices. Complex visualizations of the mystical body (e.g., of the *cakras* and symbols associated with them) and of *maṇḍalas* of divine beings are part and parcel of tantric practices. Construing a deity in this way may involve embodying it and experiencing its mental states. A good example is Tibetan deity yoga, in which a person visualizes a chosen divine being, identifies with it, and adopts the attitudes associated with it, such as wisdom and compassion.

While meditating, yogis might have had ultimate aims—such as experiencing the true character of reality, attaining absolute consciousness, and unifying with or embodying gods—on other occasions, their goals were more temporary and pragmatic. Yogic meditative focus was also seen as a way to attain magical powers (*siddhi* or *vibhūti*). The third part of the *Pātañjalayogaśāstra* is an enumeration of assorted special powers (from becoming infinitely small or light, through extrasensory perception, up to varieties of superhuman knowledge) that can be attained by meditating on particular (physical or abstract) objects.

While modern transnational yoga may be associated primarily with āsana practice, in fact, the first modern forms of yoga practice introduced to non-Indian audiences were of a contemplative nature. The stilling of the breath, the senses, and the mind was represented as a gateway to profound introspection that would bring the practitioner to a realization of their true self. One of the forefathers of modern yoga, Swami Vivekananda, described yoga as a method of analyzing one's own mind and, as a result, directly experiencing one's own pure, indestructible, and divine soul. At the same time, meditative introspection would grant the practitioner understanding and control over their physiology. Vivekananda claimed that a skilled yogi could observe and control their nerve currents, thus achieving perfect control of their body.

In the twentieth century, despite the emergence and growing popularity of postural yoga practices, strands of modern yoga focused on meditative practices kept emerging. The Self-Realization Fellowship of Swami Yogananda founded in the 1920s and postwar movements such as Transcendental Meditation and Sahaja Yoga are among many examples of yoga systems advocating primarily meditative practices. However, notions of meditation are also associated with modern postural yoga practice. Postural yoga instructors often claim that āsana practice itself is a form of meditation. In more static forms of postural practice, focusing attention on the positioning of various body parts is construed in terms of dhāraṇā and dhyāna. In dynamic, "flow" varieties of practice, movement itself may be the object of meditative focus. Control over the body achieved in āsana is seen as a gateway to experiencing a state of focused contemplation, which is believed to make postural yoga more than just "physical practice."

About the author

Matylda Ciołkosz is an assistant professor at the Institute of Religious Studies, Jagiellonian University in Kraków. She earned her PhD in culture and religion studies in 2019 for her research on the meaning-making role of kinesthetic experience in the practice of modern postural yoga. In her research, she draws from cognitive approaches to the study of religions to explore the influence of sensory, motor, and social contexts on the formation and application of religious concepts.

Suggestions for further reading

In this book

See also chapters 13 (Do yogis want to transcend or transform the body?) and 54 (Who was Swami Vivekananda?).

Elsewhere

De Michelis, Elizabeth. "Modern Yoga: History and Forms." In *Yoga in the Modern World: Contemporary Perspectives*, edited by Mark Singleton and Jean Byrne. Routledge, 2008.

Federman, Asaf. "Meditation and the Cognitive Sciences." In *Routledge Handbook of Yoga and Meditation Studies*, edited by Suzanne Newcombe and Karen O'Brien-Kop. Routledge, 2020.

O'Brien-Kop, Karen, and Newcombe, Suzanne. "Reframing Yoga and Meditation Studies." In *Routledge Handbook of Yoga and Meditation Studies*, edited by Suzanne Newcombe and Karen O'Brien-Kop. Routledge, 2020.

34
What is *kuṇḍalinī*?

Ruth Westoby

Kuṇḍalinī, and how she can be understood and experienced, has excited and perplexed scholars and practitioners not only in the last few hundred years but also across the last two thousand. What does it mean that kuṇḍalinī is a snake coiled at the base of the torso? Is kuṇḍalinī cosmic consciousness? Sonic reverberation? Interiorized beloved? And then for nerds like me, is she coiled eight times or three and a half? Or is it three and three-quarters?

This entry is definitely not an attempt to answer what kuṇḍalinī is materially or substantially—that is, from the ontological perspective. In gesturing toward what kuṇḍalinī is or could be experienced as, I will start where I am most familiar, in the *haṭha* sources, before considering her tantric precursors and what this means for haṭha's adaptive reuse of kuṇḍalinī. Finally, I touch on kuṇḍalinī in the contemporary period.

Kuṇḍalinī is Sanskrit for "she who is coiled." A *kuṇḍala* is a coil, a *kuṇḍalin* is one who possesses coils, and *kuṇḍalinī* is the female-gendered "she" who possesses coils. The term *kuṇḍalī* is also used in the haṭha texts as a synonym for *kuṇḍalinī*. I use feminine pronouns for *kuṇḍalinī* to reflect her grammatical gender and her association with *śakti*, the female-gendered divinity or power, and her association with cosmogonic procreation in tantric sources. However, I acknowledge that the use of the female pronoun can impute a permanent feminine essence that neither I nor the sources as I understand them intend.

The concept of the coiled, snakelike kuṇḍalinī, who awakens and rises upward during yoga, is intrinsically connected with yoga in the modern and premodern periods. In the early haṭha corpus of the eleventh to fifteenth century, she occurs in all sources that teach the physical practices of yoga as defined by the *Haṭhapradīpikā*—except the *Amṛtasiddhi*. Her importance increases over the corpus: In *Vivekamārtaṇḍa* (31–39), all the seals (*mudrās*) work on kuṇḍalinī, and in the *Haṭhapradīpikā* (3.1), kuṇḍalinī supports all yoga practices just as the lord of snakes supports the cosmos. The awakening and forceful rising upward of kuṇḍalinī, by which she breaks through the energetic vortices (*cakras*) and locks (*granthis*), is definitional of *haṭhayoga*: the yoga of force.

In the haṭha materials, *kuṇḍalinī* is a synonym for *śakti*, female-gendered power, and just like śakti, kuṇḍalinī is a goddess. In Indian cosmology, Ādiśeṣa or Ananta, the primordial snake, supports the cosmos on his stable coils. Yogic body physiology is based on an interiorization of the outer world, such as rivers, mountains, and gods—and the cosmic serpent is equated with kuṇḍalinī.

The *Gorakṣaśataka* has an extensive description of kuṇḍalinī that gives an evocative sense of kuṇḍalinī. Once kuṇḍalinī has risen to the head, she dries up and consumes the bodily or experiential nectars, including the usually cool white fluid thought to be in the head that is now hot. As the esoteric moon in the head becomes hotter, the fluid flows more rapidly until kuṇḍalinī embraces Śiva and disappears. In some sources, she descends back down the body to her home in the base, drenching the body with nectar as she does so.

In the Śaiva sources, kuṇḍalinī is a key creative or cosmogonic principal, especially in accounts of creation that use the alphabet as a creative sequence. Kuṇḍalinī's correlate in esoteric or Tantric Buddhism, Vajrayāna, is *caṇḍālī*. In both Śaiva and Vajrayāna sources, kuṇḍalinī and caṇḍālī derive from rituals internal to the body of the practitioner and external to the body—that is, in the outer, social world.

In Śaiva sources such as the six-to-seventh-century *Sārdhatriśatikālottaratantra* (12.1–2), there is an early reference to kuṇḍalinī as a primordial coil in the heart possessed of moon, fire, and sun and flowing with nectar. The *Skandapurāṇa* of the same period has a serpent-shaped power in the channels (*nāḍīs*) in the three states of waking, sleeping, and deep sleep. These three states reference the older Upaniṣadic schema of consciousness and associate the awakening of kuṇḍalinī with the awakening of the yogi to ultimate reality while also utilizing kuṇḍalinī as a cosmogonic principle. We find this reference too in the eighth-century *Tantrasdabhāva*, where kuṇḍalinī is described as curved and the power (śakti) in the heart in the form of a snake. In some sources, kuṇḍalinī has a creative or cosmogonic role. In the sixth-to-ninth-century *Brahmayāmala*'s first chapter and similarly in the *Bhairavāmaṅgalā* of the same period, she is shaped like a coil in the alphabet beginning with the vowels and voids and creates all following the will of Śiva.

Contrasting with the majority of haṭha sources in which kuṇḍalinī is a dynamic force that pierces upward, in the tenth-century *Vaiṣṇava Pādmasaṃhitā*, kuṇḍalinī is a coiled obstruction that must be straightened with heat to allow breath to rise upward through the body. Vajrayāna or Tibetan Buddhist sources have a non-serpentine correlate of kuṇḍalinī as caṇḍālī, such as in *Hevajratantra* (1.1.31).

The haṭha sources have adapted their models of kuṇḍalinī from earlier Śaiva and Vajrayāna material and creatively reworked it. The haṭha sources are economical with a metaphysic explanation but selective in the elements that compose the yogic body. How should we understand the ways in which the physical practices of haṭhayoga engage with kuṇḍalinī to effect liberation? The easy option is to see kuṇḍalinī as mediating between body and mind but herself unreal, a mere mesocosmic device. I would prefer to emphasize the experiential and affective aspects of kuṇḍalinī to understand her role in the process of haṭhayoga. Kuṇḍalinī effects the central purpose of haṭhayoga, which is to interrupt and reverse the process of aging and death. This is not brought about through the rejection of the body, the rendering of the body inconsequential to a cerebral transcendence. Rather, the body is the vehicle, the crucible, and kuṇḍalinī is that vibrant matter that thwarts the dictates of time and death. Kuṇḍalinī is adapted to the physical emphasis of haṭhayoga. Kuṇḍalinī is awoken by physical practices—breathing—for the cultivation of personal soteriology. Kuṇḍalinī is the synecdoche, the correlate of the real-world beloved, and the central paradigm of haṭhayoga, the yoga of force, with kuṇḍalinī instrumentalized for the forceful attainment of yoga.

Kuṇḍalinī has proved fascinating in the modern period. Scholars and practitioners have adopted and adapted Indian materials and sought to practice and teach kuṇḍalinī. The English John Woodroffe, also known as Arthur Avalon, together with the Bengali intellectuals who enabled his work, published *The Serpent Power* in 1918. Vasant Rele published *The Mysterious Kundalini* in 1927, arguing that kuṇḍalinī is the vagus nerve. The Swiss psychoanalyst Carl Jung, erstwhile protégé of Sigmund Freud, integrated kuṇḍalinī into his work, giving a series of lectures in 1932 later published as *The Kundalini Yoga* in 1933.

Many styles of yoga abound in the modern period, and that which is referred to as Kundalini Yoga is usually the school popularized by Yogi Bhajan, also known as Harbhajan Singh Khalsa. Yogi Bhajan was the spiritual director of the 3HO foundation and popularized his version of Kundalini Yoga in North America. Of course, kuṇḍalinī yoga is not confined to that school but is an element of many contemporary schools, whether central and clearly articulated or marginal and enigmatic.

About the author

Ruth Westoby is a doctoral candidate at SOAS University of London, and she teaches for SOAS Yoga Studies Online. Her thesis is a historical textual study of the yoga body in Sanskrit sources on early *haṭhayoga* identifying the functional paradigms of the body that explain how yoga works. As a practitioner, she has collaborated on the reconstruction of historical textual sequences of postures, contributing to the development of a new methodology: embodied philology. Her 2021 article, "Raising *Rajas* in *Haṭha* Yoga and Beyond," appears in *Religions of South Asia*, also published by Equinox Publishing Ltd. Her research interests include yoga, the body, gender, textual history, and critical theory.

Suggestions for further reading

In this book

See also chapters 19 (Does yoga give you extraordinary powers?) and 41 (What is the *Haṭhapradīpikā*?).

Elsewhere

Deslippe, Philip. "From Maharaj to Mahan Tantric: The Construction of Yogi Bhajan's Kundalini Yoga." *Sikh Formations* 8, no. 3 (2012): 369–387.

Hatley, Shaman. "Kuṇḍalinī." In *Encyclopedia of Indian Religions*, edited by Arvind Sharma. Springer, 2015.

35
What is a *yoginī*?

Ruth Westoby

Like many yoga practitioners, I originally thought that *yoginī* simply referred to female practitioners of modern postural yoga. I was therefore very surprised to come across this definition of a yoginī in Venkatesananda's edition of the *Yogavasiṣtha*: "The class of people known as *yoginī* (NOTE: the practitioners of 'black' arts) are fallen into the pit of drinking and eating like uncultured people." How could this account be so different from my earlier assumption? Was there any truth to it? What *is* a yoginī?

The Sanskrit term *yoginī* is the grammatically feminine version of a male *yogin* or *yogī* (*yogin* is the stem form, and *yogī* is the masculine nominative). The term *yogin* or *yogī* in the *haṭhayoga* texts of the second millennium refers to a male practitioner of yoga postures, breathing techniques, meditation, and other practices associated with yoga. The term usually implies proficiency or mastery of these practices. The term *yoginī* is occasionally used in *haṭha* sources, but it does not necessarily encompass the range of techniques that are applicable to its male counterpart. Instead, women who are successful in certain practices become yoginīs when they acquire "superhuman" powers. We find this, for example, in the circa 1450 *Haṭhapradīpikā*. Elsewhere in the haṭha corpus, the term is used to threaten and instill fear: In the fourteenth-century *Khecarīvidyā*, the reader is warned that if they make the text public, they risk being eaten by yoginīs on the order of Śiva.

The term *yoginī* in the haṭha corpus appears to be consistent with earlier tantric usages of the term rather than the female correlate of *yogi*. In the tantras, the term is much more common than in haṭhayoga. Here it emerges in the second half of the first millennium to characterize a semidivine figure who transmits the tantric doctrine and helps practitioners obtain supernatural powers. Yoginīs occur in the context of male practitioners propitiating them for their powers and their protection. Less articulated is whether human female practitioners might become yoginīs or be known as yoginīs.

The meaning of the term *yoginī* varies considerably according to context. The scholar István Keul describes how the term *yoginī* includes all the following different definitions: a class of tantric goddesses, a designation for the Great Goddess, intermediary beings / demigoddesses, ghosts, witches, female ascetics, tantric practitioners, women consecrated to a deity, and persons with a special affinity for Indian religion.

Shaman Hatley, in Keul's edited volume, offers a definition of *yoginī* via a cluster of seven characteristics, all or some of which define a yoginī. He derives these definitions from his work on the seventh-century tantric text the *Brahmayāmala*. These definitions are (1) multiplicity; (2) manifestation in or as mortal women; (3) organization into clans; (4) theriomorphism; (5) danger, impurity, and power; (6) protection and transmission of esoteric teachings; and (7) flight. We see from the tenth century that yoginīs appear in groups, especially groups of sixty-four, and are characterized more by their multiplicity than their individual identities. The category of the yoginī blurs the boundary between human and divine: They can be deities or goddesses or human women who embody the deity. Yoginīs, whether deities or human practitioners, are organized into clans and associated with the goddesses known as the Seven and Eight Mothers. Yoginīs are theriomorphic or shape-shifting, taking the form, for example, of birds, lions, and snakes. A key characteristic of yoginīs is their danger, impurity, and power. Practitioners seek to propitiate yoginīs to partake in their awesome powers through transactional encounters, but the costs of failure are high: As the *Khecarīvidyā* notes, the yoginī might eat you. The power of yoginīs is associated with impure or antinomian offerings, and they often inhabit cremation grounds and wear skull ornaments. Yoginīs both transmit and protect esoteric tantric teachings. Finally, because yoginīs are sometimes associated with the power of flight, their temples are hypaethral or roofless to enable them to ascend and alight.

This polythetic description of yoginīs highlights their different components. The enigmatic nature of yoginīs is such that their human and divine manifestations overlap. For example, human female participants in Kaula cults are ritually identified as yoginīs.

Yoginīs who move through the air (*khecarīs*) are contrasted with those who walk on the ground (*bhūcarīs*) in the tantras. Yoginīs are, alternatively or simultaneously, understood as internal to the yogic body, both within *cakras* and as aspects of consciousness. In systems such as the Krama, one of the Kālī cults of the Northern transmission of the Kula or Way of the Goddess, these two categories are joined by *dīkcarīs* and *gocarīs*, representing the fourfold manifestation of consciousness, and are thus inner faculties rather than external humans or divinities. Here, yoginīs are understood to manifest as consciousness.

The early modern period in India sees widespread evidence of depicting, or perhaps documenting, yoginīs in art. This is the case in the Mughal style from the sixteenth century onward and into the schools of Bengal and Awadh when images of yoginīs became increasingly common in the later eighteenth century. These images represent yoginīs at court, in hermitages, and in the forest. Yoginīs are represented as undertaking ascetic practices such as standing on one leg while leaning on a swing. Yoginīs are also represented as teachers (gurus) receiving devotees and guests. Does this fascination amount to fetishization or factual representation? The answer to this is unclear, but it is clear that the fascination with yoginīs continues into the modern period. In recent decades, ethnographers have taken up the study of female practitioner communities in India. Such practitioners tend to be called not *yoginīs* but, for example, *sādhvī*, the feminine form of *sādhu*.

This historical survey of the meanings of the term *yoginī* might suggest that the term is not applicable to contemporary practitioners of global, or glocal, modern postural yoga. However, this entry has indicated the multiple meanings of the term *yoginī* over the many centuries. The application of the term *yoginī* to female-identifying practitioners of modern postural yoga is yet another manifestation of the term's multivalency, adaptation, and enduring intrigue.

About the author

Ruth Westoby is a doctoral candidate at SOAS University of London, and she teaches for SOAS Yoga Studies Online. Her thesis is a historical textual study of the yoga body in Sanskrit sources on early *haṭhayoga* identifying the functional paradigms of the body that explain how yoga works. As a practitioner, she has collaborated on the reconstruction of historical textual sequences of postures, contributing to the development of a new methodology: embodied philology. Her 2021 article, "Raising *Rajas* in *Haṭha* Yoga and Beyond," appears in *Religions of South Asia*, also published by Equinox Publishing Ltd. Her research interests include yoga, the body, gender, textual history, and critical theory.

Suggestions for further reading

In this book

See also chapters 5 (Is yoga atheistic, nontheistic, or theistic?) and 53 (Where did all the women come from?).

Elsewhere

Dehejia, Vidya. *Yoginī Cult and Temples: A Tantric Tradition.* National Museum, 1986.

Keul, István, ed. *"Yoginī" in South Asia: Interdisciplinary Approaches.* Routledge, 2013.

How do you study yoga?

36

Do you need to practice yoga to understand it?

Laura von Ostrowski

One simple answer to this question would be the following: There are aspects of what runs under the name "yoga" that cannot be understood without intellectual endeavor and a broad range of study, and there are other aspects of yoga that cannot be approached without directly experiencing them.

However, this reflection should begin with a historical framing of the issue of practice versus theory. At its core, the question at stake revolves around an old discourse and dichotomy in the history of yoga. The statement that yoga must be practiced to be truly understood came to international fame through the Indian monk Swami Vivekananda (1836–1902), became a basis of modern yoga in the twentieth century, and is still prevalent in twenty-first-century understandings of yoga.

Earlier than Vivekananda but less famous, his contemporary Manilal Nabhubhai Dvivedi (1858–1898), author, Sanskritist, and theosophist, stated that "yoga is more a practical than a theoretical science." Scholastic approaches to yoga have had a negative reputation from early on in yoga history. Dvivedi and Vivekananda were referring to their own understanding of Patañjali's yoga and understood breathing, concentration, and meditation exercises as practical approaches to it. They did not refer to those physical yoga practices that shaped yoga in the twentieth century and continue to shape it today. Nonetheless, early medieval *haṭhayoga* traditions that built the foundation of many of today's physical yoga styles employed a discourse that also emphasized the importance of practice over theory, like the thirteenth-century text *Dattātreyayogaśāstra*: "[If] diligent, through practice everyone, even the young or the old or the diseased, gradually obtains success in yoga. . . . Success happens for he who performs the practices—how could it happen for one who does not? Success in any form does not arise merely by reading the scriptures."

Such historical foundations shaped not only Dvivedi's and Vivekananda's discourses but also modern postural yoga. The dichotomy at stake is reflected by a quote from the late twentieth-century yoga teacher Pattabhi Jois, who is often associated with the dictum "Yoga is 99% practice and 1% theory." The first part of the original title of Matthew Remski's book *Practice and All Is Coming: Abuse, Cult Dynamics, and Healing in Yoga and Beyond* refers to another quote of Jois, who has been credibly accused of abusing a number of his students.

Building on such historical and contemporary reflections, the question arises with new urgency: Does one need to practice yoga to understand it? To approach the answer from an academic point of view, three aspects of the question at stake must be investigated thoroughly: First, what is meant by "yoga"; second, what by "practice"; and third, in which ways can yoga be understood, and are they more or less valid?

When it comes to "yoga," one can distinguish between Pātañjalayoga, tantric yoga, *haṭhayoga*, and modern yoga, among many other historic expressions of yoga that have developed in Indian thought. For each of them, practice refers to something different, but practicing is always related to certain performative acts, thus to mental or physical activities.

Indeed, according to the fourth-to-fifth-century text *Pātañjalayogaśāstra* (1.7), knowledge gained through direct experience (*pratyakṣa-pramāṇa*) is of higher value than knowledge gained through logic (*anumāna-pramāṇa*) or tradition (*āgama-pramāṇa*). This highlights an ancient debate between Nyāya, the philosophical system of Indian intellectual history that is committed to logic, and the yoga of Patañjali. Accordingly, the *Pātañjalayogaśāstra* equates yoga with *samādhi* (i.e., a psychophysical state of intense absorption) in the commentary section (*bhāṣya*) of *sūtra* (1.1). When it comes to states of consciousness of any sort, these need to be experienced directly to truly understand them. Nevertheless, when it comes to talking about special mental states like *samādhi*, it is also very important to consider *āgama-pramāṇa*—that is, what is written in scriptures—in order to have an intellectual framework for such experiential knowledge.

Generally speaking, the act of understanding always implies the acquisition of new knowledge. Knowledge can be roughly divided into two major categories: propositional or explicit knowledge—that is, knowledge that can be put into words—and nonpropositional or implicit knowledge, which remains performative and largely escapes verbalization. A common and simple example is the taste of an apple. One can describe it as "sweet," "sour," "juicy," and so on, but the experience of its taste in all its complexity cannot be understood without the act of eating the apple. When yoga is associated with a set of practices, like *bandha*, the *ujjāyī* breath, or the performance of *āsanas*, one indeed needs to practice them in order to gain implicit knowledge about how to approach them successfully so that a certain muscular contraction, a certain sound of breath, or a certain bodily shape can be achieved.

Still, from a historical and cultural studies point of view, it is difficult to assume that one would have gained a complete understanding of yoga only by practicing certain techniques. Beyond the practice, there is the acquisition of theoretical knowledge about yoga. Especially in the late modern era, as the history of yoga is already well advanced, theoretical knowledge about yoga is important to be able to enhance one's own experiences with added cultural and social context.

In a nutshell, to truly understand and teach practices associated with yoga, such practices should be performed and experienced. But to understand yoga as the historical, multifaceted phenomenon that it is requires theoretical study.

About the author

Laura von Ostrowski received her PhD in religious studies in 2021. The book to her PhD thesis was published open access under the title *A Text in Motion* in 2022. Her areas of research include modern and contemporary yoga, the reception of the *Yogasūtra*, the history of German yoga and the physical culture movement, contemporary religion, aesthetics, and embodiment. Since 2007, she has worked as a yoga teacher, including running her own yoga studio in the center of Munich since 2018 and teaching the history of modern yoga at the German online education portal Yogastudien.

Suggestions for further reading

In this book

See also chapters 26 (What life does the ideal yogi lead?) and 38 (Is yoga only an individual endeavor?).

Elsewhere

Hariharānanda Āraṇya, Swāmi. *Yoga Philosophy of Patañjali*. Rev. ed. State University of New York Press, 1983.

Remski, Matthew. *Surviving Modern Yoga: Cult Dynamics, Charismatic Leaders, and What Survivors Can Teach Us*. North Atlantic Books, 2024.

37 How do academics study yoga?

Karen O'Brien-Kop

In the past several decades and in line with the rapid expansion of globalized meditation and yoga, there has been a correlative increase in academic studies of yoga and yogic meditation from a range of perspectives. Recent research has not only expanded from the more historical perspectives that are often bound up with colonialism but also extended into newer approaches in the humanities, social sciences, and sciences. The increased academic interest reflects that yoga and meditation studies is significantly shifting from a submerged subfield within selected disciplines to a visible field of study in its own right, one that is both multidisciplinary and interdisciplinary, as well as increasingly transregional. Arguably, as its global distribution and development proliferate, yoga is becoming a topic and phenomenon that can be approached through almost any academic lens, discipline, or method that looks at human beliefs, practices, thoughts, or cultures in history or today.

Until the latter parts of the twentieth century, much academic research on yoga was concentrated on historical methods. With outsider roots in the European colonial project, Western scholarship tended to be located in Orientalism. Through "classically" inflected fields of inquiry such as "Indology" or "Oriental studies," yoga was scrutinized primarily through the study of ancient texts, philology, and translation. Textual histories took the shape of religious studies (generating the "world religions" paradigm), literary studies (focused on epic texts such as the *Mahābhārata* and the "classical" language of Sanskrit), or philosophical studies (often framed as comparative philosophy with the European tradition as the benchmark). Today, historical methods are still popular, including translation, textual analysis, and art historical study, but age-old paradigms are also being transformed through new methods such as digital humanities or corpus linguistics. One growth curve for yoga is the recognition of its wider contribution to the history of philosophy but also to contemporary ethics.

From the mid-twentieth century onward and following the contentious work of Mircea Eliade, there was an increased interest in phenomenology, the study of consciousness and experience—often from culturally outsider perspectives. Yet as one of the six *āstika* schools of thought in early South Asia, Pātañjalayoga has always been part of the philosophy of South Asia and continues to be a popular component of philosophical studies in higher education in India today. More recently, a growing approach to the study of yoga, both within South Asian scholarship and also more internationally, has been through theological and insider research. Yoga has been inherent to theology and the study of religion in South Asia through its dispersion into many branches of Hinduism, including Vaiṣṇavism, Śaivism, and Tantra. Yet today there are deep layers of nuance and complexity to the many insider/outsider identities of scholarship, with researchers sometimes identifying as scholar-practitioners. Such scholar-practitioners can be insiders to yoga but outsiders to Hinduism, thus generating critical questions about their relation to the topic of study. Secular or religious insiders may carry out studies of their own experiences using various bracketed, phenomenological, or auto-ethnographic methods. Good research practice invites critical reflexivity on one's own positionality and situatedness in the research field.

The humanities and the social sciences are increasingly absorbing and generating critical theory, including perspectives on the power dynamics of gender, race, and class/caste, as well as the theory and practice of decolonization. As in the humanities, anthropological and sociological approaches to yoga can be traced back to the days of the European empire and the formation and control of knowledge about colonized cultures. However, in the late twentieth century, the spread of yoga to different societies and cultures outside South Asia also produced new regional foci and approaches in the social sciences. Anthropological approaches tend to be largely qualitative, developing fieldwork through selectively purposeful methods such as ethnography, participant observation, and small-scale interviews to observe and richly describe yoga at close hand in both religious and secular settings. Sociological methods can employ both quantitative and qualitative methods to analyze the social context of yoga and the larger structures and patterns through which it operates, such as demographics, locale, transnational institutions, migration, social hierarchies, public space, or communications technologies. Sociological methods can range from data gathering to media studies, discourse analysis, interviews, focus groups, and surveys. More recently, political science is being used to explore topics as diverse as yoga's relation to political theology and mainstream global politics, the role of yoga in conspiracy movements, or yoga's role in promoting care and respite for groups engaged in social justice campaigns, anti-racism, or supporting survivors of sexual abuse—all the while analyzing yoga's complicity in social infrastructures of inequality.

Since the early twentieth century and the work of Indian biomedical researchers Kuvalayananda (1883–1966) and Yogendra (1897–1989), there has been a sustained effort to demonstrate the physical and health benefits of yoga and yogic meditation using empirical scientific methods. Kuvalayananda's laboratory research sought to highlight the measurable characteristics of yoga in psychophysiology. Employing advanced equipment, such as X-ray machines, he published extensively on his biomedical findings. During the 1960s–1970s, the scientific trend assumed a more international dimension through new transnational organizations such as Maharishi Mahesh Yogi's (1918–2008) Transcendental Meditation brand, which sought to bolster its own credibility and influence through alignment with science. Although not a match for the rapid growth of Western scientific research on Buddhist meditation, particularly mindfulness, there has been a rapid channeling of global research funds into the psychophysiology of yoga and yogic meditation during the past few decades. Health science investigations into the benefits of yoga and yogic meditation have been used to construct public health interventions, resulting in an increasing rollout of national health-care provisions. The integration of research on yoga as therapy is increasingly used both to build compelling case studies for efficacy and to demonstrate beneficial cost impacts on health-care markets. There now exists a wide-ranging body of studies published in the psychological sciences, including cognitive science and neuroscience, with findings focused on aspects of mental health, cognitive function, and happiness indices.

The current interest in yoga as a social and cultural phenomenon has also produced studies that employ multidisciplinary methods as well as cross-disciplinary or interdisciplinary approaches. For example, sound studies can be employed to investigate religious practice, ethnography can be used to support the translation of illustrated manuscripts, or cognitive science can be used to engage philosophical concepts. One growing area of methodological interest is the health humanities, where researchers are theorizing the body using somatic perspectives on embodiment, such as interoception, as well as affect theory and sensory studies to extrapolate new avenues for public health applications. Future directions of interest also lie in studying how yoga relates to technology through the impact of apps, artificial intelligence, digital religion, and more niche developments such as EEG meditation headsets and consciousness implants.

About the author

Karen O'Brien-Kop is Lecturer in Asian Religions at King's College London and acquired her PhD from SOAS University of London. She researches philosophy of mind, asceticism, and Sanskrit texts in Buddhist and Hindu traditions. Her books include *Rethinking "Classical Yoga" and Buddhism: Meditation, Metaphors and Materiality* (Bloomsbury, 2022) and *The Philosophy of the Yogasutra* (Bloomsbury, 2023) and the coedited volume *The Routledge Handbook of Yoga and Meditation Studies* (Routledge, 2021).

Suggestions for further reading

In this book

See also chapters 20 (Is yoga safe?) and 37 (How do academics study yoga?).

Elsewhere

Newcombe, S., and K. O'Brien-Kop, eds. *The Routledge Handbook of Yoga and Meditation Studies*. Routledge, 2020.

38

Is yoga only an individual endeavor?

Daniela Bevilacqua

One prerequisite that seems quite necessary for practicing the various steps of yoga is finding the right place. Since Vedic times, seekers or dispensers of a "higher truth" have been associated with secluded places, often the jungle, where they could practice without being disturbed or distracted by other individuals. Isolation, therefore, seems to be an indispensable condition for spiritual improvement, and this appears to be well established with reference to textual sources on yoga. While Patañjali devotes his fourth *pāda* to the isolated state (*kaivalya*), which seems to be a state of mind rather than a physical space, Svātmārāma in his *Haṭhapradīpikā* (ca. fifteenth century) says that the *haṭhayogī* should live in a secluded hut (1.12) and should not talk too much or socialize lest his practice be compromised (1.15), and he will succeed in solitude (1.16). This description, which is echoed by other Sanskrit texts such as the *Gheraṇḍasaṃhitā* (5.5), advises the practitioner not to leave his place but to concentrate on his practice, enclosing himself in what is almost a small fort. The author of the *Caurāsī Āsana*, a vernacular text in Hindi written around the end of the nineteenth century, Brahmacārī Śrī Narsiṃha Śarmā, states, "One should practise *āsanas* in a hidden place. One should not sit and show oneself here or there to anyone passing by, because that too can cause problems," because "only by practising *ekānt*, alone, can one attain the fruits of yoga."

From these examples, it would therefore seem that the practice of yoga is indeed an individual endeavor. However, one should look not only at the information provided by institutions or texts but also at the ways in which ordinary people share, enact, and adapt knowledge. Therefore, it is necessary to look at practices as they are lived rather than as represented.

Textual sources often briefly mention but never describe an important moment: the moment of learning. In fact, although the texts emphasize the importance of the guru, they never describe the important moment when the practitioner, or yogi-to-be, actually learns the techniques and practices described in the textual sources. Yoga has to be considered a praxis, hence a practice that needs time and instructions, most of which occur through oral transmission and visual examples. Instead, the presence of a guru during the practice is often forgotten. It is true that the practice per se—that is, the exact moment when the individual is able to practice independently—is to be spent alone, but before and after that, the individual is connected with his guru and with other practitioners, as well as with other gurus. We cannot imagine yoga practitioners as isolated figures who begin their practice alone. Yoga is antisocial and completely individual when performed "proficiently," but its trainings and some of its practices do not take place in an antisocial context because the experience of the teaching community is part of *sādhanā*.

In fact, the practice always begins with a shared endeavor: that of the guru/master who teaches and that of the disciple/student who learns. The guru is the one who, having already gone through yogic practices and experiences, can guide another individual on the path.

This relationship is vital to ascetic society, and it is considered the main source of knowledge for ascetics: More important than books are the words of one's own guru and the words and examples of all the experienced gurus and *sādhus* whom an individual encounters on his or her learning path. Indeed, the practitioner may meet other masters than their guru to improve their practice or learn further techniques. Furthermore, we must not forget the presence of the guru's other disciples with whom the practitioner can share their efforts and their results.

This very important pedagogical moment is present not only in the context of ascetic practitioners but in all places where yoga is taught. A modern yoga instructor has the same role as an ascetic guru, as he or she shares his or her experience and teaches students directly. A student may also take several training courses and refer to different teachers to improve their practice. Again, the moment of learning yoga can take place within a shared endeavor.

Considering that different "yogas" may have different objectives or goals, for those who aspire to practice the more internal practices of yoga and have learned to do so, the phase of putting into practice what has been learned on an individual basis begins. It is at this point that yoga effectively becomes an individual endeavor.

Those who have achieved the ultimate goals of yoga do so in a state of isolation that can be physical or mental. An intense yoga practice—that is, a meditative practice—occurs in isolated places that can be imagined as a *guphā*, or "cave." India still presents us with many such sites, scattered across its various states, that echo the stories of isolated yogis or generations of yogis who have occupied places that, thanks to their presence, not only are believed to have accumulated a special spiritual power and are often called *tapo bhūmi*, lands of *tapasyā* (austerity), but continue to be known to house practitioners. However, the guphā can also be symbolic of any place where the practitioner takes refuge to focus on yoga practice.

In summary, we can say that yoga is both a shared and an individual endeavor depending on the level of the practitioners and the goal of the practice.

About the author

Daniela Bevilacqua is an Indianist specialized in Hindu asceticism, investigated through an ethnographic and historical perspective. She received her PhD in civilizations of Africa and Asia from Sapienza University of Rome and in anthropology from the University of Paris Nanterre. She worked as a postdoc research fellow at SOAS for the ERC-funded Haṭha Yoga Project (2015–2020). She is currently a researcher at CRIA (ISCTE-IUL) in Lisbon. She has authored *Modern Hindu Traditionalism in Contemporary India* (Routledge, 2018) and *From Tapas to Modern Yoga: Sādhus' Understanding of Embodied Practices* (Equinox Publishing Ltd., 2024), edited volumes, and written several articles and book chapters on topics related to Hindu religious tradition, gender, and embodied practices.

Suggestions for further reading

In this book

See also chapters 40 (What do the words *sampradāya* and *paramparā* mean?) and 43 (What do we know about the teaching of yoga?).

Elsewhere

Hauser, Beatrix. *Yoga Traveling, Bodily Practice in Transcultural Perspective.* Springer, 2013.

Langien, J. Lars. "Yoga, Change and Embodied Enlightenment." *Approaching Religion* 2, no. 2 (2012): 27–37.

Newcombe, Suzanne. "Spaces of Yoga: Towards a Non-Essentialist Understanding of Yoga." In *Yoga in Transformation: Historical and Contemporary Perspectives,* edited by K. Baier, P. Mass, and K. Preisendanz. V&R unipress, 2018.

39

Does a yogi need to be part of a lineage?

Theodora Wildcroft

As far as we can tell, the most authoritative texts of premodern yoga agree that a teacher, or guru, is needed for advancement in most forms of yoga. In so far as orthodoxy can be determined, the orthodox view was that a student should choose a teacher carefully, but once the right teacher was chosen, the student should be devoted to them and to their service uniquely. A wise teacher was, by definition, more advanced in the practice and also able to see and correct faults in the student. Thus to an extent, a teaching lineage is one in which the will of each student is sublimated to that of their teacher, forming an ongoing chain of service not just to the personal development of each practitioner but also to the transmission of the practice through time.

If every student has a teacher, or every disciple has a guru, then logically, every student is part of a lineage of teachers, at least in theory. In practice, the relationship between student and teacher can be more complex. A student might become disillusioned with one guru and find another. A practitioner might be more or less reliant on the teachings they receive. Practices evolve and are adapted by each practitioner over time. A practitioner might even have reason to inflate the significance of their relationship with a particular teacher as a way of borrowing some of that teacher's authority for themselves. Behind this question, therefore, lie more difficult questions to answer: what it means to be "part of" a lineage and, indeed, what it means to be a student of a specific teacher over many decades of practice. In many cases, any difference between the ideal student-teacher relationship and the pragmatic reality of interpersonal practitioner relationships is erased by the lack of corroborative evidence available to us.

If premodern texts agree that each yoga student must find their teacher, it is in the twentieth century CE that the idea of belonging to a lineage gathers more semantic power. The claiming of a lineage begins to afford significant authority to the practitioner, especially if they wish to be seen as an authoritative teacher themselves. Lineage in this context means more than just the chronological inevitability of a series of interpersonal bonds between student and teacher. As modern yoga developed, the practice, its intentions and perceived benefits, the media and transmission forms it utilized, and even the demographics of its average practitioners radically and rapidly changed. One point of continuity that modern practitioners could hold to was a perceived line of transmission from themselves back to Indian gurus, back to premodern gurus, and even back to ancient sages. The idea of lineage is more transferable than heritage, more adaptable than tradition. Yoga might not be a practice that was culturally common for your family. Yoga might not be the same as it was a century ago. Yet modern yoga could still benefit from an aura of ancient authenticity and authority by claiming a chain of memory to a premodern era on a different continent.

Many of the most prominent teachers who developed modern postural yoga in India as part of the fight for independence sought to connect their new renaissance of the practice to ancient roots. They did so by claiming the authority of premodern texts but also by claiming a direct connection to lineages of gurus. The biographies and hagiographies of figures such as Pattabhi Jois and B. K. S. Iyengar make reference to ancient texts but also delineate the lineages of their teachers. Their senior students in turn added their own names when describing their own lineages of practice to their students, and it is still common for yoga teachers to connect themselves to the "family tree" of modern yoga in this way. It should, however, be noted that in a number of documented cases, and perhaps unsurprisingly, the connections to teachers and gurus thus described are known to be somewhat exaggerated or even invented. Some practitioners have claimed that their primary teacher or guru is someone they met only once or twice. Others have claimed a link to lineage on the basis of gurus and saints appearing to them in dreams and meditation.

The truth of such claims to lineage is less interesting than the uses to which such claims are put. To what end do we as humans seek to claim that a practice is more consistent with tradition than is historically factual? Lineages of teachers' names become litanies that their own students and their students' students can add their own names to, and the chains of memory that result become genealogies in which every student in turn finds a place. Indeed, contemporary yoga practitioners will still talk of the direct connection between teacher and student as a connection to the "roots" of yoga. A direct line of transmission to the founder of a well-known lineage is one sign of a teacher's authority or a practitioner's authenticity, no matter how many generations of names it contains.

Nonetheless, there have always been radicals and rebels in the transmission of yoga. Arguably, many of the prominent founders of modern yoga were themselves practicing in ways that would be unrecognizable to their own teachers. This level of innovation and adaptation from what they were themselves taught did not seem to invalidate their claims to lineage. Since the latter quarter of the twentieth century CE, more and more yoga teachers have come to prominence who overtly reject not only their own teaching lineage but the idea of deference to lineage entirely. In response to uncovering or experiencing abuses at the hands of senior teachers and founders of many modern yoga schools, practitioners have disavowed their teachers, the brands associated with them, or the practice they were taught. Others have maintained a more complex relationship with the people and the practices that they were taught and, in many cases, still bring them comfort and benefit.

A wider reckoning has spread from these individual cases of abuse, and contemporary practitioners have begun to question the place and implicit power of modern yoga lineages. As the schools of modern yoga grew into industry brands with a global reach, simple lineages of teachers and students were transformed into complex hierarchies of power and authority, dependent on the reputation of one or a small handful of charismatic teachers at their peak. Some practitioners and some researchers have drawn parallels with similar systems of religious and cultural authority, describing the ways by which charismatic hierarchies silence victims and enable further abuse at an institutional level.

Both outside and alongside lineage systems, more horizontally organized, informally organized, and pragmatic systems of authority have arguably always existed in yoga, albeit with less cultural value attached to them. Such post-lineage networks are now seen as a more legitimate source of knowledge about the practice. But the idea of lineage—the dream of an unbroken, somehow unchanging line that reaches from teacher to student over thousands of years, somehow intimate and yet also universal—still retains a certain mythological power.

In simple terms, almost every yoga student has a teacher, whether they study with them for years or only follow their practice on social media. Thus every yogi has their lineage. And yet when practitioners make claims about being "part of" a lineage, they mean something much more, something perhaps ultimately undefinable.

About the author

Theodora Wildcroft, PhD, is a researcher investigating the democratization and evolution of physical practice as it moves beyond both traditional and early modern frameworks of relationship. Her PhD was a significant advance in the analysis of contemporary yoga pedagogies. Her research continues to consider the democratization of yoga post-lineage and meaning making in grassroots communities of practice. She is an associate lecturer at the Open University, UK; a former coordinator of the SOAS Centre of Yoga Studies; an editor of the *BASR Bulletin*; an honorary member of the British Wheel of Yoga; a member of the IAYT; and a continuing professional development trainer and consultant for Yoga Alliance (US). Her monograph *Post-Lineage Yoga: From Guru to #MeToo* is available from Equinox Publishing Ltd. (2020).

Suggestions for further reading

In this book

See also chapters 40 (What do the words *sampradāya* and *paramparā* mean?) and 47 (What is a guru?).

Elsewhere

Hervieu-Léger, Danièle. *Religion as a Chain of Memory*. Rutgers University Press, 2000.

Singleton, Mark, and Ellen Goldberg. *Gurus of Modern Yoga*. Oxford University Press, 2013.

Wildcroft, Theodora. *Post-Lineage Yoga: From Guru to #MeToo*. Equinox Publishing Ltd., 2020.

40

What do the words *sampradāya* and *paramparā* mean?

Daniela Bevilacqua

Hinduism is characterized by different religious approaches, philosophies, and theologies often organized into religious orders/communities called *sampradāyas*.

Etymologically, the word *sampradāya* refers to an act of transfer. In general, in religious contexts, it indicates received doctrines or teachings, hence a religious tradition or system. The most important feature of a *sampradāya* is the *paramparā*, the unbroken chain of knowledge transmission. *Paramparā* most commonly means "one after another." In its adjectival meaning, it is used to indicate something that is inherited from the past. Paramparā is thus the succession from gurus to disciples that creates a spiritual chain through which the body of knowledge is transmitted. In the composite term *guru-śiṣya-paramparā* (transmission from guru to disciple), it acquires the meaning of "established institution through transmission" and indicates the various lineages present in a sampradāya. Each transmission is a trace of a strategy through which the religious order has reinterpreted its past to compete more effectively. Indeed, the *guru-śiṣya-paramparā* is often established retrospectively and traced back to a divine origin. The human founder then becomes a representative of divine teachings that are then passed on to his disciple.

A sampradāya is thus the assemblage of all these lineages, through which theories, practices, and rules proposed by a guru are transmitted and further developed or modified by subsequent gurus based on their own practices and achievements.

From a historical point of view, the rise and institutionalization of sampradāyas are far from clear, but we can relate them to the broader processes of socioeconomic and cultural changes that took place in India between the fifth century BCE and the eighth century CE, when the Brahmanical tradition was challenged and various religious orders began to offer alternative interpretations of rituals, life, and most importantly, religious goals. Sampradāyas proliferated over the centuries, becoming the organizational repository of various religious approaches (Śaiva, Vaiṣṇava, Tantric, devotional, and so on) and were embodied in places such as *maṭhas* (monasteries) and temples, thus becoming fundamental elements in the lives of Hindus, both ascetics and laypeople who frequented these religious centers, following their doctrines, rituals, and teachings.

The economic support, land grants, and respect that gurus gained from donors, especially kings, determined the development of monastic institutions and, by consequence, sampradāyas. We can infer that sampradāyas with a broader social appeal attracted the attention of rulers and their donations, to such an extent that religious centers could have various patrons from different geographical areas. This created a mutual dependence between royal and religious authorities: The royals relied on religious authorities to implement their agenda, while the religious authorities benefited from royal patronage to promote their teachings. However, because of this mutual dependence, tensions between these two spheres of power were not unusual.

The charisma and value placed on a guru were important vehicles for the dissemination of religious beliefs. It was through the gurus' charisma and the subsequent centers or monasteries they (or their successors) were able to establish that sampradāyas and paramparās could be transmitted and codified.

Changing historical contexts often pushed sampradāyas toward a more precise definition of their identity in comparison to other groups and communities. This favored the systematization of Hindu religious orders throughout India, leading to their institutionalization in the sixteenth century, which was promoted also through a vast production of texts in regional languages and hagiographic works.

Over the centuries, some sampradāyas have developed subgroups (also on the basis of geographical distinction) that may follow different religious disciplines. The presence of several subgroups in a sampradāya emphasizes the importance of lineages of transmission but can be caused by several reasons. After the death of a guru, most often, a selected disciple is entitled to become his successor in the main center, while others leave to establish their own monastic institutions. Other disciples may explore other religious practices, even developing "new" aspects to follow the religious "trend" of the time, introducing new teachings or practices on becoming a guru while maintaining their affiliation to the sampradāya. Because of this segmented and decentralized structure, a sampradāya may have more than one representative and heads of institutions. The members of a sampradāya are nonetheless bound by a spiritual kinship, and members of different teaching lineages regard one another as spiritual relatives.

Several paramparās that may correspond to different religious approaches within the same sampradāya give the individual seeking a religious path the chance to access different opportunities present in the religious environment, while the absence of a strict centralization allows the boundaries of each sampradāya to be fluid. What mattered was and is the religious quest. Individuals could learn different teachings and practices from different teachers, even from different sampradāyas.

This *sampradāyik-paramparik* aspect of Hindu religions was and still is very much distinctive and meaningful because it allowed and allows for constant innovation: Teachings could be redefined and revised by each successive generation of gurus. The transmission of a tradition did not (and does not) remain static, and as a consequence, the tradition and teachings were and are constantly updated.

Although sampradāyas are diverse, common features can be recognized: the importance given to founders, often evidenced by the fact that sampradāyas are named after them (e.g., the Rāmānandī sampradāya, named after guru Rāmānanda); the importance of affiliation that is conferred through initiation (it is during initiation that the disciple is bestowed with a specific mantra, a new name, and other characteristics that demonstrate his or her affiliation); the presence of canonical texts supporting specific philosophical-theological doctrines; the establishment of centers often at a pan-Indian level; and the importance of lineages of transmission.

About the author

Daniela Bevilacqua is an Indianist specialized in Hindu asceticism, investigated through an ethnographic and historical perspective. She received her PhD in civilizations of Africa and Asia from Sapienza University of Rome and in anthropology from the University of Paris Nanterre. She worked as a postdoc research fellow at SOAS for the ERC-funded Haṭha Yoga Project (2015–2020). She is currently a researcher at CRIA (ISCTE-IUL) in Lisbon. She has authored *Modern Hindu Traditionalism in Contemporary India* (Routledge, 2018) and *From Tapas to Modern Yoga: Sādhus' Understanding of Embodied Practices* (Equinox Publishing Ltd., 2024), edited volumes, and written several articles and book chapters on topics related to Hindu religious tradition, gender, and embodied practices.

Suggestions for further reading

In this book

See also chapters 46 (Who were Gorakṣanātha and Matsyendranātha?) and 48 (Are the teachers of yoga enlightened?).

Elsewhere

Burghart, Richard. "Renunciation in the Religious Traditions of South Asia." *Man* 18, no. 4 (1983): 635–653.

Kasturi, Malavika. "Asceticising Monastic Families: Ascetic Genealogies, Property Feuds and Anglo-Hindu Law in Late Colonial India." *Modern Asian Studies* 43, no. 5 (2009): 1039–1083.

Malinar, Angelika. "Sampradāya." In *Brill's Encyclopedia of Hinduism Online*, edited by Knut A. Jacobsen, Helene Basu, Angelika Malinar, and Vasudha Narayanan. Brill, 2018.

Squarcini, Federico. *Tradens, traditum, Recipiens, Studi Storici e Sociali sull'Istituto della tradizione nell'Antichità Sudasiatica*. Società Editrice Fiorentina, 2008.

Thapar, Romila. "Imagined Religious Communities? Ancient History and the Modern Search for a Hindu Identity." *Modern Asian Studies* 23, no. 2 (1989): 209–231.

41
What is the *Haṭhapradīpikā*?

Nils Jacob Liersch

The *Haṭhapradīpikā*, often known as the *Haṭhayogapradīpikā* in the secondary literature, is a practical guide to the form of yoga known as *haṭhayoga* (yoga of force), written in Sanskrit verse. Due to its immense popularity and impact on the entire genre, the *Haṭhapradīpikā* is considered a milestone in yoga literature. Svātmārāma likely composed the *Haṭhapradīpikā* in the first half of the fifteenth century CE.

Svātmārāma acknowledges the multitude of opinions on yoga prevalent during his time. This diversity is reflected in his *Haṭhapradīpikā*, which compiles verses from at least twenty earlier yoga source texts. He aims to resolve their contradictions by merging the various teachings into a coherent soteriological system, which he calls *haṭhayoga*. The method primarily incorporates postures (*āsana*), breath retention (*kumbhaka*), physical techniques known as seals (*mudrā*), and the fusion of the mind with the inner resonance (*nādānusandhāna*).

The ultimate goal of Svātmārāma's haṭhayoga is the attainment of *rājayoga*. Rājayoga is a non-dual meditative state generally known as *samādhi* characterized by the dissolution of the mind.

The *Haṭhapradīpikā*'s success was enormous. All subsequent Sanskrit compilations and commentaries on haṭhayoga revolve around its doctrine, accepting Svātmārāma's definition as authoritative. Many hundreds of copies have survived, the text has been widely printed and translated into multiple languages, and it remains a standard reference for yoga teacher training.

Various versions of the text have survived, exhibiting significant differences. The Light on Haṭha project (2021–2024)—conducted by the University of London (SOAS), the University of Oxford, and the University of Marburg—has reconstructed a critical edition of the *Haṭhapradīpikā*. The project recognizes distinct recensions of the text, categorized by the number of chapters (*upadeśa*) they contain: three, four, five, six, and ten. Notably, these recensions can differ considerably regarding their verse count and overall structure.

The three-chapter recension is found in the oldest surviving manuscript of the *Haṭhapradīpikā* and is dated 1496 CE. However, the Light on Haṭha project suggests that the scribe intentionally excluded the fourth chapter. It is highly likely that Svātmārāma's work originally comprised four chapters, although significant structural variations exist among the four-chapter manuscripts. The Light on Haṭha project was able to identify at least seven main groups, some with their own subgroups. The four-chapter recension is by far the most widely used.

It was also one among the four-chapter recensions that were first printed in 1893, along with the most significant commentary on the *Haṭhapradīpikā*, the *Jyotsnā* of Brahmānanda, which was composed in the late 1820s. The recension of the *Haṭhapradīpikā* within this printed edition evolved into the Vulgate, becoming the standard text version of the twentieth century.

The following content outline is based on the new critical edition of the *Haṭhapradīpikā* with four chapters and highlights the various recensions' structural differences.

The first chapter primarily focuses on the first key element of Svātmārāma's method—namely, the practice of yoga positions (āsana). With fifteen out of a total of eighty-four yoga positions attributed to Śiva, the *Haṭhapradīpikā* not only describes significantly more yoga positions than any previous yoga text, but it is also the first yoga text to present positions as dedicated techniques of haṭhayoga. The practice of postures promises stability of body and mind, health, and fitness. Svātmārāma describes a total of eight seated postures and seven nonseated postures. Among these, five postures are complex ones: *kukkuṭāsana*, *uttānakūrmāsana*, *dhanurāsana*, *matsyendrāsana*, and *mayūrāsana*.

In the second chapter, Svātmārāma begins by elucidating the prerequisites and fundamental techniques for breath control (*prāṇāyāma*), the next component in his interpretation of haṭhayoga. To purify the network of bodily channels, Svātmārāma prescribes the practice of alternate nostril breathing accompanied by breath retention. For three months, this practice should be performed eighty times a day, twenty each in the morning, midday, evening, and midnight. Once the channels are clear, the practitioner should be able to retain breath effectively.

For individuals who find this practice too challenging due to excess fat and phlegm, Svātmārāma recommends performing the six therapeutic interventions (*ṣaṭkarma*). Interestingly, these six techniques have not been found in earlier works. Svātmārāma then elaborates on eight types of deliberate (*sahita*) breath retention (*kumbhaka*). The repeated practice of these kumbhakas results in effortless breath retention (*kevalakumbhaka*), wherein one can hold one's breath for as long as desired.

The third chapter teaches yogic seals (mudrā). These are physical techniques that, in the case of the *Haṭhapradīpikā*, serve to awaken the dormant *kuṇḍalinī* at the entrance of the central channel. Upon her awakening, the entrance to the central channel becomes unobstructed, allowing the breath and kuṇḍalinī to flow into the central channel and ascend. This chapter provides detailed descriptions of ten mudrās: *mahāmudrā*, *mahābandha*, *mahāvedha*, *khecarīmudrā*, *jālandhara*, *uḍḍiyāna*, *mūlabandha*, *viparītakaraṇī*, *vajrolī*, and *śakticālana*. Svātmārāma also mentions *yonimudrā* in passing. In some recensions, the section on *vajrolīmudrā* is either placed at the very end of the text, making that section a separate fifth chapter, or removed altogether. This repositioning or exclusion was presumably because vajrolīmudrā involves sucking liquids through the genitals utilizing a bamboo tube, which was a clear violation of the social norms of some sectors of the population at that time. Another striking difference in some recensions is the addition of a whole section containing extra information about khecarīmudrā.

The fourth and final chapter explores the state of rājayoga or samādhi. Here, Svātmārāma teaches the mental component of his method, which first stabilizes and ultimately dissolves the mind. In order to stabilize the mind, Svātmārāma initially teaches *śāmbhavī mudrā*: The yogi stares at the tip of the nose with eyes half open, looking outward and focusing inward. Subsequently, to facilitate the dissolution of the stabilized mind, the yogi should practice the fusion of the mind with inner resonance (nādānusandhāna). This involves attentively listening to the inner resonance in the right ear. The mind focused on this sound becomes one with resonance and dissolves into the space of consciousness. It is at this precise moment that the yogi attains rājayoga.

This fourth chapter exhibits considerable variations in the number and arrangement of verses. Some later versions of the four-chapter recensions feature substantial insertions concerning samādhi through khecarīmudrā (*khecarīsamādhi*) and an extended section appended to the chapter, addressing topics such as knowledge of the time of death (*kālajñāna*), salvation after death (*videhamukti*), and the art of cheating death (*kālavañcana*).

Also noteworthy is a hitherto unedited, extremely long recension of the *Haṭhapradīpikā*. This text survives in a single manuscript from 1708 CE and is called *Haṭhapradīpikā Siddhāntamuktāvalī*, with a total of six chapters and 1,553 verses. The text offers a wealth of additional information and practical insights into the original text. The āsana chapter, for example, describes over ninety-six postures.

Finally, there is a ten-chapter recension of the *Haṭhapradīpikā*, which has undergone critical editing by the Lonavla Yoga Institute together with the commentary known as the *Yogaprakāśikā* of Bālākṛṣṇa. This recension contains a description of a yoga system with six limbs (*ṣaḍaṅgayoga*), a separate chapter on the six therapeutic interventions (*ṣaṭkarma*), and chapters on withdrawal of the senses (*pratyāhāra*), concentration (*dhāraṇā*), and meditation (*dhyāna*). Notably, this recension also offers an extensive discussion on *cakras*, adding another dimension to the text.

About the author

Nils Jacob Liersch is a research assistant involved in the Light on Haṭha project at the University of London (SOAS), the University of Oxford, and the University of Marburg. This project aims to produce a critical edition of the *Haṭhapradīpikā* between 2021 and 2024. In addition to his role in the project, he is currently pursuing a PhD at the Institute for Indology and Tibetology at the University of Marburg under the supervision of Jürgen Hanneder. His PhD research focuses on preparing a critical edition and annotated translation of Rāmacandra's *Yogatattvabindu* (possibly also called *Tattvayogabindu*), a yoga textbook from the sixteenth to eighteenth century that systematizes fifteen different yogas. This particular text was likely compiled for a nonascetic and courtly audience.

Suggestions for further reading

In this book

See also chapters 50 (What is the difference between *haṭhayoga* and Hatha Yoga?) and 56 (How do modern practitioners relate to ancient texts?).

Elsewhere

Birch, Jason. "Haṭhayoga's Floruit on the Eve of Colonialism." In *Śaivism and the Tantric Traditions: Essays in Honour of Alexis G. J. S. Sanderson*, edited by Dominic Goodall, Shaman Hatley, Harunaga Isaacson, and Srilata Raman. Brill, 2020.

Birch, Jason. "Rājayoga: Reincarnations of the King of All Yogas." *International Journal of Hindu Studies* 17, no. 3 (2013): 401–444.

Gharote, M. L., and Parimal Devnath, eds. *Haṭhāpradīpikā*. With *Yogaprakāśikā* commentary by Bālakṛṣṇa. Lonavla Yoga Institute, 2001.

Mallinson, James, Jason Birch, Jürgen Hanneder, Mitsuyo Demoto, and Nils Jacob Liersch, eds. *Haṭhapradīpikā*. Critical Edition and Annotated Translation. École française d'Extrême-Orient, forthcoming.

42 Who are the *siddha yogis*?

Adrián Muñoz

In a very general way, a *yogi* is someone who practices yoga, and a *siddha* is someone who has accomplished (usually religious and ascetic) perfection: Literally, *siddha* means a perfected or accomplished one. The problem lies in how yoga is defined, as some of the chapters of this volume discuss. Across different traditions, contexts, and texts, the formulas *yoga siddha* and *siddha yogi* feature frequently, although there is not a single, concrete referent. In other words, whether a practitioner is called a yogi or a siddha does not depend on their specific religious identification. Whether they endorse a Śaiva, a Śākta, or a Buddhist faith, they can still be called a *siddha yogi* because what is crucial here is a mastery of various techniques aimed at perfecting the practitioner at various levels. In South Asian literature, yogis and siddhas are often portrayed as possessors of supernatural powers or faculties (*siddhi* in Sanskrit), such as clairvoyance, levitation, invisibility, and so forth. As the circa fourteenth-century *Yogabīja* states, a real *yogasiddha* is one who is equipped with siddhi.

A circa ninth-century composition, the *Akulavīratantra*, addresses the Hindu god Śiva as Siddhanātha (Perfect Master or Master of the Siddhas). This allusion resorts to a common trope of Śiva as a tantric preceptor and the head of different yogic lineages. The *yogi* is a key and essential figure of South Asian religious imagery and folklore. Yogis are commonly associated with different ascetic practices, renunciations, and pilgrimage sites across the Indian subcontinent. Far from constituting a unified group, yogis comprise a vast array of orders, lineages, sects, and branches, of which the Nāth Yogīs have gained relevant prominence in recent years.

In different oral and written sources (in both classical and vernacular Indian languages), there are many accounts of lists of yogis and siddhas. The most common are the list of the Nine Nāths and the list of Eighty-Four Mahāsiddhas, all of which, in a sense, can be categorized as yogis. These lists are means of shoring up the symbolic purport of these characters, more than attempts at establishing definite lineages; for example, there are also lists of Eight Nāths or Four Yuga Nāths. Some names appear in more than one list, and usually, no two lists are identical.

See, for example, the circa 1500 CE *Haṭhapradīpikā*, a famous *haṭhayoga* treatise with no single affiliation. It provides a list of thirty reputed teachers (HP 1.4–9): Ādinātha, Matsyendra, Śābara, Ānandabhairava, Cauraṅgī, Mīna, Gorakṣa, Virūpakṣa, Bileśaya, Manthāna, Bhairava, Siddhi, Kanthaḍi, Koranṭaka, Surānanda, Siddhapāda, Carpaṭī, Kānerī, Pūjyapāda, Nityanātha, Nirañjana, Kāpālin, Bindunātha, Kākacaṇḍīśvara, Allāma Prabhudeva, Ghoḍācolin, Tiṇṭini, Bhānukin, Nāradeva, and Khaṇḍa Kāpālika. Clearly, many of these names evince a Śaiva affiliation (Ādinātha [= God Śiva], Kāpālin, Bhairava, etc.), while others are obviously Buddhist in affiliation (Buddha, Virūpakṣa). In the yogic world, one particularly relevant figure—also included in this list—is Gorakṣanātha (although he is more commonly known in the Hindi form, Gorakhnāth). He is the putative founder of the order of the Nāth Yogīs, proverbially linked to the propagation of haṭhayoga. Even though this relationship is dubious, the symbolic relation of the Nāth Yogīs, haṭhayoga, and powers is key to a plethora of legends and folktales all over South Asia. Apart from Gorakhnāth, other proverbial yogis who often feature in these lists are Matsyendra, Jālandhar, or Gopīcand; they are also main characters in said legends.

Because yogis can be very powerful, they can also appear as valuable allies to monarchs. This is a recurrent motif in literature but has more than one equivalent in South Asian recorded history. Apart from the proverbial support from religious figures to kings, there are many recorded examples of yogis acting as ministers in different courts across the ages. Some historians have discussed how even non-Hindu and non-Buddhist monarchs have been fascinated by siddhas and yogis, as was the case for many Muslim Mughal dignitaries. There are tales of kings or princes who become yogis (Bhartharī, Gopīcand), legendary yogis counseling kings (Gorakhnāth, Jālandharnāth), or actual yogis allying with historical political figures (Āyas Deonāth in Rajasthan, Bhagavantnāth in Kathmandu). It is believed that yogis can provide counsel and power through their channeling of supernatural energies.

The interplay between yoga and Tantra has also been pervasive. There is a great deal of tantric imagery and lexicon in some forms of yoga, including haṭhayoga. Thus, Matsyendra, Gorakhnāth's teacher, has been associated with the tantric cult of powerful, fierce female beings in the form of a school known as Yoginī Kaula, and evidence of this relationship can be found in many doctrinal, geographical, and linguistic contexts. Siddhas and yogis have often been intimately associated with Tantra, sometimes with shifting identities. Buddhists, Sahajiyā Vaiṣṇavas, Kaulas, and other Tantra-driven groups have shared idioms and soteriologies. At the same time, some yogis and siddhas can be associated with black magic and, therefore, deemed dangerous.

For all these reasons, the characterization of yogis is by no means monovalent. They can appear either as benevolent and wise renunciants or as fierce and vengeful personages. As the recurrent appeal of these yogis in oral and written sources shows, the response toward them shifts from fascination and awe to distrust and dread. In many South Asian villages, people fear curses from yogis, which can be terrible and inevitable. Even children are often compelled to behave, lest a yogi may take them away. In folklore, the yogi is usually not far from a tantric siddha, both a miracle broker and a granter of boons.

About the author

Adrián Muñoz is faculty member at the Centre for Asian and African Studies, El Colegio de México. His main areas of research are premodern religious movements and yogic hagiography and literature. He is currently leading a collective project on the history and practice of yoga in Latin America. Among other titles, he has coauthored *Historia mínima del yoga* (2019) and coedited *Yogi Heroes and Poets: Histories and Legends of the Nāths* (2011). He has also contributed to *The Routledge Handbook of Yoga and Meditation Studies* (Routledge, 2021) and *The Routledge Handbook of South Asian Religions* (Routledge, 2021).

Suggestions for further reading

In this book

See also chapters 19 (Does yoga give you extraordinary powers?) and 35 (What is a *yoginī*?).

Elsewhere

Bouillier, Véronique. *Monastic Wanderers: Nāth Yogī Ascetics in Modern South Asia*. Routledge/Manohar, 2018.

Dowman, Keith. *Masters of Mahamudra: Songs and Histories of the Eighty-Four Buddhist Siddhas*. State University of New York Press, 1985.

Pinch, William R. "Mughal *Yogis*." In *Warrior Ascetics and Indian Empires*. Cambridge University Press, 2006.

White, David Gordon. *Sinister Yogis*. University of Chicago Press, 2009.

How do you teach yoga?

43 What do we know about the teaching of yoga?

Theodora Wildcroft

There are limits to what can be known through research. In particular, our evidence for premodern practice is defined by the evidence available. Much of the most accessible and enduring evidence of cultural practices such as yoga takes the form of physical texts, art, and sculpture that illustrate and idealize as much as they explain the practice and its practitioners. It is, of course, also true that of all the texts that have been written about yoga, many have not survived into the modern era, and many others have not yet been subjected to rigorous philological and critical study. As a result, it is possible that our understanding of premodern yoga teachers—how they understood the practice and what practices they recommended and why—is representative only of a subset of experts who wrote or who were written about by others.

Increasing numbers of such texts are being translated into the kind of critical editions that other researchers can access, however. These premodern yoga-related texts most often take the form of collections of aphorisms, philosophical discussions, or guides to practice. Simply put, premodern guides to yoga consist of instructions for practice but also assume that the reader will have a teacher to support them in understanding and implementing the knowledge they contain. Throughout its history, yoga has most often been a lived practice that involved a living teacher-student relationship of some kind. Many premodern practice guides make specific reference to the need for a teacher to support the student's progress, and some even offer guidance on how to choose such a teacher, yet very few texts have been found that discuss pedagogical methods or theory.

More substantial evidence of premodern pedagogies may well emerge. What we can reasonably assume about the teachers of premodern or modern yoga so far is that they are practitioners as well as teachers of yoga. Evidence strongly suggests that the premodern teachers of yoga would therefore have been of a particular caste, gender, and social position, consistent with the profile of yoga practitioners in general. We can probably also assume that certain aspects of a teacher's lifestyle would be consistent with their advice to students. Therefore, any conclusion that is drawn elsewhere in this volume about who practices yoga can also be provisionally applied to answer the question of who teaches yoga.

If we turn our attention to the modern era in particular, much of the historical research into modern yoga began by profiling some of the most prominent yoga teachers who wrote widely or were written about and therefore left behind a significant quantity of evidence to analyze. For a long time, this has given the impression that modern yoga was shaped by very few people, most of them the founders of modern transnational lineages. Much of the biographical data available is also produced by the communities of practice that developed around the well-known teacher in question and can be more hagiographical in tone rather than historically accurate.

This is changing. Research now exists that profiles less well-known figures in the development of yoga. Each research project that is published tells a new and fascinating story. Suzanne Newcombe has detailed the negotiations between local educational authorities and the founders of the British Wheel of Yoga. Philip Deslippe has uncovered a cohort of Hindu religious teachers who traveled to America in the early twentieth century. Similar research is underway that describes the localization of modern yoga to countries in Europe, South America, and East Asia. One of the shared aims for the future of the yoga studies field is revealing the rich specificity of yoga's development in different times, places, and communities. The stories of many such yoga teachers have been told, but many others are still unheard.

Again, however, much of the most enduring evidence takes the form of guides to practice written by already well-known yoga teachers. In contrast, in the latter half of the twentieth century, as the number of yoga teachers was climbing worldwide, a new genre of yoga-related texts and products arose to support yoga teachers themselves. Conferences by membership organizations, educational courses, teacher-training manuals, and magazines proliferated. We begin to see more substantial evidence of who was teaching modern yoga, how, and why, beyond the most prominent figures with a global reputation.

We can be sure as a result that the modern transnational yoga teacher has a very different demographic profile from the premodern practitioner. Yoga teachers are still expected to model a "yogic" lifestyle, but that lifestyle has evolved just as much as the practice it supported. By the end of the twentieth century CE, like their students, most yoga teachers were likely to be white, Western, affluent but probably not rich, and above all, mostly female. They largely conform to a profile known in religious studies as "spiritual but not religious" (SBNR) or New Age seekers. They are also householders rather than ascetics, balancing their practice and their profession with multiple roles and responsibilities.

It is still possible to supplement textual and cultural evidence of modern yoga teaching with interviews and other sociological evidence. The development of modern yoga is, in many cases, still in living memory, but research into contemporary yoga benefits from the possibility of more direct anthropological study. Multiple methodologies from diverse disciplines are now used to profile and understand contemporary yoga teaching communities of practice.

A wave of research is now underway that examines the reality of yoga teaching in contemporary contexts. We can map, for example, the fears and concerns of yoga teachers, which often revolve around issues of appropriation, exploitation, and abuse. We can map precarious working conditions and complex professional identities. A number of other researchers are considering the continuities and ruptures between ancient and contemporary practices, and part of that work necessitates investigating how yoga teachers themselves understand their practices and pedagogies within a global and historical context. Multiple researchers are also innovating new methodologies to investigate the more ineffable aspects of practice and pedagogy. We are discovering what can be known, or at least inferred, about the relationship between practice and identity, between self- and co-regulation, between pedagogy and practice within yoga teaching relationships.

Almost every aspect of modern yoga instruction—postural analysis, physical adjustment, and the narration and visual recording of practice—is necessarily a modern development. One of the greatest differences between premodern and contemporary yoga teaching is the application of teaching to larger and larger groups, both in person and, more recently, online. Understanding modern and contemporary yoga pedagogy, therefore, is also a matter of investigating group entrainment, somatic expression, charismatic storytelling, and embodied philosophy, as well as the impact of modern media on transmission.

Finally, more and more contemporary yoga teachers are engaging in higher educational study associated with the practice. Yoga is a subject of interest in classes in economics and medical therapeutics sponsored by the Indian government. MA courses in yoga studies exist in the UK, US, and Europe, bringing together premodern philology with contemporary anthropology and other disciplines. Yoga teachers are not just a legitimate target of research but can be students and researchers within the academy themselves. As a result, a new category of scholar—the practitioner-researcher—also emerges to complicate the answer to the question of who teaches yoga. No statistics yet detail the prevalence of yoga studies scholars who are also not just practitioners but also teachers of yoga, but anecdotally, many exist.

About the author

Theodora Wildcroft, PhD, is a researcher investigating the democratization and evolution of physical practice as it moves beyond both traditional and early modern frameworks of relationship. Her PhD was a significant advance in the analysis of contemporary yoga pedagogies. Her research continues to consider the democratization of yoga post-lineage and meaning making in grassroots communities of practice. She is an associate lecturer at the Open University, UK; a former coordinator of the SOAS Centre of Yoga Studies; an editor of the *BASR Bulletin*; an honorary member of the British Wheel of Yoga; a member of the IAYT; and a continuing professional development trainer and consultant for Yoga Alliance (US). Her monograph *Post-Lineage Yoga: From Guru to #MeToo* is available from Equinox Publishing Ltd. (2020).

Suggestions for further reading

In this book

See also chapters 37 (How do academics study yoga?) and 49 (Does a yoga teacher need to be an advanced practitioner?).

Elsewhere

Deslippe, Philip. "The Swami Circuit: Mapping the Terrain of Early American Yoga." *Journal of Yoga Studies* 1 (2018): 5–44.

Newcombe, Suzanne. *Yoga in Britain: Stretching Spirituality and Educating Yogis*. Equinox Publishing Ltd., 2019.

Wildcroft, Theodora. *Post-Lineage Yoga: From Guru to #MeToo*. Equinox Publishing Ltd., 2020.

44

Who was the first teacher of yoga?

Daniela Bevilacqua

Considering that the first evidence we have of a soteriological method called yoga appears in the Upaniṣads, the question of who the first teacher of yoga was should start from there. In the *Kaṭha Upaniṣad* (ca. fifth century BCE), which is the first text to mention yoga as a soteriological method, the yoga teaching is given by Yama, the deity of death, to Naciketas, the son of the sage Vājaśravas, to answer his question about what happens after a person dies. A similar situation can be found in the *Maitrāyanīya Upaniṣad*, in which the sage Śākāyanya answers a series of questions posed by King Bṛhadratha about the nature of the self, and in the sixth *prapāṭhaka* (appendix), he teaches a sixfold yoga.

In the Upaniṣads, therefore, we find several sages teaching practices that aim to develop *jñānayoga*, the method recommended for obtaining salvific knowledge based on the realization of the relationship between *ātman* and *brahman* through breathing and meditative practices.

Different literary contexts present a wider range of teachers, as they relate to different ideas of yoga. In the *Mahābhārata* (MBh), for example, there are several passages on yoga, especially in the twelfth book, the *Śāntiparvan*, and more specifically in its third subsection, the *Mokṣadharmaparvan* (MBh 12.168–353). Here, the behaviors and rules for attaining *mokṣa* are described by referring to various yogic ideas. Once again, we read of the yoga teaching given by sages such as Yājñavalkya, who popularized the science of the *yogis*, to Janaka; Vyāsa in MBh 12.232 and Vasiṣṭha in MBh 12.294.15–25. But in MBh 12.337.60, Kapila and Hiranyagarbha are said to have originated two different methods: *ṛṣi* Kapila that of Sāṃkhya, while Hiranyagarbha, a form of the sun god, that of yoga. Should we then consider the latter the first teacher of yoga?

The layers of stories, teachings, and information present in the Epics do not allow us to do so. In the Epics, yoga practices appear in contexts similar to that of *tapas* (austerity), and tapas and yoga were frequently subsumed into a single concept: *Tapasvins* are referred to as yogis, and their practice of tapas is frequently designated as yoga. The yogi is one who breaks the bonds of *karma* with the strength (*bala*) or willpower he accumulates through yoga, an understanding that clearly recalls the meaning of tapas as ascetic fervor.

In the Epics, yoga is a loose set of practices closely linked to tapas, and both are recognized as methods of achieving spiritual and worldly goals through the manipulation of the powers they produce. The presence of powers in yoga is fundamental to its association with deities. Such powers of yoga were mythically attributed to various deities. In the early centuries CE, the practice of yoga began to be associated with Hindu deities who, as such Epics became more popular, began to be depicted as masters of the discipline. Of note are the figures of Viṣṇu and Śiva, who both became represented as *yogeśvara*, Lord of Yoga, using their ascetic practices as instruments of cosmogonic creation. We can therefore speak of several divine yoga teachers.

The most renowned Vaiṣṇava yoga teacher who is also divine is Kṛṣṇa. In the *Bhagavadgītā* (BhG), Kṛṣṇa explains different forms of yoga, and in BhG 18.75, he is called *yogeśvara*. Kṛṣṇa gives predominance to *karmayoga* and especially *bhaktiyoga*. Hence, we may consider Kṛṣṇa as the first teacher of bhaktiyoga and the first to have taught a form of yoga that can be followed outside of an ascetic environment.

The link between yoga and asceticism is strong in the case of Śiva, the epitome of the divine ascetic. Already in the *Śvetāśvatara Upaniṣad*, Rudra, an early and terrifying manifestation of Śiva, is the source of grace and object of meditation for the yoga practitioner. In Hindu Śaiva mythology, Śiva is indeed the god of destruction, but he is also the yogi who lives in the Himalayas, with his body covered by ash and matted hair. At the time of the *Purāṇas* (ca. fourth to thirteenth century), the legends of Pārvatī, Śiva's wife, come to the fore. This divine couple is also associated with the teaching of yoga.

In the *Śivapurāṇa* (ca. tenth century), the sage Nārada describes Śiva living on Mount Kailāsa as a naked yogi with Pārvatī, the most beautiful woman in the universe (2.5.18.44–51). We know that Pārvatī is a yoginī because the same text tells us that Śiva could only marry someone who could be a yoginī when he was doing yoga (2.2.16.39). In the *Śivasaṃhitā* (ca. thirteenth to fifteenth century), Śiva actually teaches yoga to Pārvatī, and several texts use this topos to introduce teachings through their dialogues. From the tenth century onward, Śiva appears in his Ādinātha form, and in the *haṭhayoga* tradition, the origin of yoga is specifically attributed to him and not to Hiranyagarbha (*Śivasaṃhitā* 1.2–3). In the haṭhayoga tradition, Śiva's teaching of Pārvatī is accidentally heard by Matsyendranātha (see the *Skandapurāṇa*, *Nāradapurāṇa*, and other texts). Matsyendranātha, traditionally the first guru of the Nāth *sampradāya*, then passed this knowledge on to his disciple Gorakhnātha, who further developed it, particularly the practice of haṭhayoga. Therefore, Gorakhnātha was said to be the first human teacher of haṭhayoga. Several works in Sanskrit are attributed to him, including the *Vivekamārtaṇḍa*, the *Gorakṣaśataka*, and the *Siddha Siddhānta Paddhati*—which can be considered technical guides to the theory and practice of haṭhayoga—as well as works in vernacular languages, such as the *Gorakh Bodh* and the *Gorakh Bānī*, metaphorical poems that attempt to express the experience of the Absolute. Generally speaking, by the turn of the first millennium, prominent gurus and yogis had become canonized as divine incarnations, thanks to codified *paramparā* that linked them directly with the teaching of a deity.

If, on the other hand, we consider who the first yoga teacher in the Western world was, we could attribute this title to Swami Vivekananda, who, after attending the Parliament of the World's Religions in Chicago in 1893, became one of the first international gurus to teach yoga. His book *Raja Yoga* (1896) influenced the history of modern transnational yoga. By reworking the *Pātañjalayogaśāstra* with some practical yoga techniques and a more scientific medical approach, he paved the path for many of the later developments in the history of yoga in India and in the West.

About the author

Daniela Bevilacqua is an Indianist specialized in Hindu asceticism, investigated through an ethnographic and historical perspective. She received her PhD in civilizations of Africa and Asia from Sapienza University of Rome and in anthropology from the University of Paris Nanterre. She worked as a postdoc research fellow at SOAS for the ERC-funded Haṭha Yoga Project (2015–2020). She is currently a researcher at CRIA (ISCTE-IUL) in Lisbon. She has authored *Modern Hindu Traditionalism in Contemporary India* (Routledge, 2018) and *From Tapas to Modern Yoga: Sādhus' Understanding of Embodied Practices* (Equinox Publishing Ltd., 2024), edited volumes, and written several articles and book chapters on topics related to Hindu religious tradition, gender, and embodied practices.

Suggestions for further reading

In this book

See also chapters 45 (Who was Patañjali?), 46 (Who were Gorakṣanātha and Matsyendranātha?), 54 (Who was Swami Vivekananda?), and 55 (Who was Krishnamacharya?).

Elsewhere

Briggs, George Weston. *Gorakhnāth and the Kānphaṭa Yogīs*. YMCA Publishing House, 1938.

Cohen, Signe, ed. *The Upaniṣads: A Complete Guide*. Routledge, 2018.

De Michelis, Elizabeth. *A History of Modern Yoga: Patañjali and Western Esotericism*. Continuum, 2004.

Mallinson, James. *The Shiva Samhita: A Critical Edition*. YogaVidya.com, 2007.

Sears, Tamara. "From Guru to God: Yogic Prowess and Places of Practice in Early-Medieval India." In *The Art of Transformation*, edited by Diamond Debra. Washington, DC: Arthur M. Sackler Gallery, 2013.

45

Who was Patañjali?

Karen O'Brien-Kop

The *Yogasūtra*, also known as the *Pātañjalayogaśāstra* or *Yogaśāstra*, was composed around the second century CE, with current approximations for the final redaction as the fourth century to early fifth century CE. Certainly, parts of the text may have been in circulation for centuries before this, but analysis of how the text relates intertextually to other works (particularly Buddhist texts) suggests that it postdates Vasubandhu's *Abhidharmakośabhāṣya*. Pātañjalayoga is both conservative and innovative; it adopted the Sāṃkhya system of formal reasoning and combined it with the more intuitive contemplative methods of the Upaniṣads, the structured meditation techniques of Buddhism, a pan-Indian ethical code, and some archaic vestiges of embodied asceticism.

Authorship of the *Yogasūtra* is attributed to "Patañjali," which was already an authoritative name in scholastic circles since the time of the renowned grammarian of the same appellation. The grammarian Patañjali wrote a treatise called the *Vyākaraṇa Mahābhāṣya* in the second century BCE (which was a commentary on the foundational grammar *Aṣṭādhyāyī* of Pāṇini). The two Patañjalis (of the grammar and yoga treatises) are clearly separate figures. What is unclear, however, is whether the *Yogasūtra* was the work of one "author" or, more likely, several composers and editors over some centuries, all grouped under the credible name of "Patañjali." Hence, the *Yogasūtra* is most likely a combination of ancient oral material with some newer and original compositions.

The *Yogaśāstra* can be regarded as a stand-alone composition by Patañjali or part of a larger text containing a commentary also by Patañjali (and hence an "auto-commentary"), with both texts combined as the *Pātañjalayogaśāstra*. However, there are differing views in scholarship on this issue, and many academics maintain that this commentary should be attributed to a later author called Vyāsa, who wrote a century or so after the *Yogasūtra*.

The *Pātañjalayogaśāstra* comprises 195 aphorisms, or *sūtras* (in most critical editions), which are divided into four chapters, or *pādas* (which may be later editorial interventions). The sūtras are terse teachings designed for mnemonic use, and the commentary (*sūtrabhāṣya*) unpacks those teachings in detail and context. The work is, on the whole, a philosophical treatise and follows the format and scope of other philosophical compendia of the period (the root texts of the *āstika* or Hindu philosophical tradition).

It is largely unproductive to speculate about the personal identity of Patañjali and the degree to which he may have been a practitioner of meditation as well as a scholar. The two roles were not strictly divided in early Indian philosophy (since philosophy was also oriented to rational reflection and contemplation). Yet given that the author or editors "Patañjali" knew Sanskrit and were working in the erudite genre of *śāstra*, we can establish that Patañjali was well educated. In two places, the commentary addresses Brahmans (PYŚ 2.30 and 4.29), and so we may suggest that Patañjali was a member of the male Brahman community—that is, the social group authorized to study Sanskrit and the Vedas. Moreover, the many references to Buddhist and Jain ideas reflect that Patañjali was widely read or learned and was possibly engaged in (or at least witnessing) public or courtly debates of the period, involving figures such as the Sāṃkhya philosopher Vindhyavāsin and the Buddhist scholar Vasubandhu.

Over history and as the reputation of the *Yogasūtra* grew, Patañjali's identity was elaborated until his reputation achieved mythic status. The first development was the elevation of Patañjali as a guru not just of the *yogaśāstra* but also of the grammar *śāstra* and even of the discipline of medicine (*āyurveda*)—although little proof exists for uniting these textual traditions under one author. By the end of the first millennium CE, Patañjali became associated with a divine serpent or *nāga* called Ananta or Śeṣa, and artists fashioned new representations of Patañjali in a half-human, half-serpent form. During this period, Patañjali began to assume the status of a saint or semidivine figure. In the text of the twelfth-century *Cidambaramāhātmya*, for example, Patañjali is presented as a semidivine being associated with the famed dance of Śiva at the Naṭarāja temple of Cidambaram in South India.

Gradually, the various profiles of Patañjali were interwoven in his iconography, and nāga features remained particularly strong in South India, even today. Veneration of Patañjali was prevalent in modern yoga developments, and the Krishnamacharya lineages of Iyengar and Jois retained a key place for the text and figure of Patañjali in their teaching curricula and practice environments, be it through iconography, recitation, or ethics.

Scholarly opinion varies as to whether Patañjali should be associated with northern or southern traditions of South Asia. Due to the interactions of Patañjali's text with key ideas from Sarvāstivāda Abhidharma, there may be some basis to argue for an association of the Pātañjala tradition with early northern strongholds of Buddhist philosophy such as Kashmir or Gandhara.

About the author

Karen O'Brien-Kop is Lecturer in Asian Religions at King's College London and acquired her PhD from SOAS University of London. She researches philosophy of mind, asceticism, and Sanskrit texts in Buddhist and Hindu traditions. Her books include *Rethinking "Classical Yoga" and Buddhism: Meditation, Metaphors and Materiality* (Bloomsbury, 2022) and *The Philosophy of the Yogasutra* (Bloomsbury, 2023) and the coedited volume *The Routledge Handbook of Yoga and Meditation Studies* (Routledge, 2021).

Suggestions for further reading

In this book

See also chapters 8 (Are there sacred texts in yoga?) and 16 (What are the *yamas* and *niyamas*?).

Elsewhere

Bühnemann, G. "*Nāga*, *Siddha* and Sage: Visions of Patañjali as an Authority on Yoga." In *Yoga in Transformation: Historical and Contemporary Perspectives*, edited by K. Baier, P. Maas, and K. Preisendanz. V&R unipress, 2018.

Gokhale, P. *The Yogasūtra of Patañjali: A New Introduction to the Buddhist Roots of the Yoga System*. Routledge, 2020.

Maas, P. A. "*Pātañjalayogaśāstra*." In *Brill's Encyclopedia of Hinduism Online*, edited by K. A. Jacobsen, H. Basu, A. Malinar, and V. Narayanan. Brill, 2020.

46
Who were Gorakṣanātha and Matsyendranātha?

Lubomír Ondračka

Gorakṣanātha and Matsyendranātha (known also as Gorakṣa and Matsyendra) have multiple identities in various South Asian sources. They are Śaiva tantric yogis, Buddhist tantric masters, alchemical experts, Hindu and Buddhist gods, authors of learned Sanskrit treatises and vernacular poetry, and Muslim saints, to name some of their most prominent roles. Their stories were—and in places still are—known throughout India, Nepal, Bangladesh, and Tibet. However, since there are no reliable historical documents about either of them, it is impossible to say when and where they lived or even to confirm with certainty that they were indeed real historical figures. The great diversity of sources on Gorakṣa and Matsyendra, composed in different South Asian languages over many centuries, does not allow us to construct coherent stories of them.

Therefore, the answer to the question of who Gorakṣa and Matsyendra were depends on the source, place, time, and religious milieu we are looking at. There are, however, a few themes common to most stories about both characters. First, Gorakṣa and Matsyendra have extraordinary abilities that they fully use in their marvelous stories: They can fly through the air, transform their bodies, overcome death, control natural processes, and so on. These miraculous powers represent tantric *siddhis* and thus demonstrate the tantric background of both figures. Second, they are often called "yogis" and are thus associated with various yogic traditions, usually with a tantric flavor. And third, in various lists, Matsyendra comes first, and if both characters appear together in a story, then Matsyendra is almost always the teacher of Gorakṣa.

Matsyendra begins to appear under various names in Sanskrit texts in the tenth century. All forms of his name contain the word "fish." At first, he was probably known as "The Fisherman," but then the name "Lord of the Fish" (Matsyendra or Matsyendranātha) prevailed. Its common synonym, Mīnanātha, later came to refer to a different person, so in some lists and stories, Mīnanātha and Matsyendra are two distinct characters (although sometimes related—for example, as brothers). All early references to Matsyendra come from texts belonging to Kaulism, a group of tantric traditions of Śākta-oriented Śaivism having a strong antinomian character (including sexual rituals). In fact, Matsyendra, along with his partner Koṅkuṇāmbā ("The Goddess" from the Konkan), is considered to be the founder of this tradition in the current fourth age (*kaliyuga*) of the cosmic cycle. As for his region of activity, in early sources, he is sometimes linked with Assam but predominantly located in Deccan, and therefore, we can assume that Matsyendra may have lived there sometime in the ninth or tenth century.

In almost all the narratives, Matsyendra is in some way associated with a fish. In what is probably the earliest story about him, recorded in the *Kaulajñānanirṇaya*, Matsyendra is identified with the god Śiva, who has to put aside his Brahmanhood and take the form of a fisherman in order to catch a gigantic fish that has devoured a scripture containing the Kaula doctrine. In the more popular and better-known story, Matsyendra, who either is in the belly of a large fish or is himself transformed into a fish, secretly listens to a teaching that Śiva is giving to his partner Pārvatī on an isolated island in the sea. Śiva eventually discovers that he has an unintended disciple and punishes Matsyendra for this presumption by making him forget this teaching once he needs it. This indeed happens later, when Matsyendra reigns in the kingdom of women, fully enjoying the erotic life, but because he has forgotten how to preserve the nectar of immortality (i.e., semen), he almost dies. Luckily, his pupil Gorakṣa saves him.

In today's South Asia, there are not many places where Matsyendra is worshipped. The exception is Nepal, where his cult is very popular. Matsyendranātha is identified with the ancient Newar deity Buṅgadyaḥ here, as well as with the *bodhisattva* Avalokiteśvara. He is worshipped in two forms (as Red and White) by both Buddhists and Hindus. His chariot processions held annually in Kathmandu and Patan are among the most important religious festivals in Nepal.

The second figure, Gorakṣa (or Gorakṣanātha), is more famous in the yogic milieu and is indeed more important for the history of yoga. The first sporadic references to him begin to appear in various types of sources in the thirteenth century. This early evidence and some later facts point to the Deccan region, so we can assume that Gorakṣa might have been active there sometime in the twelfth century. This would imply, however, that the traditional view seeing Gorakṣa as a disciple of Matsyendra cannot be true because they were separated by two or three centuries.

Gorakṣanātha is the Sanskrit form of his name; vernacular languages use other forms, often Gorakhnāth, but also simply Gorakh, Gorkha, and so on. The name Gorakṣa means "The Protector of Cows" and refers to one of several versions of his birth. A barren woman asked for help from the god Śiva, who gave her ashes to eat. She did not do so and threw them on a pile of cow dung (or in a cow shed). From these ashes, a boy was born, whom Śiva (or Matsyendra) discovered twelve years later and named Gorakṣa.

Probably the most popular story describes how Gorakṣa saved his teacher Matsyendra. As we know, Matsyendra almost died because of his excessive sex life and the loss of the nectar of immortality, which he could not preserve because he was punished by forgetting the teachings of Śiva. Overcoming many obstacles, Gorakṣa finally reached his guru, reminded him of the relevant doctrine, led him away from the kingdom of women, and thus saved him from death. This story is important because it demonstrates two very different ways of practice within one lineage of yoga masters. Matsyendra represents the Kaula tradition, which includes sexual rituals, while Gorakṣa is an ascetic practicing strict celibacy. This image of Gorakṣa as a celibate yogi, with a strong misogynist flavor, is attested to in many sources and is normative today.

Gorakṣa is a key figure for the Nāth *sampradāya*. He is considered the founder and the supreme guru of this tradition, and its members are also called Gorakhnāthīs. Besides this, the Nāths claim that Gorakṣa is the founder or inventor of *haṭhayoga*. This is somewhat paradoxical, since the Nāths were not practitioners of this yogic tradition, but the fact is that several haṭhayoga texts in Sanskrit are attributed to Gorakṣa (this is, however, the result of the successful usurpation of haṭhayoga by the Nāth order). In addition to haṭhayoga works, Gorakṣa is credited as the author of a large number of other texts of various genres composed in different Indian languages.

Today, Gorakṣa is fully identified with the god Śiva and is seen as one of his forms. There are not many temples dedicated to him, and their distribution is uneven in South Asia. Gorakṣa's temples are concentrated both in areas with a strong presence of householder Nāths and in places that are important to the ascetic Nāth lineage, the most popular temple being in Gorakhpur in North India. Nowadays, Gorakṣa is completely stripped of his tantric background, many of his original stories are sanitized, and he is worshipped as an archetypal yogi in the bhakti way typical of Hinduism today.

About the author

Lubomír Ondračka is a publisher, independent researcher, and occasional lecturer at the Department of Philosophy and Religious Studies, Faculty of Arts, Charles University in Prague. Currently, he is a research fellow at Balliol College, University of Oxford. His research is focused on the history of yoga, death, and dying in India and on the religions and culture of Bengal.

Suggestions for further reading

In this book

See also chapters 19 (Does yoga give you extraordinary powers?) and 42 (Who are the *siddha yogis*?).

Elsewhere

Bagchi, Prabodh Chandra. *Kaulajñāna-nirṇaya and Some Minor Texts of the School of Matsyendranātha*. Metropolitan Printing & Publishing House, 1934; pp. 6–32 (on Matsyendra).

Briggs, George Weston. *Gorakhnāth and the Kānphaṭa Yogīs*. YMCA Publishing House, 1938; pp. 179–207 and 228–250 (on Gorakṣa).

Dyczkowski, Mark S. G. *Manthānabhairavatantram: Kumārikākhaṇḍaḥ; the Section Concerning the Virgin Goddess of the Tantra of the Churning Bhairava*. Introduction, vol. 2. Indira Gandhi Centre for the Arts and D. K. Printworld, 2009; pp. 303–328 (on Matsyendra in Kaula sources).

47
What is a guru?

Jens U. Augspurger

A guru is a venerable and revered teacher or guide. Historically, the guru concept derives from spiritual, religious, or artistic disciplines of pan-India (e.g., Hinduism, Jainism, Sikhism, and Buddhism) and was used to refer to a teacher of an elevated standing. Today, the word *guru* retains this honorific meaning in religious and traditional settings, but beyond, it is also used more colloquially to refer to a personal guide or leader.

The term *guru* is a Sanskrit word with several meanings. As an adjective, it can be translated as "heavy" or "weighty." It is also often translated as "the remover of darkness," following an esoteric etymology according to which the syllable *gu* is associated with the meaning "ignorance" and *ru* interpreted as "dispeller." The trope that a guru is a remover of darkness refers to the Vedic understanding of knowledge (*vidyā*) being the counterpart of ignorance, or absence of knowledge (*avidyā*), metaphorically symbolized by light and darkness.

Besides its linguistic meaning, gurus and guru-disciple relationships have found mention in numerous ways in ancient and contemporary literature, producing a plethora of descriptions of the guru and his or her relationship to the student, or *śiṣya*. The actual meaning of the guru concept might therefore vary by context and ultimately also depend on personal beliefs and experiences. Joel D. Mlecko writes, "If the word 'guru' means many things, it is because the guru is many things" (1982, 34). There is no formal requirement or process for becoming a guru. One of the few exceptions is when a guru nominates one or more students in order to maintain a *paramparā*—that is, a specific line of tradition. In more practical terms, therefore, guruhood is granted mainly by recognition from others, making it closely connected to charisma and popularity.

Historically, gurus had an important role in the *gurukula* (house of the guru) education system, which was described in the ancient Indian scriptures and served as a popular model for the upper classes of India from 800 to 1000 BCE. In lieu of religious or artistic unified organizations or monolithic frameworks in charge of maintaining tradition, gurus were the bearers of knowledge and tradition. In the gurukula system, gurus passed on their knowledge mostly in oral form. Many Hindu traditions today consider such education to be essential for personal evolution and to understand *karma* (one's destiny) and *dharma* (religious law). India's ancient scriptures describe the guru's responsibilities for the holistic education of his or her students, or śiṣyas. The śiṣyas traditionally lived with the guru or nearby and were not only students but also disciples, devotees, and servants. Śiṣyas were usually recruited from higher classes—for instance, from the Brahman class—to stay with, serve, and revere the guru in exchange for their knowledge.

The guru concept remains a significant figure in many pan-Indian traditions. In some traditions or rituals, it is also customary to refer to certain deities as gurus and, likewise, to one's parents as the first respected teachers in one's life. In religious settings, a guru might also be considered an enlightened being or an *avatāra*, or anthropomorphic incarnation of the divine. Sometimes, an enlightened teacher is referred to as a *satguru*, *sat* meaning "truth" in Sanskrit. And many Hindus, Jains, and Buddhists observe the holiday of Guru Pūrṇīmā in worship of all spiritual and academic teachers. Guru Pūrṇīmā is dated to the full moon of the month of Āṣāḍhā of the Hindu calendar, which is also said to be the birthday of Vyāsa, a sage in Hindu mythology, considered to be the author of the *Mahābhārata*. The festival usually takes place in June or July of the Gregorian calendar.

In South Asian religious settings and artistic traditions, the term *guru* may refer to a venerable teacher but does not necessarily designate a teacher who is part of the system of gurukula.

With the emergence and growing popularity of many new religious movements since the 1970s/1980s and their presence in contemporary pop culture, the guru figure has become more widely conventionally known and often decontextualized. In modern transnational yoga, the concept of the guru is commonly used to refer to a respected head teacher, leader, innovator, or brand propagator of a certain yoga lineage, style, or brand. Guruhood is de facto granted by reputation and is therefore not an official title or recognition. Authority can thus be earned through charisma and popularity. In other Hindu-related new religious movements, the necessity of having or finding a guru is still a prerequisite. Many of these traditions present themselves based on a guru lineage, or paramparā, although they rarely emerge from an uninterrupted succession or long-standing tradition, as paramparā would imply, but rather showcase a contemporary guru as the start of their (sub)tradition or particular innovation in religious practice. This is, for instance, the case with T. Krishnamacharya, who is widely regarded as the "father of modern yoga," and many of his students, all of which left a large following, are considered to be modern gurus, each marking the starting point of a distinct postural yoga tradition.

Some contemporary groups have also adapted, or at least paid lip service to the gurukula system in constructing residential training programs for yoga teachers, particularly in places like *āśrams* or seminar houses. Some of these groups also value other traditional aspects of the guru-disciple relationship; the group demands respect and obedience toward their guru, dead or alive, as well as service to the leaders and the community, often termed *karmayoga*, in order for an individual to receive the grace of the guru through blessings or benevolence. This unique power structure paired with the popular idea of the guru's infallibility is potentially harmful. Many former members of such structures have since made credible allegations against contemporary gurus of fraud, sexualized violence, and physical, psychological, and financial abuse. In many cases, the existing hierarchy has advantaged the accused, and allegations have been historically silenced. Some contemporary guru figures have even been convicted of abuse but continue to attract a large following.

Other prominent gurus of the last century included, for instance, Maharishi Mahesh Yogi, who became widely known as the "Beatles' Guru" for having taught the Beatles Transcendental Meditation during their stays with him, and Satchitananda, who was also referred to as the "Woodstock Guru" for having spoken at the music festival in 1969. The appropriation, decontextualization, and exploitation of (traditional) ideas about the guru role within the commodified market logics of postindustrial societies have also enabled successful businesspeople to appropriate religious content more deeply into the market logics of capitalism. Often, these businesspeople brand themselves as "gurus" and run "spiritual businesses" that effectively conceal or justify their underlying monetary interests pursued through selling products such as advice, merchandise, books, self-help guides, and other materials to devotees, students, and disciples who are often unaware that they are simply clients. Their enterprises are widely perceived as benevolent religious or spiritual organizations, and their leaders are thought to be disseminators of wisdom or providers of alternative medicine. This system becomes particularly problematic when adherents, unaware of their own status as clients, are willing to give free labor (disguised as karmayoga) to the organization or guru, helping the leader/guru accrue even more wealth.

Lastly, due to the popularity and evolution of the guru concept, the term is now used outside of religious or cultural traditions of India in several ways. Sometimes people refer to any personal guide or leader with whom they entertain a direct or indirect relationship as their guru. Indeed, the word *guru* has become a loanword in English for anyone who is considered to have a certain expertise, knowledge, or insight—for instance, a *computer guru*. This usage has been lexicalized into other languages as well, though not always with positive connotations.

About the author

Jens U. Augspurger is a PhD candidate in the Department of Religions and Philosophies at SOAS University of London. His research and teaching focus on modern transnational yoga and spiritual movements, as well as their respective intersections with politics. He is also a recovering yoga teacher and the cofounder of Project SATYA, a community movement that supports survivors of sexualized violence and advocates for accountability and truth in the yoga industry. Considering spiritual tourism as a journey for self-discovery, his ethnographic dissertation project explores yoga tourism in India and the complex relationships the yoga tourist builds while journeying (toward) the destination.

Suggestions for further reading

In this book

See also chapters 20 (Is yoga safe?) and 49 (Does a yoga teacher need to be an advanced practitioner?).

Elsewhere

Lucia, A. J. "The Contemporary Guru Field." *Religion Compass* 16, no. 2 (2022).

Mlecko, J. D. "The Guru in Hindu Tradition." *Numen* 29, no. 1 (1982): 33–61.

48

Are the teachers of yoga enlightened?

Amelia Wood

What it means to be enlightened—in the context of yoga—and the path to achieving such an accolade have varied over time and across philosophical and religious traditions and cultural contexts. Whether the teachers of yoga, in any context, are enlightened beings is questionable.

In premodern yoga texts, there is no single word that can be directly translated to mean "enlightenment": There were many paths and many goals to liberation for the yogic seeker. To be enlightened, in modern yoga, is a broad idea that refers to spiritual success. Teachers of modern yoga have taken on and adapted the language of liberation found in premodern texts to lend authority and authenticity to their teachings. Not all modern teachers have upheld the ethical standards that they preached were vital steps on the path to this goal. Given such disparities between the language associated with enlightenment and the actions of the (apparently) enlightened, we must consider the following: Are teachers of yoga knowledgeable beings and on the path to spiritual salvation? Is the former a prerequisite to the latter? What are the indicating factors of such states? For practitioners today, is an enlightened yoga teacher an asset?

Liberation in premodern traditions was most often achieved beyond one's lifetime, in death. The methods of reaching such freedom evolved over the centuries and can be traced in texts. Around 500 BCE, ascetics, known as *śramaṇas*, strove for liberation (*mokṣa*) from the inherent suffering of the cycle of rebirth, or to extinguish the self (*nirvāṇa*). This goal was achieved through the practice of austerities (*tapas*). The early Upaniṣads characterize a doctrine on salvation and liberation through a chariot metaphor: If the mind can control the senses—that is, rein in the horses and drive the chariot on the right path—one will not be reborn but attain the highest state, known as *puruṣa*. According to the *Pātañjalayogaśāstra* (fourth century CE), the goal is isolation, or *kaivalya*. Achieving isolation from the material (*prakṛti*) and total identification with *puruṣa* can only happen in death. The step or limb (*aṅga*) prior to *kaivalya*—known as *samādhi*—while not the ultimate goal, can also be considered akin to enlightenment. *Samādhi* is understood to be a continual state rather than something one moves in and out of, which, again, makes the idea of being living, liberated, and able to teach others unsustainable. In premodern tantric teachings, *samādhi* is understood as a process of dissolution into the supreme reality, and thus yoga, or union, is achieved. Tantric teachings are often theistic (rather than atheistic), and therefore the practitioner's goal exists in relationship with God. One aims to realize union with God or, conversely, distinction from God, being an attendant to God, or superior to a particular God. Again, such states can be understood as a kind of liberation and can only occur in death.

In postmedieval India, ideas of living, embodied liberation—or *jīvanmukti*—gained traction but remained contentious. For some, living liberation was debated as a possibility, but in actuality, it remained philosophically theoretical or contradictory. Non-dual schools of thought rejected the possibility. In a living, embodied state, one is bound to materiality; therefore, one cannot have knowledge of God. Other yogis were able to transcend the binary notion of life and death, consciousness and absence of consciousness, and for them, therefore, embodied liberation was, on some level, possible. There are stories of yogis entering other's deceased and living bodies, existing on multiple plains within the universe, and enjoying supernatural powers (*siddhi*) attained by liberation, but again, this remained theoretical to the majority of practitioners.

In modern transnational yoga, there is both a sense of continuity in and a shift from what it means to be enlightened. Typically, modern yoga teachers use the language of salvation found in premodern texts, teaching that the goal of practice is to become united with God or the universe, achieve a state of bliss, and gain special insight or supernatural powers. Some yoga teachers, however, have claimed to have reached enlightened states and lived as enlightened beings prior to death. Some have taught that enlightenment is also attainable for their followers in this lifetime. Consequently, their disciples believed they gained significant spiritual insight due, firstly, to their proximity to an enlightened teacher and, secondly, to the practices and lifestyles they followed under their teachers' instruction.

There is enough evidence, however, for us to now reasonably call into question the legitimacy of such claims. Some yoga teachers seriously harmed others in search of their own liberation, gained wealth and power through dishonest means, and abused their position of power. The following examples are drawn from both mid-twentieth-century teachers popular in the New Age milieu and teachers who can be considered innovators of modern postural yoga.

Swami Muktananda (1908–1982), founder of Siddha Yoga, was believed to be a *jīvanmukta*—a living embodiment of liberation. He taught that God dwells within oneself and offered *śaktipat* initiation—a transmission of divine energy, or *śakti*—through his touch. It was revealed in the 1980s, however, that Muktananda was not celibate (as he professed) but engaged in what he considered to be esoteric sexual tantric rituals with women and girls. Sexual rituals can, in theory, be part of tantric initiation, but spiritual success is contingent on consent from all parties. Multiple firsthand accounts confirm that consent was not sought or received, and those subjected to these apparent "rituals" were left traumatized.

Similarly, followers of Satyananda Yoga considered their leader, Swami Satyananda, and his appointed head of the Australian ashram at Mangrove Mountain, Swami Akhandananda, to be godlike figures. The 2013 Australian Royal Commission into Institutional Responses to Child Sexual Abuse heard testimonies that Akhandananda physically and sexually assaulted a number of children throughout the 1970s and 1980s. The commission also heard that on a visit to India in 1985, one devotee disclosed the sexual assault to Satyananda. Instead of removing Akhandananda from power, Satyananda asserted that any perceived problem resided in the victim's own mind and what happened was for her spiritual enlightenment. Removing Akhandananda from power would have exposed Satyananda as a less than omniscient being in appointing him. Instead, the swami chose to maintain the status quo and his own power.

From 2013 onward, several legal cases were brought against the founder of the Hot Yoga franchise, Bikram Choudhury, which included accusations of physical and sexual violence. When questioned by media outlets about the accusations, he has consistently claimed that women love him because he is "God." Proclaiming association with the divine is not the same as being genuinely enlightened.

More recently, both before and after the popularization of the #MeToo movement in 2017, there have been allegations of abuse perpetrated by prominent yoga teachers, including but not limited to Pattabhi Jois, who founded Ashtanga Vinyasa Yoga; Svami Vishnudevananda, who popularized and disseminated Sivananda Yoga; and the founder of Kundalini Yoga, Yogi Bhajan.

While most premodern practitioners of yoga sought liberation beyond their lifetime, some teachers of yoga in modern contexts have sought to attain power, wealth, and status within this one. For these teachers, the means to gain and maintain power has been justified with the language of liberation to the detriment of many of their students.

About the author

Amelia Wood is a PhD candidate at SOAS University of London researching modern yoga, specifically spiritual abuse in modern yoga. She received an MA from SOAS in the traditions of meditation and yoga, during which she researched the roles and representations of women in premodern yoga.

Suggestions for further reading

In this book

See also chapters 12 (Does yoga liberate or constrain?) and 47 (What is a guru?).

Elsewhere

Caldwell, Sarah. "The Heart of the Secret: A Personal and Scholarly Encounter with Shakta Tantrism in Siddha Yoga." *Nova Religio: The Journal of Alternative and Emergent Religions* 5, no. 1 (2001): 9–51.

Pankhania, Josna. "The Ethical and Leadership Challenges Posed by the Royal Commission's Revelations of Sexual Abuse at a Satyananda Yoga Ashram in Australia." *Research in Ethical Issues in Organizations* 17 (2017): 105–123.

49

Does a yoga teacher need to be an advanced practitioner?

Theodora Wildcroft and Barbora Sojková

In contemporary mainstream discourse, yoga is unequivocally associated with physical exercise, which is generally understood to be a practice of specific poses known as *āsana*. In early texts on yoga, the word *āsana* denoted simply a seat or a way of sitting, such as in the *Pātañjalayogaśāstra*. Over the centuries of yoga's development, the word has come to include other bodily exercises—namely, complex nonseated postures. Among the earliest is the so-called *mayūrāsana*, the peacock pose, a challenging arm balance in which the practitioner holds their body horizontally over their hands, first described in the tenth-century Vaiṣṇava text *Vimānārcanākalpa*. Physical exercises such as the peacock pose became increasingly more prevalent in yoga, and by the end of the nineteenth century, āsanas were among the most important and best-documented yogic practices. Aside from āsanas, yogic practice has included other aspects of physicality such as breath work (*prāṇāyāma*), relaxation, and purifications of the body.

Given the prominence of physicality in modern yogic practice, many conflate a healthy body and a physical ability to perform āsana with a general mastery of yoga. But even for more well-informed practitioners of contemporary yoga, this association often holds value. This is because any practice of yoga is done *with the body*, and thus mastery of the body is associated with self-discipline more generally. In many ways, the physical practice of yoga has somaticized many of the broader aims of yoga, and this reflects a change in the goal of many modern yoga practitioners from liberation *from* existence to liberation *within* it.

Premodern yoga texts see the ultimate goal of yoga as liberation from *saṃsāra*, the cycle of rebirths. Physical activity in the form of āsana is among the tools used to attain such liberation, alongside breath work and meditation. According to the fifteenth-century *Haṭhapradīpikā*, āsana practice brings about good health, steadiness, and lightness of limbs. Other physical aspects of yogic practice, such as purifications of the body, bring about other bodily improvements: They are said to remove all diseases and imbalances. Prāṇāyāma enhances the body even further; according to the *Dattātreyayogaśāstra*, the yogi who devotes themselves to the breath exercises looks like the god of love. Thus physical mastery of the body is an outcome as well as a prerequisite for advanced practice.

Not all yoga practice is, of course, physical and external. In fact, physical exercises primarily seem to serve as a prerequisite to more advanced stages of yoga, preparing the body for the arduously long meditative and mantra-based practices. These internal practices are performed in varying states of physical stillness. These practices, however, are also said to have an effect on the practitioner's body. According to the *Vasiṣṭhasaṃhitā*, the feces and urine of an adept who practices the meditative practice known as *pratyāhāra* (withdrawal) will diminish within a year. Thus even for the authors of premodern yoga texts, the body naturally comes into a perfect state of self-mastery as a result of the discipline of the practitioner. A perfected body becomes the signifier of regular practice and mastery over yoga, but only to a certain extent. Once the practitioner attains their goal of liberation from saṃsāra, their body will perish. Mastery exemplified by bodily perfection is therefore not permanent in most premodern practice.

Premodern forms of bodily "perfection" may also be remarkably alien to the modern practitioner. One ideal result of practice is to attain the status of an "adamantine" or impervious body: one that does not move, sleep, or even breathe, as the practitioner endures eternal and unchanged by their environment. There are still gurus to this day whose bodies are said to be "living" in this way, semi-mummified but apparently able to regain consciousness at any time. Other, more obscure premodern texts describe long and arduous preparations for a form of ritually pure yogic suicide (*utkrānti*) that enables the practitioner to remove themselves entirely from the cycle of reincarnation.

Such forms of physical "mastery" may seem at odds with the photographs of charismatic modern yoga gurus in postures of extreme athleticism or the very similar images of contemporary yoga teacher-influencers that accompany any interviews or promotional materials that feature them. Nonetheless, a common thread emerges: Physical mastery of the body is a prerequisite for more advanced or internal practices, and the less tangible goals of yoga are often signified or performed by physical mastery itself. Thus a practitioner who can hold an uncomfortable posture for long periods is demonstrating perseverance, one who balances effortlessly is demonstrating equanimity, and so forth. In other words, an authentic contemporary yoga practice is the result of mastering qualities that may be invisible or internal, but one visual signifier of such qualities is mastery of the postures and, by extension, one's senses, one's health, and one's general well-being. The eventual aim of contemporary practice is much more likely to be longevity within rather than liberation from the body. But the more implicit assumption that is also continuous among premodern, modern, and contemporary forms of yoga is less recognized. This is that mastery of the practice signifies the authority to teach others.

The development of modern yoga brought a much wider audience to modern yoga gurus than their premodern counterparts. The person of the guru was still associated with mastery over the practice, which was assumed to signify both their spiritual advancement and their authority to lead the practice of others, but in the modern era, this afforded them an unprecedented rise in pedagogical and spiritual authority. In some cases, this authority was exploited abusively. But even when it was not, this set the firm foundations for according significant authority to practitioners who can perform the ideal qualities of contemporary yoga practice—be that health and well-being or abundant ease—with apparently effortless charisma in yoga-related mainstream and social media. As Pattabhi Jois was fond of saying, "Do your practice, and all is coming" indeed.

About the authors

Theodora Wildcroft, PhD, is a researcher investigating the democratization and evolution of physical practice as it moves beyond both traditional and early modern frameworks of relationship. Her PhD was a significant advance in the analysis of contemporary yoga pedagogies. Her research continues to consider the democratization of yoga post-lineage and meaning making in grassroots communities of practice. She is an associate lecturer at the Open University, UK; a former coordinator of the SOAS Centre of Yoga Studies; an editor of the *BASR Bulletin*; an honorary member of the British Wheel of Yoga; a member of the IAYT; and a continuing professional development trainer and consultant for Yoga Alliance (US). Her monograph *Post-Lineage Yoga: From Guru to #MeToo* is available from Equinox Publishing Ltd. (2020).

Barbora Sojková holds a DPhil in Asian and Middle Eastern studies (Sanskrit) from the University of Oxford, where her research focused on human-animal relationships in Vedic Sanskrit literature. She works as an academic librarian at the All Souls College, Oxford, and as a Sanskrit cataloger at the Bodleian Library, Oxford. She is a certified yoga teacher and trainer focusing on the history and philosophy of yoga.

Suggestions for further reading

In this book

See also chapters 13 (Do yogis want to transcend or transform the body?) and 23 (Are all yoga practitioners flexible?).

Elsewhere

Ciołkosz, Matylda. *Thinking in Āsana: Movement and Philosophy in Viniyoga, Iyengar Yoga, and Ashtanga Yoga*. Equinox Publishing Ltd., 2022.

Von Ostrowski, Laura. *Ein Text in Bewegung. Das Yogasūtra als Praxiselement im Ashtanga Yoga. Eine historische, empirische und religionsästhetische Studie*. Georg Olms-Verlag, 2022.

Wildcroft, Theodora. *Post-Lineage Yoga: From Guru to #MeToo*. Equinox Publishing Ltd., 2020.

How did modern yoga develop?

50

What is the difference between *haṭhayoga* and Hatha Yoga?

James Mallinson

Were I to go to my local yoga studio in England and introduce myself as a novice practitioner with no knowledge of modern yoga's many different styles, it's likely that I would be encouraged to start off by trying Hatha Yoga, a phrase that is an anglicized version of the Sanskrit compound *haṭhayoga*, its *th* pronounced as an unvoiced dental fricative, like in "think." Hatha Yoga is a system of postural practice consisting of a few basic and gentle poses, in contrast to the more vigorous and demanding sequential posture routines of, for example, Ashtanga or Hot Yoga.

On the other hand, were I to have wandered the 2021 Kumbh Mela festival in India in search of a practitioner of *haṭh yog* (the Hindi form of *haṭhayoga*, in which the *ṭh* is pronounced as an unvoiced aspirated retroflex, like the *t* in try, followed by an *h*), I might have been pointed to the camp of Phalāhārī Jī, a Hindu ascetic who, in addition to living off a diet restricted to certain specific fruits and vegetables, practices ancient *tapasyās* (austerities), such as sitting in the midst of smoldering cow dung fires under the burning sun of the North Indian summer or having a constant stream of freezing water poured over him in the chilly nights of winter.

In scholarly parlance, meanwhile, both that of Sanskrit authors from about the thirteenth century onward and that of academics today, *haṭhayoga* has a technical meaning that lies somewhere between these two extremes: It denotes a system of yoga practice in which physical methods—ranging from easy to very difficult—predominate.

An etiology of the Sanskrit compound *haṭhayoga*—a slippery term, hence my writing it in uncapitalized italics, in contrast to today's more firmly established Hatha Yoga—will allow for an understanding of all these usages. A prima facie interpretation of *haṭhayoga* would align it most closely with Phalāhārī Jī's austerities; *haṭha* means "force" or "stubbornness," so *haṭhayoga* is yoga by means of force or stubbornness or simply the application (*yoga*) of force or stubbornness. This meaning also makes sense in *haṭhayoga*'s earliest usages, found in tantric Buddhist texts from the eighth century CE in which it is an unorthodox method of achieving success in sexual yoga. The male practitioner uses force (*haṭha*) to make the breath enter the central channel in order to stop himself from ejaculating. The details of how he does this are not specified, but it may be that it is by using a method of urethral suction taught in later non-Buddhist *haṭhayoga* texts as *vajrolīmudrā*, the "Seal of the tantric Buddhists."

The first text to teach any of the methods that constitute *haṭhayoga* in any way resembling the yoga practiced around the world today was the *Amṛtasiddhi*, which was composed in South India in the eleventh century CE, also in a tantric Buddhist milieu, but one in which sexual ritual is rejected—the *Amṛtasiddhi*'s teachings are for celibate male ascetics. The *Amṛtasiddhi* did not, however, use the term *haṭha* for its yoga, which consists of three physical techniques used in series to make the breath enter the central channel.

The first text to use *haṭha* to denote a system of physical yoga was the circa twelfth-century *Amaraugha*, which was probably composed in Mangalore in southwest India. This short Śaiva work teaches four different types of yoga: *mantra*, *laya*, *haṭha*, and *rāja*. Its *haṭhayoga* consists of the practices taught in the *Amṛtasiddhi*, so it appears that, despite the differences in their practical contexts, the author of the *Amaraugha* took the name *haṭhayoga* from tantric Buddhist texts, perhaps because it too made the breath enter the central channel.

Over the following two centuries, texts teaching the new techniques of physical yoga proliferated, and *haṭhayoga*'s scope widened. The circa 1200 CE *Dattātreyayogaśāstra* used the term to denote the three methods of the *Amṛtasiddhi* and *Amaraugha*, supplemented by six more techniques for manipulating the vital energies, including *vajrolīmudrā*, *viparītakaraṇī* (an inverted posture), and *khecarīmudrā*, in which the tongue is turned backward and inserted above the soft palate in order to drink the nectar of immortality. Then, in about 1400 CE, Svātmārāma compiled the *Haṭhapradīpikā*, in which he names *āsana* (posture), *kumbhaka* (breath control), *mudrā* (methods for manipulating the vital energies corresponding to the techniques taught in the *Dattātreyayogaśāstra*), and *nādānusandhāna* (concentration on the inner sounds that arise in the course of yoga practice) as the four components of *haṭha*. Svātmārāma's definition became the blueprint for physical yoga in most subsequent texts and established *haṭhayoga*'s dominance as the scholarly name for a method of yoga in which physical techniques predominate, in contrast to other methods such as *mantrayoga* or *bhaktiyoga*.

The name *haṭhayoga* has never been universally accepted, however. Several texts that teach its distinctive methods, from the twelfth-century *Vivekamārtaṇḍa* up to the circa eighteenth-century Old Hindi *Jogpradīpakā*, do not use it. There are various reasons for this: an unwillingness to associate with the traditions that had introduced the name *haṭhayoga*; an understanding—which survives to this day—that there was only one kind of yoga, so there was no need to distinguish it; and the name *haṭhayoga*'s implication of strenuous practice and asceticism, which are explicitly forbidden in, for example, the *Haṭhapradīpikā*. This connotation is responsible for *haṭhayoga*'s earliest usages always being at least a little pejorative—in tantric Buddhism, in which unforced (*sahaja*) methods are best, *haṭhayoga* was a method of last resort. Some texts employ the term but redefine it to avoid these negative implications. Thus, in a definition that is commonly repeated, a secondary recension of the *Yogabīja* says that *haṭhayoga* is so called because it brings about the union (*yoga*) of the *ha*, "sun," and *ṭha*, "moon," sun and moon referring to aspects of the yogic body.

Like the term *haṭhayoga*, the status and scope of physical yoga itself have long been contested. The texts of the early corpus composed in the eleventh to fourteenth century define it in different ways and value it differently in their hierarchies, with some condemning it outright and others seeing it as the only means to liberation. The *Haṭhapradīpikā* may have set its methods in stone, but its status continued to be contentious, with the nineteenth-century Hindu reformer Swami Vivekananda, for example, condemning *haṭhayoga* as being mere gymnastics.

The physical yoga practiced by ascetics of established lineages in India today is very similar across traditions and matches closely the *haṭhayoga* of Svātmārāma's *Haṭhapradīpikā*. Such ascetics call their practices simply "yoga," however, with no qualifier; for them, as we have seen, *haṭhayoga* denotes extreme physical austerities. Meanwhile, over the course of the last 150 years, modern globalized yoga has developed into a multitude of very different systems, with a range of brand names distinguishing one variety from the next, such as Iyengar Yoga, Ashtanga Yoga, and Bikram Yoga. The majority of modern practitioners, however, engage in a generic relaxation-oriented yoga that is not associated with any specific lineage or school and, if it needs to be differentiated from yoga's branded forms, has, by default, come to be denoted by Hatha Yoga, an anglicized form of *haṭhayoga*, the Sanskrit technical term for physical yoga.

About the author

James Mallinson is the Boden Professor of Sanskrit at the University of Oxford and author of a range of books and articles on yoga, including *The Khecarīvidyā of Ādinātha* (Routledge, 2007), *Roots of Yoga* (with Mark Singleton, Penguin Classics, 2017), and *The Amṛtasiddhi and Amṛtasiddhimūla* (with Péter-Dániel Szántō, IFP, 2022). From 2015 to 2021, he was the principal investigator of the SOAS-based ERC-funded Haṭha Yoga Project.

Suggestions for further reading

In this book

See also chapters 32 (Why do yogis go upside down?) and 41 (What is the *Haṭhapradīpikā*?).

Elsewhere

Birch, Jason. "Haṭhayoga's Floruit on the Eve of Colonialism." In *Śaivism and the Tantric Traditions: Essays in Honour of Alexis G. J. S. Sanderson*, edited by D. Goodall, S. Hatley, H. Isaacson, and S. Raman. Brill, 2020.

Olivelle, Patrick. *Language, Texts, and Society: Explorations in Ancient Indian Culture and Religion*. Anthem, 2011.

51
How has modern yoga developed around the world?

Firdose Moonda

In yoga's millennia-long history, the modern chapter is the shortest and most globalized. It refers to the period between 1849, when the first Western practitioner of yoga was recorded, and the present day and to the types of yoga that emerged from Western interactions with Indian teachers. In general, modern and contemporary yoga differ from the premodern practice because they are not necessarily aimed at the liberation of the soul from a perpetual cycle of rebirth but are viewed as a practice that can contribute to an individual's physical and mental health as well as influence the ways in which they interact with the world around them. Yoga today typically includes *āsana* (postures), *prāṇāyāma* (breath work), *dhyāna* (meditation), and observation of the self.

Swami Vivekananda's 1896 book *Raja Yoga*, which combined the classical yoga of Patañjali with a selection of *haṭhayoga* techniques, is still regarded as signaling the foundation of modern yoga. The ideas in Vivekananda's work were particularly appealing to the growing occultist movement in the United States in the late nineteenth century. In the 1960s, the Western world saw the rise of the New Age movement, which explored alternative spiritual and lifestyle practices in various fields, including medicine. Its practitioners promoted holistic forms of healing, rather than biomedicine, and encouraged personal growth. For the New Age, yoga was part of a privatized form of religion and a means of self-development that could allow practitioners to connect with the metaphysical world through continued and dedicated practice.

Indra Devi (born Eiženija Pētersone) opened her first yoga studio in Hollywood in 1948. Her teachings were secular and emphasized the benefits of yoga as exercise, setting the tone for the versions of yoga that boomed in popularity in subsequent decades. From the 1960s onward, yoga as a physical practice gained in popularity through a series of high-profile teachers. B. K. S. Iyengar introduced an alignment-based, eponymous style of postural yoga to the adult education system in Britain and elsewhere, and the British Wheel of Yoga (BWY) was one of many national organizations established by Westerners with an interest in yoga. Most such organizations were established as umbrella bodies governing a number of smaller schools, and many of them, including the BWY, still exist today. On the other side of the Atlantic, forms such as Pattabhi Jois's flow-style Ashtanga Vinyasa and Bikram Choudhury's self-titled yoga consisting of a sequence of twenty-six postures in a hot room became popular in the 1980s. They were followed by a proliferation of styles and brands, such as Jivamukti Yoga, founded by Sharon Gannon and David Life in the 1980s, and John Friend's Anusara Yoga in the 1990s. Most of these forms of yoga were associated with an Indian lineage but made celebrities of their Western founders. In the 2000s, the death of Iyengar and Jois arguably marked the end of the age of the guru in the West, and yoga teaching has since become more democratic. Most such yoga today is taught in post-lineage communities of practice, organized around mostly white female students who have become largely disillusioned with the excesses and abuses of modern, guru-led systems. Such communities still need institutions, however, and in 1999, Yoga Alliance was formed in the United States, taking on a similar role to the BWY. Yoga Alliance, the BWY, and similar national and international professional associations have, over the years, reached an uneasy consensus on a minimum standard for yoga teacher training, informally known as the two-hundred-hour yoga teacher training. Yoga Alliance today has a more global reach than many such organizations, and over seven thousand yoga schools and more than one hundred thousand yoga teachers from around the world are registered with Yoga Alliance.

The 1990s onward also saw a boom in consumer culture, and yoga did not escape this. In popular culture, yoga is a consumer good, sold through clothing, equipment and accessories, food, and other wellness products, arguably more often than an actual practice. Yoga-related products are today sold to many people who will rarely or never practice yoga. But even as a commodified practice in the West, yoga is largely the domain of middle-class, able-bodied, white women, although there are growing movements to push back against this and position contemporary yoga as inclusive, accessible, and body positive.

In its geographic birthplace, in the Indian subcontinent (which also covers the countries of Pakistan, Afghanistan, and Bangladesh), the multiplicity of yoga's history is often reduced by politicians and pundits alike to a linear history that plays into a Hindu nationalist narrative. In this story, India is the only recognized territory of origin, and yoga is the country's gift to the world. In 2014, India's Prime Minister Narendra Modi successfully campaigned at the United Nations General Assembly for a day of recognition for yoga as an intangible cultural heritage. The idea was supported by 175 countries, and International Day of Yoga (IYD) has been celebrated annually on June 21 since that year. The now global support for IYD is an example of the scale of soft power Modi has been able to exert through yoga to promote a Hindu nationalist agenda.

Modi's conservative Bharatiya Janata Party (BJP) constructed a common yoga protocol that must be adhered to on IYD and in it included the *sūryanamaskār* sequence of postures. Many non-Hindus in India see this sequence as a Hindu practice of devotion to a Hindu deity. Their opposition to mandating this sequence has been met with resistance from BJP members, including Yogi Adiyanath (the chief minister of the most populous state in India, Uttar Pradesh), who said those who do not want to perform the sequence should "drown themselves in the sea." Widespread protests eventually led to sūryanamaskār being removed from the IYD protocol, but the tensions between Hindu nationalists and minority groups remain.

In Latin America, no Indian yogis had arrived on the continent before 1950, but yoga was known in the region from the early 1900s. This meant that Latin America developed its own form of yoga, which was based on not postural practice but rather a non-dualistic, religio-philosophical worldview. It evolved into a form of hybrid esoteric spirituality, including references to Egyptian philosophy. Similarly, in East Asia, and specifically Japan, another type of hybrid practice developed in the 1900s by combining yoga, martial arts, and Indigenous forms of meditation.

There is a gap in the current research on the history of yoga in Africa, despite the east of the continent being home to Indian migrants for almost two hundred years. In South Africa, the history of yoga can be traced back to the Divine Life Centre, which opened in 1956, and to white, female students of Iyengar in the 1960s. No traceable mention is made of yoga when Indian migrants first arrived in the country in 1860. Further investigations into this hidden history are ongoing.

Contemporary yoga has been influenced by the global reach of the practice and shape-shifted in its passage through different regions intersecting with local culture and interests. In practice, most contemporary yoga is postural, with variations found in different schools and brands. This form of yoga has also found a place in health provision and is offered as a social prescription by the United Kingdom's National Health Service, among others. It is also taught in some schools, workplaces, and prisons as a means of managing stress and encouraging present-moment awareness, body positivity, and self-acceptance.

While postural yoga has dominated contemporary conceptions of yoga, meditation also has its place. Transcendental Meditation was pioneered by Maharishi Mahesh Yogi in the 1950s in India and transported into the mainstream by the Beatles, among others. Yogic practices of meditation have also blended with the various modern interpretations of Buddhism that have emerged in the last century and have established footholds in parts of the West.

About the author

Firdose Moonda is a PhD candidate at the University of Cape Town in South Africa and is working on a doctoral project provisionally titled Yoga, Politics and Possibilities for Social Justice. She completed her MA in traditions of yoga and meditation at the School of Oriental and African Studies in 2019 and works as a journalist and yoga teacher trainer. She is interested in research areas including the politics of the body, decolonization, and the intersection of yoga and Islam.

Suggestions for further reading

In this book

See also chapters 6 (Has yoga always been associated with Hinduism?) and 54 (Who was Swami Vivekananda?).

Elsewhere

Michelis, Elizabeth De. *A History of Modern Yoga: Patañjali and Western Esotericism*. Continuum, 2008.

Singleton, Mark. *Yoga Body: The Origins of Modern Posture Practice*. University Press, 2010.

Wildcroft, Theodora. *Post-Lineage Yoga: From Guru to #MeToo*. Equinox Publishing Ltd., 2020.

52

Why did yoga start being practiced in the Western world?

Philip Deslippe

Currently, yoga is practiced by an estimated three hundred million people throughout the world and generates annual revenue in the tens of billions of dollars, but in the late nineteenth century, relatively little was known about yoga outside of India. The spread of yoga to the Western world and its dramatic transformation into a global phenomenon over the last century and a half was the cumulative result of several key reformers and teachers, transnational metaphysical movements, cultural changes, and the use of media and technology.

Yoga as it is understood and practiced around the world is largely the consequence of the *haṭhayoga* renaissance in early twentieth-century India. In this movement, yoga was codified through a combination of pre-existing yogic practices and ideas with Western forms of physical culture, gymnastics, and bodybuilding and explained through modern medical science and related to practical, worldly benefits. Yoga could strengthen the body, cure illness, and make a person more energetic, efficient, and successful in their daily life. While this was a product of large historical and cultural forces, it was also due to key individuals, particularly reformers such as Swami Kuvalayananda and Shri Yogendra, who founded research centers for yoga and shaped how it was seen and understood, and teachers such as Tirumalai Krishnamacharya, whose students became the most influential and significant proponents of modern yoga.

Before the *haṭha* renaissance took hold outside of India in the late 1930s, there was little consensus as to what yoga actually was in the West, and it was primarily pursued by metaphysical seekers. Yoga was primarily seen as mental and magical, and when yoga was physical, it was mostly a matter of breathing exercises and diet reform. There was perhaps no greater promoter of yoga in the West during this time than the Theosophical Society, founded in New York in 1875, with its headquarters established in Adyar, India, in 1882, whose stated aims were to "form a nucleus of universal brotherhood"; promote the comparative study of religion, philosophy, and science; and "investigate unexplained laws of nature and the powers latent in man." Branches and members of the Theosophical Society, as well as its students and sympathizers, studied yoga and translated and distributed premodern and contemporary books on yoga around the world, including Europe, Russia, and Latin America.

Physical postures started to become central to an understanding of yoga outside of India around the time of the Second World War. In response to the mystique and misunderstandings of yoga held in the West, numerous teachers, both Indian and Western, taught forms of yoga in Europe and the Americas that were described as accessible and appropriate for Westerners. One of the ways this was done was through printed instruction manuals, usually with photographs and detailed descriptions of postures and exercises along with their purported benefits. No manual was more influential than the 1966 *Light on Yoga* by B. K. S. Iyengar, which has sold over three million copies and been translated into more than twenty-three languages. In 1961, Richard Hittleman became the first yoga teacher in the United States to have a television program. His *Yoga for Health* inspired Lilias Folan, who began her own program titled *Yoga and Yoga* in 1970, which was aired nationally on public television for almost three decades for a total of nearly five hundred episodes. Television was a powerful force in popularizing yoga, and it helped domesticate yoga, figuratively and literally, in America by allowing large numbers of people to take regular, weekly classes in the privacy of their own homes.

Large numbers of spiritual seekers in the hippie counterculture of the late sixties looked to yoga and spiritual teachers from India as a source of mystic wisdom, creating another upwelling of visibility and popularity of yoga in the West that continued through the New Age movement of the following decades. There were other more mundane movements and institutions that assisted the popularity of yoga. In postwar Britain, yoga found a home within adult education classes, which not only made yoga more popular but helped develop its reputation as a public good and shape its methods of instruction and certification. In the United States, there was a physical fitness boom during the late 1970s that soon saw the creation of several massive nationwide gym chains throughout the subsequent decades. Gyms and health clubs became a common site for yoga classes and put the practice squarely in the context of health and physical fitness for many, while the increasing mainstream acceptance of holistic health and alternative medicine allowed for the inclusion of yoga as a tool for stress reduction and the prevention and treatment of chronic diseases.

In the nineties, yoga became more organized and professionalized. Previously, many were authorized to teach directly by their own teachers, and length of practice was often the most important credential, but during this time, many schools of yoga codified the training of teachers, and a consensus emerged more broadly about standards and credentialing. Teacher-training programs were open to the public and resulted in a massive increase in the number of teachers. The magazine *Yoga Journal* not only had increased circulation but began to host large live events in which many studio owners, teachers, and dedicated students were able to network and exchange ideas, leading to the streamlining of many practices and the rise of numerous “celebrity” yoga teachers. The advent of VHS tapes and DVDs further helped popularize and diversify yoga in the West. Like television before them, these forms of media not only allowed people to practice on their own schedule at home, but they also allowed many teachers to create classes for specific audiences and physical conditions.

Numerous detailed surveys of contemporary yoga practitioners have been conducted in the United States, Britain, and Australia as part of medical studies carried out by researchers or demographic research for commercial entities such as *Yoga Journal* magazine. The data from these surveys suggests that although a small but significant minority of practitioners in the West see yoga as a spiritual practice, the primary motivation for the majority is health and flexibility, with stress relief and relaxation as secondary motivations. Today, yoga has a popularity, mainstream acceptance, and global presence that would have been unthinkable a little over a century ago. There are not only yoga studios and practitioners in most major cities around the world, but yoga is practiced in massive numbers by millions upon millions of people as a form of physical fitness and self-improvement.

About the author

Philip Deslippe is a doctoral candidate in the Department of Religious Studies at the University of California, Santa Barbara where his research focuses on Asian, metaphysical, and marginal religious traditions in the United States. He has published numerous articles for academic journals including the *Journal of Yoga Studies* and *Japanese Religions*, and popular venues such as *Yoga Journal* and *Tricycle.*

Suggestions for further reading

In this book

See also chapters 37 (How do academics study yoga?) and 55 (Who was Krishnamacharya?).

Elsewhere

Alter, Joseph S. *Yoga in Modern India: The Body Between Science and Philosophy*. Princeton University Press, 2004.

Newcombe, Suzanne. *Yoga in Britain: Stretching Spirituality and Educating Yogis*. Equinox Publishing Ltd., 2019.

Oliver, Paul. *Hinduism and the 1960s: The Rise of a Counter-Culture*. Bloomsbury, 2014.

53 Where did all the women come from?

Suzanne Newcombe

Today, women make up the vast majority of yoga practitioners. Surveys of practitioners in the Americas, Europe, and Australasia often estimate that 75–90 percent of contemporary yoga practitioners are women—and this demographic can in most cases be further described as upper middle class and well educated. Understanding this contemporary gender imbalance requires some reflection and explanation.

It has been widely assumed that most historical yoga practitioners were male, largely because most texts appear to be written from the point of view of male practitioners. Yet yoga—however the aims and practices are understood—has never been solely accessible to males. Early Buddhist and Jain communities incorporated women as renunciates and lay practitioners. Even if female yoga practitioners are exceptional in the historical record, there are documented female ascetics and tantric practitioners. Female practitioners are also explicitly mentioned in a yoga manual possibly dating to the early seventh century, in the context of seeking liberation. A lack of evidence of premodern women practicing yoga in public spaces does not mean there were no female yoga practitioners.

Nevertheless, something specific happened with the yoga revival of the early twentieth century that made posture-focused yoga popular among women. In early twentieth-century India, Indian nationalists began to call for the revitalization of the Indian body through specifically Indian cultural traditions. Much of the focus was on vitalizing the Indian male body in the *akhāṛā* (gymnasium), the traditional training grounds of wrestling, with martial arts, *sūryanamaskār*, Indian clubs, and *mallakhamb* (exercises on a pillar or rope). While many of these activities were more popularly associated with men, others such as *sūryanamaskār* and *mallakhamb* may have been more gender neutral, at least for the young and unmarried. As yoga *āsana* entered the repertoire of Indian physical culture, Indian women were also participating in certain contexts. Shri Yogendra (Manibhai Haribhai Desai, 1897–1989) was among the first to have pioneered āsana-focused classes that became popular among middle classes worldwide. Teaching largely from a suburb of Mumbai (Bombay), Yogendra's *Yoga Asanas Simplified* (1928) became a template for future yoga books, and his wife Sitadevi (1912–2008) published *Yoga Physical Education (for Women)* in 1934. Because of the historical associations of yoga as a form of Indigenous masculinity that supported national self-rule (*swaraj*) and economic independence (*swadeshi*), yoga as a physical practice in India continues to have more male practitioners than elsewhere in the world.

The influential teacher Tirumalai Krishnamacharya (1888–1989) presided over a revival of yoga āsana at the Mysore Palace (1926–1950) and largely taught āsana to young men who gave impressive, physically demanding public demonstrations to encourage interest in the subject. But Krishnamacharya also taught yoga to female members of his family in private and encouraged his much younger brother-in-law B. K. S. Iyengar (1918–2014) to teach āsana to groups of young women. During the late 1930s, Krishnamacharya taught āsana to the Latvian wife of a Czechoslovakian diplomat, Eiženija Pētersone (1899–2002). Pētersone, adopting the name of Indra Devi, popularized a form of modern postural yoga specifically marked as an elixir of youth and beauty for women by teaching female Hollywood celebrities in the 1950s and publishing *Forever Young, Forever Healthy* (1953).

Gendered forms of physical culture in European cultures meant that the physical aspects of yoga teaching looked similar to the kinds of exercise that were socially acceptable for middle-class women. In the nineteenth century, middle-class girls were likely to have been taught Pehr Henrik Ling's Swedish Gymnastics, while boys were taught military drills and competitive games such as rugby and cricket. In Britain during the 1920s, yoga was explicitly incorporated into Mary Bagot Stack's "Women's League of Health and Beauty" and also familiarized in other forms of female physical culture such as Ruth St. Denis's (1878–1968) explorations of movement, body, breath, and spirit in the early twentieth-century United States.

Yoga in the mid-twentieth century appealed particularly to women in the Global North for many reasons. Married middle-class women generally did not need to work outside the home for economic reasons during the 1950s, but in Europe, many had been working as part of the war effort. Many women were searching for greater connections with the world outside of their homes as well as seeking psychological freedom and greater economic autonomy. Simultaneously, women in the mid-twentieth century were very much judged and valued on normative standards of youth and beauty. The emerging physical-based yoga practice was perfectly positioned to address these social and psychological desires. Popular books like Nancy Phelan and Michael Volin's *Yoga for Women* (1963) promised that yoga would defy the aging process, maintaining a youthful appearance and vitality well into the second half of life. In the 1960s and 1970s, yoga classes on television were offered during school hours and in-person classes in the evenings when children could be left with husbands. Testimonies report that women practicing yoga in this period felt physically and psychologically supported by the practices.

Yoga also was associated with the natural birth movement and second-wave feminism's discontent with the biomedical profession's treatment of women. Very often, women felt as though they were given no choice about the nature or extent of medical interventions and that their own experience of labor was less important than what the medical professionals expected to happen. The body awareness developed in yoga practice helped women validate their own embodied experiences. Frédérick Leboyer's film *Birth without Violence* (1969) and his book by the same name (1975) presented an idealized version of natural childbirth in India, which poetically championed the personhood of the newborn and the inherent ability of women to give birth without medical intervention. Yoga classes were often incorporated into female networks for prenatal and postnatal care and supported women in challenging the medical profession to incorporate more respect for women's embodied experiences into birthing practices. Many women continued to find such networks supportive of their embodied experience throughout their life cycle.

While women in Global North societies have increasingly been working outside the home and achieving more economic independence, pressures on women to maintain their youth and beauty continue. In her analysis of contemporary yoga, Andrea Jain emphasizes how neoliberalism has infused some forms of feminism and enables a consumerist model of yoga practice. Twenty-first-century visual presentations of yoga in advertising and social media have been criticized as promoting a narrow form of female beauty, with idealized white, thin, flexible bodies that do not reflect the diversity of shapes and abilities experienced by the majority of female bodies. However, a variety of female-led expressions of yoga also exist in the contemporary world and promote alternative forms of gender, racial, and environmental relationships.

About the author

Suzanne Newcombe is a senior lecturer in religious studies at the Open University and honorary director of the charity Inform, based in theology and religious studies at King's College London. From 2015 to 2020, she was part of the European Research Council–funded project "Ayuryog: Entangled Histories of Yoga, Ayurveda and Alchemy" in South Asia, which examined the histories of yoga, Ayurveda, and rasaśāstra (Indian alchemy and iatrochemistry) from the tenth century to the present, focusing on the disciplines' health, rejuvenation, and longevity practices. She is the coeditor of *The Routledge Handbook of Yoga and Meditation Studies* (Routledge, 2021) and the author of *Yoga in Britain: Stretching Spirituality and Educating Yogis* (Equinox Publishing Ltd., 2019).

Suggestions for further reading

In this book

See also chapters 35 (What is a *yoginī*?) and 51 (How has modern yoga developed around the world?).

Elsewhere

Evans, S. Y. *Black Women's Yoga History: Memoirs of Inner Peace*. SUNY Press, 2021.

Foxen, A. P. *Inhaling Spirit: Harmonialism, Orientalism, and the Western Roots of Modern Yoga*. Oxford University Press, 2020.

Newcombe, S. *Yoga in Britain: Stretching Spirituality and Educating Yogis*. Equinox Publishing Ltd., 2019.

Jain, A. *Peace Love Yoga: The Politics of Global Spirituality*. Oxford University Press, 2020.

Wittich, A., and P. McCartney. "Changing Face of the Yoga Industry, Its Dharmic Roots and Its Message to Women: An Analysis of Yoga Journal Magazine Covers, 1975–2020." *Journal of Dharma Studies* 3, no. 1 (2020): 31–44.

54 Who was Swami Vivekananda?

Gwilym Beckerlegge

For many devotees, Swami Vivekananda (1863–1902) was a great teacher in his own right and the faithful disciple of his master, Sri Ramakrishna Paramahamsa (ca. 1836–1866). By establishing the Ramakrishna Math and Mission, Vivekananda not only ensured the dissemination of Ramakrishna's teaching and his own but also provided an organizational model that other Hindu groups subsequently adopted, together with many of his ideas. Vivekananda has been credited with contributing to the resurgence of Hindu confidence during the closing years of the nineteenth century, which fed into the movement for independence. He has exercised a diffusive, sometimes indirect influence on how Hindu spirituality, and indeed "Hinduism," has come to be understood beyond India. His ideas have been selectively assimilated into countercultural and New Age movements in North America and western Europe and into yoga during its transformation over the last century into a global phenomenon.

The distinctive phases of Vivekananda's life are reflected in his teaching. Vivekananda (birth name Narendranath Datta) was born and largely raised in Calcutta (Kolkata) and expected to enter the legal profession. While receiving a European-style education at a Christian missionary college, however, he heard about Ramakrishna, whose single-minded pursuit of God-realization, manifested in changes of consciousness, and informal discourses had begun to attract followers. Emerging from a phase of religious skepticism, by the time of Ramakrishna's death, Vivekananda had become the leader of a group of largely college-educated, unmarried, young disciples who had cared for their dying master. At Vivekananda's instigation, these disciples initiated themselves (a ritual normally performed by a guru) into a life of renunciation (*saṃnyāsa*), adopting religious names and the honorific title of Swami (*svāmin*, "Lord"). This is said to be the origin of the Ramakrishna Math (*maṭh*, "monastery").

Over the next seven years, as Vivekananda traveled through India on increasingly solitary pilgrimages, he adopted the religious name

Vivekananda (bliss of discrimination) and, in his words, "hit upon a plan" to use *saṃnyāsins* (renouncers) to alleviate the plight of India's poor and oppressed through education. This plan transformed his mission, taking him to the 1893 World's Parliament of Religions in Chicago, originally in the hope of raising funds. Vivekananda became known for his vigorous defense of Hinduism at the parliament and began to draw American supporters and devotees. Invited to London, he gathered further admirers and traveled in Europe. He returned to India in 1897 when he established the Ramakrishna Mission, having already founded a Vedanta Society in New York, a title that continues to be used for the movement's branches in the United States and Europe. Vivekananda visited the United States and London again in 1899, returning to India in late 1900, by which time his health was failing. He died in his thirty-ninth year.

In India, Vivekananda is known preeminently for his popularization of *sevā*, service to those in need as divine, which was inspired by his travels through India and institutionalized in the Ramakrishna Math and Mission. While in the United States and England, Vivekananda responded to what he perceived to be the spiritual needs of his American and English audiences by giving several lectures and talks that contained what are now regarded as his key teachings. He presented Hinduism at the Parliament of Religions at Chicago not just as a "world religion" but as the "mother of religions," which embodies tolerance and universalism in contrast, he maintained, to the exclusivism of Christianity. His exposition of a universal religion most fully realized in the Hindu philosophy of Advaita Vedānta would remain central to his message. In London, he elaborated his idea of "Practical Vedanta," also anchored in the philosophy of Vedānta. Now often assumed to provide a rationale for Vivekananda's promotion of service to humanity, "Practical Vedanta" speaks primarily of "practicality" in relation to God-realization and reconciling religion and the new scientific knowledge of Vivekananda's day. In New York, Vivekananda lectured on the four yogas: *karmayoga*, *bhaktiyoga*, *jñānayoga*, and *rājayoga* ("royal yoga," the system outlined in the *Yogasūtra* attributed to Patañjali). He offered little by way of guidance about the physical practice of yoga, once declaring that he had made "very little progress" after a lifelong study of yoga, and he could be dismissive of *haṭhayoga*. His lectures on *rājayoga*, published as *Raja Yoga* in 1896, included a translation of Patañjali's "Yoga Aphorisms" (*Yogasūtra*), which focus more on quieting the mind than following a systematic program of postures.

Vivekananda continues to be revered and admired in India and was arguably the first international Hindu guru. His role in representing the Hindu tradition in a variety of settings, however, has provoked continuing scholarly debate about both the nature of the continuity between his ideas and priorities, referred to by some as neo-Hinduism or neo-Vedanta, and those of earlier Hindu tradition, including those of his master, and about the extent of the influence of Vivekananda's praise of Hindu culture on the later growth of Hindu nationalism. In his promotion of sevā, Vivekananda pointed to the teaching and example of Ramakrishna. He extolled the "path of action" (karmayoga) and formulated an ethic of service that reinterprets elements of Advaita Vedānta and passages from Hindu texts such as the *Bhagavadgītā* and the Upaniṣads. Vivekananda's critics have viewed this initiative more as a sign of his exposure to Christian influence, some questioning whether Ramakrishna would have regarded social activism as an aid to God-realization or as a distraction. Vivekananda's novel reworking of aspects of the yoga tradition has been acknowledged as having been influential in the globalizing of yoga. Although it has been suggested that here again there is evidence of Vivekananda's exposure to ideas outside the Hindu tradition, it has also been argued that Vivekananda played a major part in presenting yoga as the core of Hindu spirituality.

About the author

Gwilym Beckerlegge studied religion at the Universities of Oxford and Lancaster where he developed a particular interest in the religions of South Asia and Japan from the nineteenth century to the present. He is the author of *The Ramakrishna Mission: The Making of a Modern Hindu Movement* (Oxford University Press, 2000) and *Swami Vivekananda's Legacy of Service: A Study of the Ramakrishna Math and Mission* (Oxford University Press, 2006). In 2006/2007 he held the post of Professor of the Study of Religions at University College Cork, and in 2010 was Visiting Professor at the Centre d'études de l'Inde et de l'Asie du Sud, École des Hautes Études en Sciences Sociale, Paris. He is currently Professor Emeritus, Department of Religious Studies, The Open University, UK.

Suggestions for further reading

In this book

See also chapters 45 (Who was Patañjali?) and 51 (How has modern yoga developed around the world?).

Elsewhere

Beckerlegge, Gwilym. *Swami Vivekananda's Legacy of Service: A Study of the Ramakrishna Math and Mission.* Oxford University Press, 2006.

Killingley, Dermot. "Manufacturing Yogis: Swami Vivekananda as a Yoga Teacher." In *Gurus of Modern Yoga*, edited by M. Singleton and E. Goldberg. Oxford University Press, 2014.

Sen, Amiya P. *Swami Vivekananda*. Oxford University Press, 2000.

Sil, Narasingha P. *Swami Vivekananda: A Reassessment*. Associated University Press, 1997.

55 Who was Krishnamacharya?

Amelia Wood

Tirumalai Krishnamacharya (1888–1989) is often referred to as the father or grandfather of modern yoga. His innovations in yoga *āsana*, the international success of his students, and the importance placed on the idea of lineage within modern yoga have resulted in many yoga teachers citing him as their teacher's teacher or, at least, a significant source of inspiration. What we know about his life and own lineage is a mix of biography and hagiography: Regardless of any biographical inaccuracies, his legacy and place in the history of modern yoga remain intact, and his influence is undeniable. In this section, I will briefly cover details of Krishnamacharya's life and teachings and the prominent students who disseminated his work.

Krishnamacharya was born in 1888 in Karnataka, India, into a prestigious family of orthodox Vaiṣṇava Brahmans. He was taught by his father to chant the Vedas and to speak and write Sanskrit at a young age and later studied at Mysore University under his great-grandfather. At age eighteen, he traveled to northern India to study in Varanasi. It is believed that Krishnamacharya also traveled to Tibet, where he studied with his guru, Rammohan Brahmacari. It is understood that here, he mastered every aspect of yoga, including philosophy, āsana, and *prāṇāyāma*. After seven years, his guru instructed him to live as a householder and spread the teachings of yoga, and in 1925, Krishnamacharya married.

Specific details of his period in Tibet, where, apparently, he lived in a cave, remain inconsistent. It is possible that his guru was actually from South India, and likely, his followers repeated the myth as a mark of respect. Tibet and similarly inaccessible locations are often evoked as sites of esoteric knowledge unavailable to the ordinary individual. Regardless of the exact location, particular mode of transmission, or name of his guru, it is clear that during this time, Krishnamacharya became very knowledgeable.

In 1926, Krishnamacharya met and impressed the maharaja of Mysore—Krishnaraja Wodiya IV—in Varanasi. Under Krishnaraja Wodiya IV, Mysore was a hub of cultural, scientific, and educational innovations. He promoted physical culture in the palace and across the state, and gymnastics and Western sports became part of children's education. In 1933, the maharaja gave Krishnamacharya a wing of the Jaganmohan Palace, in Mysore, to open a yoga school, or *yogaśala*. He was tasked with promoting yoga as a desirable and—importantly—Indigenous activity. During that time, Krishnamacharya held demonstrations of yogic feats in the palace, such as stopping his pulse and performing complex āsana. The maharaja patronized the school until his death in 1940, and Krishnamacharya taught in the palace until it closed in 1950 amid the political upheaval associated with India's independence, which led to a loss of patronage.

The diverse methods that Krishnamacharya developed during his almost sixty years of teaching are evident in the approaches of those he taught and went on to establish their own lineage, brand, or style of yoga. The most prominent include K. Pattabhi Jois (1915–2009), B. K. S. Iyengar (1918–2004), Indra Devi (1899–2002), and his son, T. K. V. Desikachar (1938–2016). The notable difference between how and what these particular teachers prioritized in their own teaching is likely due to the fact that Krishnamacharya's approach to yoga was inherently adaptable and innovative. According to Desikachar, the yoga practice offered to students by his father depended on the context and requirements of the individual.

Indra Devi, unlike Krishnamacharya's other students, did not establish a yoga school or lineage but was nonetheless influential. Similarly to the maharaja, she was impressed by Krishnamacharya's heart-stopping demonstration and in 1938 asked if she could study yoga with him. At the maharaja's insistence, he took Devi on, and she became the first foreign woman to be taught at the Mysore Palace.

In turn, at Krishnamacharya's behest, Devi taught yoga when she left India, first in China in 1939 and then in America. In 1948, she opened a yoga studio in Hollywood. Devi appealed particularly to women—she sold yoga as a remedy for anxiety and the secret to retaining youth and staying trim. Her first book, published in 1953, *Forever Young, Forever Healthy*, taught a form of slow, relaxing yoga that appealed to the busy lives of office workers striving for the American dream. The location and novelty of her studio, the success of her published yoga books, and her style of teaching all contributed to her influence as a yoga teacher.

Krishnamacharya took on Pattabhi Jois as a student (aged twelve) in 1927 for two years in Karnataka and again in 1932 in Mysore. In 1934, B. K. S. Iyengar, Krishnamacharya's brother-in-law, also went to Mysore (aged sixteen) to practice yoga for his health. Both Jois and Iyengar assisted their teacher by performing yoga demonstrations to audiences at the Mysore Palace. It is possible that Jois was there when Devi first saw these yoga demonstrations, but by this time, Iyengar had moved on. Krishnamacharya sent him to Pune in 1937 to teach yoga.

Iyengar Yoga, as a method, involves static poses and the use of props. Comparatively, the style of yoga practice pioneered by Jois, known as Ashtanga Vinyasa Yoga, is dynamic and gymnastic. Āsana are performed in repetitive sequences, and poses are sometimes held for a count of five. Vinyasa Flow and Power Yoga, which the reader may be familiar with, emerged from Jois's Ashtanga Vinyasa system.

Jois claimed the *āsana* (postures) and *vinyāsa* (steps) that make up the sequences were taught to Krishnamacharya by his guru (in Tibet) from a five-thousand-year-old text called the *Yoga Kurunta*. There is no trace of even a partial transcription of this text, and no oral transmission was passed onto any disciples, which is the typical practice in Brahmanical culture. It is more likely that the sequences and *sūryanamaskār* (gymnastic prostrations to the sun) became part of yoga—as taught by Krishnamacharya—due to the influence of Western physical culture, the close proximity of the gymnasium and bodybuilding classes in the Mysore Palace, and the remit under which he taught. Classes at the yogaśala were to improve the physical well-being of the boys in attendance, and we know that his classes were categorized as exercise. This does not render particular yoga sequences as inauthentic. It demonstrates that Krishnamacharya did not teach in a vacuum but innovated and responded, as pundits did before him, to create a yoga that exists in relationship with modernity and orthodoxy.

Krishnamacharya's ability to adapt yoga to the individual is perhaps most evident in the yoga methods of his son, Desikachar. Desikachar began learning yoga in the 1960s, after working as an engineer, and went on to establish Viniyoga. The term comes from the *Yogasūtra*, and his methods include therapeutic movement, prāṇāyāma, chanting, meditation, and instruction in philosophy.

Jois, Iyengar, and Desikachar all successfully followed their teacher's request to spread the teachings of yoga. Iyengar taught his first yoga class in the UK in 1954 and visited the US for the first time in 1956, and his first book, *Light on Yoga* (1966), has sold millions of copies. In 2004, *Time* magazine named him as one of the most influential people in the world. Similarly, in the 1970s, Jois began traveling the world to teach yoga, and Westerners traveled to study directly with him in Mysore. Desikachar also traveled and taught internationally and in 1976 established the Krishnamacharya Yoga Mandiram in Madras, India, with A. G. Mohan. Students continue to travel to Pune to practice yoga with the Iyengar family and become officially certified as Iyengar Yoga teachers. Similarly, people travel to Mysore to practice Ashtanga Vinyasa Yoga with Jois's family. And the Mohans continue Desikachar's legacy through online and in-person trainings in Chennai. Despite their diversity in yoga pedagogy, Jois, Iyengar, and Desikachar are united in citing Krishnamacharya as their teacher and claimed to continue his lineage or tradition of yoga in their own work.

Krishnamacharya successfully fulfilled his guru's wishes of disseminating yoga—he did not covet fame or ever leave India, but his influence can, to some extent, be identified in almost every modern postural yoga class today.

About the author

Amelia Wood is a PhD candidate at SOAS University of London researching modern yoga, specifically spiritual abuse in modern yoga. She received an MA from SOAS in the traditions of meditation and yoga, during which she researched the roles and representations of women in premodern yoga.

Suggestions for further reading

In this book

See also chapters 29 (What is *vinyasa*?) and 48 (Are the teachers of yoga enlightened?).

Elsewhere

Mohan, A. G., and Mohan, Ganesh. *Krishnamacharya: His Life and Teachings*. Shambhala Publications, 2010.

Singleton, Mark. "T. Krishnamacharya, Father of Modern Yoga." In *Gurus of Modern Yoga*, edited by Jane Byrne and Mark Singleton. Oxford University Press, 2014.

Singleton, Mark. "T. Krishnamacharya and the Mysore *Asana* Revival." In *Yoga Body: The Origins of Modern Posture Practice*. Oxford University Press, 2010.

What does yoga look like today?

56 How do modern practitioners relate to ancient texts?

Barbora Sojková

From the early centuries before the Common Era, the Indian subcontinent has been a multilingual area, with many local languages and dialects. This suggests that yoga texts, as well as other forms of knowledge, were transmitted in various languages, both orally and in writing. Among these, the most important one is the commonly named Classical Sanskrit, an elite register of an Indo-European language that developed and flourished in South Asia from the first half of the first millennium BCE onward. At that time, Sanskrit stopped developing as a living language and was standardized by the grammarian Pāṇini. Since then, it has been used for matters of high culture, such as literature, drama, philosophy, religion, and other technical subjects, and served as a lingua franca in the Indian subcontinent as well as further afield (Tibet, China). Due to the status and function of Sanskrit in premodern South Asia, our understanding of yoga's premodern history largely rests on texts written in this language.

This does not mean, however, that Sanskrit is the only source of textual knowledge about yoga. Many texts describing yoga (or techniques and methods associated with it, such as breath control) were written in other classical Asian languages, such as Pali, various Prakrits, Persian, Tamil, Arabic, Tibetan, Chinese, and earlier forms of Sanskrit known as Vedic. While these classical languages are studied relatively frequently in academic settings, considerably less attention is given to the premodern vernacular languages of the Indian subcontinent, such as Avadhi, Braj Bhasha, Old Bengali, Kashmiri, Old Marathi, Maithili, or Assamese. In comparison to the highly technical literature in Sanskrit (and, to a certain extent, the other classical languages), texts in these vernacular languages have a tendency to reflect social reality and thus provide valuable information about the social history of premodern yoga. Yet these texts are largely overlooked in academic research, owing to the privileged status of

Sanskritic culture in South Asian history as well as the lack of resources and secondary materials for their study. In view of this, vernacular texts on yoga present an important corrective in the study of premodern yoga, and if included in its academic study, they can yield important findings.

While referencing the multiplicity of languages in which yoga was transmitted, we should not forget about the modern and contemporary history of yoga. For the most part, from the nineteenth century onward, original teachings have been composed in modern South Asian languages, particularly Hindi and Bengali, as well as in English, German, and other European languages. Taking the whole of yoga history into account, these languages are similarly important for its development.

There is as much variety in texts describing yoga practice as there is among the languages in which they have been written. At present, academics are studying close to a hundred premodern texts in numerous manuscript variants and printed editions. These texts come in many genres: We find philosophical treatises, practical manuals, meditation instructions, and religious teachings. Even within the same genre, the teachings of various texts differ enormously, providing windows on particular traditions at particular times. Furthermore, references to yoga are found in a much wider scope of texts, including literary, poetic, and dramatic works. As might be expected, these sources can offer a somewhat different view of premodern yoga than the normative instructional manuals. As an example, consider the popular story of yogi Gorakṣanātha's rescue of his guru from the kingdom of women, transmitted orally and in writing in many vernacular Indian languages, including Bengali. This mythological story features many motifs that normative Sanskrit texts often shy away from, including yogic supernatural powers (*siddhi*) and sexual relationships with women, and points us to a different, vernacular understanding of yoga.

Among practitioners, three texts usually form the "canon" of yoga texts studied within yoga teacher trainings, most often in popular editions and translations. The text of the *Pātañjalayogaśāstra*, colloquially known as Patañjali's *Yogasūtra*, has been considered uniquely important for the history of yoga. While the influence of the *Yogasūtra* on the contemporary yoga community is unquestionable, its roots are complex and point to early Western scholars of India and the late nineteenth-century religious thinker and yoga reformer Swami Vivekananda as much as they speak to the premodern philosophical tradition. Aside from the *Yogasūtra*, the *Bhagavadgītā* and the *Haṭhapradīpikā*, along with some Upaniṣads, are prescribed in teacher-training programs. Although hugely significant for yoga history, these texts barely cover the scope evidenced by the multitude of premodern yoga teachings. The wider textual sources, exposing the development of yoga practice in more nuance, are largely unknown outside of academia.

Moreover, even those practitioners who study those few premodern yogic texts within yoga teacher-training programs are seldom taught the nuance that would help them understand the wider implications of these texts. This, I believe, is caused by the difficulty of access and expertise in both academia and the wider yoga community. In particular, expertise in premodern South Asian languages is becoming increasingly marginalized in academia, and this marginalization has a ripple effect outward to the practitioner community.

To return to our question, if one were to study one of the three most commonly taught premodern yoga texts, be it in original or in translation, what would be the benefits? Many practitioners and teachers consider language and textual study to be a part of their yoga practice, often referencing the concept of *svādhyāya* (recitation, literally "self-study"), one of the observances (*niyama*) prescribed by Patañjali. In Patañjali's text, svādhyāya is specifically the study of texts on liberation, which can be substituted by the repetition of the mantra *oṃ*. In the contemporary context, it can include the study of all kinds of material associated with yoga, be it premodern or later, and it is sometimes interpreted as a tool for exploration and improvement of the self.

For many, personal study of Sanskrit or other premodern languages and yoga texts is a way of engaging with yoga's complex history. This can influence one's understanding of the past, present, and future of yoga and make one appreciate the variety, complexity, evolution, and dynamic nature of yoga. Moreover, contact with premodern texts and languages exposes practitioners to issues of translation. Premodern languages, and Sanskrit especially, are semantically rich, and since every translator has a very different goal or agenda in mind, translations can vary enormously. If one engages with a text in its original language or with multiple translations, this variety becomes very clear and can influence one's outlook on any written language and its usage. This can increase one's critical thinking skills, which, in turn, can have a positive effect on one's understanding of the development of yoga.

Furthermore, a close reading of any text of a different provenance, be it premodern or contemporary, can have a vast influence on one's understanding of the world. Beyond the development of personal practice, there are more general benefits. While studying unfamiliar and complex languages such as Sanskrit or Persian for the sake of personal yoga practice might seem like a lot of work, scientific studies show that learning any new language boosts attentional functions of the brain and might even be protective from degenerative neurological conditions.

Although these benefits will be instilled by engaging with any of the premodern yoga texts and languages, they would be exponentially increased if one studies a wider diversity of texts and languages with a wider diversity of provenance. This can lead to a much more nuanced understanding of the competing discourses of different yoga teachings and a deeper understanding of the sociopolitical reality of the time, as well as a greater appreciation of yoga's complex heritage.

About the author

Barbora Sojková holds a DPhil in Asian and Middle Eastern studies (Sanskrit) from the University of Oxford, where her research focused on human-animal relationships in Vedic Sanskrit literature. She works as an academic librarian at the All Souls College, Oxford, and as a Sanskrit cataloger at the Bodleian Library, Oxford. She is a certified yoga teacher and trainer focusing on the history and philosophy of yoga.

Suggestions for further reading

In this book

See also chapters 9 (What is Sanskrit?) and 31 (How do mantras relate to yoga?).

Elsewhere

Lubomír Ondračka. "What Should Mīnanāth Do to Save His Life?" In *Yogi Heroes and Poets: Histories and Legends of the Nāths*, edited by David N. Lorenzen and Adrián Muñoz. SUNY Press, 2011.

Sojková, Barbora. "Tools for Non-Dogmatic Yoga History." In *The Yoga Teacher's Survival Guide: Social Justice, Science, Politics, and Power*, edited by Theodora Wildcroft and Harriet McAttee. Singing Dragon, 2024.

57
Can people from all backgrounds practice yoga?

Jens U. Augspurger

"Yoga is for everyone." This slogan caught my attention as I passed by a European yoga studio a few years ago. It suggests that everyone could come and practice yoga. *But should they?*

In light of the critique of cultural appropriation, some may argue that the answer is simply no. Cultural appropriation refers to the harmful and violent exploitation of a minority culture by a dominant culture and is rooted in the colonial and postcolonial structures of Western capitalism. Its critique raises significant concern about the appropriateness of the slogan "Yoga is for everyone" and the use, profit, and exploitation of yoga by individuals or groups from dominant cultures.

But as modern transnational yoga is increasingly established as a mainstream practice at the intersections of the health, well-being, and spirituality markets, with many stakeholders involved, it is important to consider the growing complexity of this discourse. I will not provide a definitive answer to this question in this entry but rather share reflections on cultural appropriation and appreciation based on my encounters in the field.

If yoga is considered culturally appropriated, is that a blanket judgment applied to everything related to yoga, or is there potential for a nonappropriative practice? And in this context, what does yoga mean?

To consider this, I want to examine two aspects of cultural appropriation: decontextualization and disrespect. Decontextualization occurs when cultural practices and traditions are removed from their original context, most often for some form of exploitation. Some proponents of the cultural appropriation critique argue that postural or secular yoga styles should not be divorced from their spiritual roots and origins in Vedānta, Hindu religion, or Indian spirituality. Disrespectful appropriation occurs when the incorporation of a culture or context is intended to mock, degrade, diminish, or de-dignify. Examples of this include blackface as entertainment and the use of Indigenous costumes by non-Indigenous people as fashion. Many yoga practitioners would defend themselves against this accusation by saying that they hold high esteem for the tradition they consider themselves to be a part of and also for the origins of the practice. This is sometimes termed "cultural appreciation," a concept that is meant to signify a difference in intent from appropriation but that can also be used by apologists to justify what remains an appropriative practice.

Reframing the context and intent of yoga practice does not equalize or address the problems of exploitation and violence that it can entail. This is particularly relevant as emphasizing cultural contexts or enacting admiration can also be perceived as disrespectful in impact, regardless of the intent. Consider, for example, the commodification of Sanskrit mantras by white Europeans who fail to pronounce the mantras correctly and have no lived or embodied experience of the cultural context from which they derive. This can be said to be appropriative regardless of their level of appreciation for the language, sound, or deity they intend to invoke.

In response to these issues, new market strategies have emerged. Certain yoga styles have branded themselves as particularly spiritual, authentic, traditional, or Indian, claiming to alleviate but in reality bypassing the critique of cultural appropriation. This risks reinforcing harmful power dynamics, as these branded yoga styles are no less implicated in the socioeconomic systems that consume and profit from the traditions and practices of other cultures.

Today, not only the practice of yoga but also the term itself has become a bestseller, and many products marketed as yoga seem truly decontextualized from the tradition, among them things like beer yoga and yoga fitness regimes. It is always worth investigating why these practices have chosen to ally themselves with the term "yoga"—especially as affiliating newly created practices and activities with the name "yoga" also connects them to a contested legacy.

This leads to the next complexity, which is yoga's history, or more precisely, the origins of modern transnational yoga. The various attributes, such as "spiritual," "Indian," and "traditional," that are often presented as a way to contextualize and respect yoga's original cultural setting make specific claims about the origin of yoga. However, these are all terms applied to forms of transnational modern yoga, the contemporaneous, commodified, and dominant form of yoga, even when they claim to offer a more authentic practice or product. The cultural appropriation critique is entirely based on the assumption that one or a set of "original" yoga practices once existed as part of a broader culture in ancient India, implying that colonial suppression, globalization, and capitalism have destroyed this ancestral practice.

But this oversimplifies the historical evolution of yoga and is often deployed by Hindu nationalists to express their dominance and cultural ownership over anything Indian, and yoga in particular.

Scholars of modern yoga have argued that the current prevalent form of yoga only emerged at the end of the nineteenth century, in conjunction with the development of neo-Hinduism, Hindu nationalism, and the international adoption of Western fitness trends such as aerobics and bodybuilding. The yoga that is practiced and taught in India today, which is often marketed as "spiritual" or "original," is more likely the product of this reappropriation or deliberate renaissance than of local tradition.

Attempts to extract appropriative elements from contemporary yoga may prove unproductive and risk subsuming the problems of exploitation into one-dimensional perspectives. The complexities surrounding this debate may also be indicative of a broader cultural trend. Byung-Chul Han's theory of *hyperculture*, inspired by the internet's network of hyperlinks, suggests that all cultural expressions have been becoming increasingly detached from their (geographic) localities and origins. Instead, they are all connected and can exist alongside one another. In such a culture, Han suggests, there will be unrestricted access to diverse cultural expressions that can be fused together, like in fusion cuisine, which makes use of ingredients and preparation methods from various places and cultures. This, Han argues, blurs the distinctions of near and far or Indigenous and foreign and eventually strips places of their aura. If we consider transnational modern yoga in this framework, it may offer an analytical approach to understanding the arbitrary combinations of culture to which yoga is applied as well as the confusion surrounding its origin and authenticity, since both the invocation of meaning through historical context and full decontextualization are effective business strategies rather than positions that reflect historical veracity or postcolonialism.

Ultimately, even in Han's suggested hyperculture, access to cultural opportunities remains limited and often reserved for those in privileged positions. Globalization does not necessarily create more opportunities for everyone, and issues of social and distributive justice are often overlooked.

In the case of yoga, Thenmozhi Soundararajan, a Dalit activist, calls for not only a decolonization of yoga but also its de-Sanskritization and de-Brahmanization, particularly in the context of current Hindu nationalism in India. In a globalized world, injustices may appear in many places, with many faces, and are often intersectional, requiring effective addressing in multiple areas. This means yoga's embedded injustices concern not only who practices and where they practice but also how and in what form.

About the author

Jens U. Augspurger is a PhD candidate in the Department of Religions and Philosophies at SOAS University of London. His research and teaching focus on modern transnational yoga and spiritual movements, as well as their respective intersections with politics. He is also a recovering yoga teacher and the cofounder of Project SATYA, a community movement that supports survivors of sexualized violence and advocates for accountability and truth in the yoga industry. Considering spiritual tourism as a journey for self-discovery, his ethnographic dissertation project explores yoga tourism in India and the complex relationships the yoga tourist builds while journeying (toward) the destination.

Suggestions for further reading

In this book

See also chapters 17 (Does a yogi need to renounce the world?) and 20 (Is yoga safe?).

Elsewhere

Askegaard, Søren, and Giana M. Eckhardt. "Glocal Yoga: Re-Appropriation in the Indian Consumptionscape." *Marketing Theory* 12, no. 1 (2012): 45–60.

Black, Shameem. "Decolonising Yoga." In *Routledge Handbook of Yoga and Meditation Studies*, edited by Suzanne Newcombe and Karen O'Brien-Kop. Routledge, 2020.

Han, Byung-Chul. *Hyperculture: Culture and Globalisation*. Polity, 2022.

Soundararajan, Thenmozhi. *The Trauma of Caste: A Dalit Feminist Meditation on Survivorship, Healing and Abolition*. North Atlantic Books, 2022.

58
What does yoga mean to Indians today?

Marissa Clarke

It is challenging to locate the origins of yoga in one place due to the heterogeneity and complex historicity of its various traditions. In *Roots of Yoga*, James Mallinson and Mark Singleton translated and compiled over one hundred yogic texts written in various languages from 1500 BCE to the nineteenth century, which signifies the range of times and places that different "yogas" have unfolded and makes it difficult to reduce the origins of yoga to a single place or structure. There is certainly no denying that archaeological, anthropological, and textual evidence confirm yoga's prominence in South Asia. Yet in contemporary discourse, yoga is often represented as a distinctly Indian tradition. Whether this is entirely accurate is up for debate. Thus, it is reasonable to critically consider the politics of placing yoga as an Indian phenomenon.

A popular theory is that yoga originated in the Indus Valley Civilization (ca. 3300–1300 BCE), a site that spanned northeast Afghanistan to Pakistan and northwest India. The famous Paśupati Seal is speculated to be an early yogic artifact from this era. The director general of the Archaeological Survey of India, Sir John Marshall, posited that the figure depicted in the seal resembles the Hindu god Śiva sitting in a yoga posture surrounded by animals. Other seals from the same era also show figures that appear to signify various yoga postures. However, Geoffrey Samuel has argued that the interpretations of these artifacts as yogic are dependent on reading later practices into the material and that the people of the Indus Valley Civilization were not all essentially Vedic. Some of the seals are preserved in Pakistan, where there are different interpretations of the figures. Debates concerning the cultural roots of the people and places of ancient civilizations inevitably differ; hence the theories concerning the relationship between yoga and the Indus Valley Civilization remain speculative.

Another theory is that yoga originated in the ancient Sapta Sindhava (Land of the Seven Rivers) in northwest India and adjoining parts of Pakistan. This is where the oldest Vedic text, the *Ṛgvedasaṃhitā* (ca. 1500–1000 BCE), was said to be written. The text contains the earliest written record of the Sanskrit word "yoga," but overall, it is a collection of hymns about cosmologies, rites, rituals, and deities. It was common for traditions to be orally transmitted in the South Asian subcontinent, so although this is the first written account of yoga, it also means there was the possibility that different forms of yoga were evolving outside of texts. The type of yoga understood in the *Ṛgveda* is not like the yoga comprehended as a set of techniques for working with the body. Geoffrey Samuel notes that ascetic traditions of yoga evolved among the non-Vedic *śramaṇic* culture of Greater Magadha, which opposed Vedic Brahmanical traditions and influenced the growth of Buddhism, Jainism, and the Ājīvika movement. The plurality of practices influencing conceptions of yoga throughout prehistory suggests that the origins of yoga cannot be mapped solely onto an expansionist Vedic civilization in India or be ring-fenced to belong solely to any single religious tradition, such as ancient Vedism.

Despite the varied prehistory and heterogeneity of yoga in South Asia, it has become known as a distinctly Indian phenomenon rooted in a Hindu identity. Jyoti Puri elucidates that romanticist Orientalism and anticolonialist nationalism have been influential in historicizing yoga as an Indian and Hindu phenomenon because both interpretations connoted ideals of an ancient Vedic civilization that was abundant in spiritual wealth. Swami Vivekananda (1863–1902) played a key role in asserting yoga as an anticolonial Hindu ideology. Yoga was conflated with a national, yet universal, ideal of "spirituality" that was presented as superior to the Western materialism that Britain had brought to India. This nationalist discourse continues today in the idealized (masculine) Hindu body partaking in physical yogic training regimes mandated in various public institutions such as in government, schools, and the military. Yoga is lobbied by key players in the ruling Bharatiya Janata Party (BJP) and on the global stage via Prime Minister of India Narendra Modi's officiation of International Day of Yoga, championed by the United Nations.

In the postcolonial context, Modi and proponents of Hindutva and the BJP utilize earlier yogic tropes from figures like Vivekananda to help "saffronize" India as a Hindu state at the expense of the cultural and religious pluralism of the country. In 2014, Modi famously announced that "yoga is an invaluable gift of ancient Indian tradition." This continues an epistemological paradox from previous generations in the sense that yoga is presented as a universal good for humanity but also as a distinct cultural product of India. As a national brand, yoga conveys the ideal image of a physically and emotionally skillful state that is stable, strong, scientific, and spiritually secular. As a soft power, yoga supports the state's political influence and global aspirations toward neoliberal economic development and increased militarization. Jyoti Puri observes how this contrasts with earlier anticolonial stances insofar as India now seeks to unite with the West on the shared "war on terror" issue, a strategy that helps distance the Indian "Hindu" state from the "Islamic" state of Pakistan.

Other initiatives that support yogic national branding include the Government of India's Ministry of AYUSH. The ministry seeks to authenticate yoga and alternative health practices, such as āyurveda, as Indigenous forms of medicine in the Indian health-care system. However, the institution has faced significant criticism for the poor quality of research and the promotion of pseudoscience. Meera Nanda's scholarship has long explored the connections among Hindutva, postcolonialism, and the promotion of Vedic "science" by institutions like AYUSH. Following the officialization of the ministry by Modi in 2014, UNESCO declared yoga as a distinctly Indian "intangible cultural heritage of humanity." Both endeavors homogenize yoga into a singular cultural commodity of Indian heritage while at the same time strengthening Hindutva ideology. As Jyoti Puri contends, the appropriation of yoga by the Hindu Right serves a larger political project to "saffronize" India while eliminating cultural pluralities and minority groups.

In the global consumptionscape, yoga is also marketed and consumed as an Indian commodity. Western practitioners have been critiqued by scholars such as Véronique Altglas and Amanda Lucia for cultural appropriation and religious exoticism through their uncritical consumption of yoga and their ambivalence toward the sociopolitical realities of the cultures they endeavor to embody. Indian and Indigenous practices are romanticized as offering ancient, mystical, and spiritual antidotes to the problems of modernity. This is problematic when considering unequal power dynamics in social relations, as such discourses can promote racial stereotypes and cultural misrepresentation. Lucia argues that such power imbalances relate to colonial legacies of oppression, particularly when linked to the "stealing" ethos of white possessivism. Yet despite the onto-epistemological differences between Hindu nationalists and Western practitioners, they often share the same yogic texts, rituals, and practices to build identities. Ultimately, both fail to critically understand the historicity and heterogeneity of yoga in South Asia (and beyond).

Recent scholarship by Anya Foxen postulates an alternative "Western" genealogy of yoga, suggesting that "yoga" has become a lingua franca for spiritualized-breath-movement practices of many kinds. In more speculative scholarship by Muata Ashby, yoga is also alluded to have origins in ancient Egypt, resonating with the African diaspora. Locating the origins of a malleable and diverse practice like yoga will always present difficulties in interpretation. However, critical thinking about the political events of the past can help contextualize the perceptions of the present. One can recognize interpretations of why yoga may be considered Indian, why the Indian state seeks a cultural monopoly on the name of yoga, and why Western practitioners can be critiqued for acts of cultural appropriation. On the other hand, one can also acknowledge the multiplicity of people, practices, and places that shape cultures, whether they are premodern or living in the present.

About the author

Marissa Clarke is a PhD candidate at the University of Edinburgh (2021–2025) and visiting doctoral researcher at Universidade Federal do Rio Grande do Sul (2024). Her research explores the phenomenology of yoga, the body, and sound. She has an interdisciplinary background in marketing studies, religious studies, and health research. Her work is funded by the Scottish Graduate School for Arts & Humanities AHRC Doctoral Training Partnership.

Suggestions for further reading

In this book

See also chapters 6 (Has yoga always been associated with Hinduism?) and 7 (Is yoga Indian?).

Elsewhere

Altglas, V. *From Yoga to Kabbalah: Religious Exoticism and the Logics of Bricolage*. Oxford University Press, 2014.

Nanda, M. "'Owning' Yoga: How 'Hindu' Is This Modern Version?" *Himal* 24, no. 1 (2011): 53–54.

Puri, Jyoti. "Sculpting the Saffron Body: Yoga, Hindutva, and the International Marketplace." In *Majoritarian State: How Hindu Nationalism Is Changing India*. Oxford University Press, 2019.

Samuel, Geoffrey. *The Origins of Yoga and Tantra: Indic Religions to the Thirteenth Century*. Cambridge University Press, 2008.

59
What is the relationship between race and yoga?

Sheena Sood

Like other cultural phenomena that circulate as a commodity on the global market, yoga is enmeshed in a system of racial hierarchy. While yoga is popularly regarded as a practice that promotes physical and spiritual well-being, access to its healing properties is often stratified by interlocking categories of race, class, gender, and sexuality. A range of social and systemic theories of race and colonialism help conceptualize the relationship between race and yoga. In this entry, I will focus on how Edward Said's framework of Orientalism simultaneously illuminates yoga's susceptibility to cultural appropriation as it also absolves its weaponization by Desi far-right cultural nationalists and religious supremacists.

The late cultural critic and postcolonial scholar Edward Said coined the term "Orientalism" to illuminate the worldview that the West fabricated to mark itself as superior to the civilizations of the "Far East" (Said 1978). In juxtaposition with stereotypes of the West as scientific, logical, and civilized, the Orientalist logic stereotypes the East as timeless, mystical, and spiritually rich. According to Said, Orientalism has served to justify imperial and colonial brutalities by European and US empires such as land and resource theft, capitalist exploitation, genocide and violence, war, and anti-immigration policies.

The framework of Orientalism continues to operate as a weapon of imperialist logic. One significant evolution, however, is that the perpetrators of colonial and imperial repression are not simply of the West; they are also of the East. Said forewarned the risk of Orientalism being internalized by those in the East: "My hope is to illustrate the formidable structure of cultural domination and, specifically for formerly colonised peoples, the dangers and temptations of employing the structure upon themselves" (1978, 33). When internalized, Orientalism lends itself to a type of identity politics—one that flattens the historical identities of colonizers and colonized people. This inclination to appropriate understandings of Orientalism and thus present a flattened analysis of race, ethnicity, and religion is relevant when considering the relationship between race and yoga.

Fortunately, there has been a mainstreaming of critical conversations on the topic of race and yoga in recent years. Practitioners and scholars have cultivated awareness around issues of cultural appropriation, whitewashing, and diversity and inclusion in yoga spaces. Such conversations, couched in a "representation Orientalist" lens, invite the public to consider the enduring legacy of colonial and racist logics and how they shape the ways in which yoga is taught, shared, and marketed as a popular cultural phenomenon that is either stripped from or stereotyped within its South Asian lineage. Critical voices of this lens offer solutions that aim to honor and appreciate yoga's ancient roots.

In contrast to the representation Orientalist framework, the "anti-imperial Orientalist" frame understands the racialization of yoga as connected to an interlocking system of imperialism, capitalist exploitation, and religious supremacy. Critical of how the representation Orientalist lens presumes Indian culture to be rooted in an unbroken monolithic lineage, the anti-imperial Orientalist frame scrutinizes essentialist explanations of yoga's South Asian roots. Cautioning against depictions of yoga as an exclusively Hindu practice belonging to a homogenized, ancient Indian identity, proponents of the anti-imperial Orientalist frame suggest that the racialized appropriation of yoga is not limited to a white and Western appropriation of yoga's history. They purport that yoga has been historically appropriated by upper-caste Hindus, more recently by the Hindu Right to advance ethnonationalist and neoliberal agendas. Instead of situating solutions to racial issues regarding yoga in romanticized interpretations of an "ancient past," critics using an anti-imperial Orientalist frame recognize yoga's weaponization by people of all racial, religious, and ethnic backgrounds. In order for yoga to be rooted in an anti-oppressive, racially liberatory potential, critics who use the anti-imperial Orientalist frame suggest practitioners be honest about yoga's oppressive history and its malleability and vulnerability as a neutral cultural phenomenon that is easily molded toward agendas of various ideologies—be they ideologies of anti-racist liberation or ones that advocate for racial (or ethnic) purity.

Structuring the conversation along a representation Orientalist to anti-imperial Orientalist continuum reveals the limitations of campaigns that advocate for identity-based rather than material solutions to issues of racial oppression. The continuum also allows us to witness the dynamism of yoga as an evolving cultural phenomenon, not a static essence.

A central aspect of the relationship between race and yoga concerns the cultural roots of yoga. The spiritual philosophy of yoga originates in South Asia—as do aspects of the modern postural practice. Considerable evidence suggests the modern postural practice emerged as a result of the hybridization of a diversity of Indigenous South Asian and also Swedish and Western calisthenic cultural processes. However, as yoga has become a pervasive part of New Age spiritual movements in a global system of white supremacy, these cultural roots have been either erased or temporarily obscured by Western practitioners. Across modern yoga spaces, contemporary practitioners either wholly displace yoga's South Asian roots or, in crediting its origins, reduce such delineations to exotified representations.

Individuals who view modern yoga through the lens of Orientalist representation generally regard such spaces as colonial and Orientalized instances of "cultural appropriation." Western culture and its prototypical yogis, who often lack a cultural connection to yoga's roots, have commodified yogic culture and philosophy in ways that have not only erased South Asian visibility but also manufactured it into a multibillion-dollar industry that excludes other racially marginalized communities from access to yoga spaces. The typical yoga studios in the West Orientalize South Asian yogic culture as a "mystical" tradition by appropriating Sanskrit phrases like *namaste*, showcasing cultural relics of Buddha and Gaṇeśa in bathrooms and studios, and blasting devotional hymns during class sessions. As a paradigm, the representation Orientalist lens has raised the public's consciousness about the racial impact of cultural appropriation by explaining the experiences of colonialism and racism in yoga.

However, the cultural appropriation lens lacks a material focus and leans on flattened notions of identity in its depiction of race through a distorted "nation-state" lens. Consider the often uncontested claim that "Sun salutations (*sūryanamaskār*) are a five-thousand-year-old tradition" or "Yoga is an ancient Indian tradition." These claims, offered by practitioners of all racial backgrounds, including far-right Hindu nationalist Prime Minister of India Narendra Modi, trap India in an essentialized place of the past. By assuming yoga to be born into a static, monolithic culture, these claims are easily co-opted by the Indian state for projects of Hindutva—a political ideology of Hindu nationalism. Religious studies scholar Andrea Jain contends that although it cloaks itself as a "decolonial" movement, the Indian state's promotion of spirituality represents a politics of Hindu nationalism. Since being elected as prime minister of India, Modi has advanced a culturally nationalist campaign to essentialize ethnic, racial, and religious ownership over yoga in an Indian identity and a Hindu narrative, what Jain identifies as the "Hindu Origins position."

We saw this campaign emerge when Modi traveled to New York in 2014 to propose a United Nations resolution for an International Day of Yoga, a holiday that recognizes India as the birthplace of yoga.

According to anti-casteist Bahujan activist Prachi Patankar, holidays like the International Day of Yoga erase the diversity of Indigenous cultures and spiritual practices, within and outside South Asia, that have contributed to the systematic development of yoga on a broader scale. The voices that claim yoga as authentically Hindu are "rooted in the chauvinistic Hinduism among some sectors of the upper-caste minority. . . . [They] claim yoga as their homogenous culture—in ways that obscure the caste, class, and religious diversity and injustices among South Asians" (Patankar 2014). Hence, although the representation Orientalist lens offers us a window into the legacy of harm as it relates to race and yoga, it also perpetuates Hindu fundamentalism, Brahmanical casteism, and anti-Muslim violence.

The anti-imperial Orientalist lens illustrates how Orientalist logic, when internalized by a frame that constructs Hinduism and India as a fixed racial identity, advances ethnonationalism in the name of yoga. Consider that one of the most globally revered yoga teachers of Indian descent, Sadhguru of the Isha Foundation, is celebrated for being an "authentic" South Asian yogi. Sadhguru's Instagram page records upward of 9.4 million followers. Sadhguru proudly boasts about habitually teaching yoga on International Day of Yoga to the Indian Armed Forces, the same Indian military that is responsible for reinscribing colonial borders, terrorizing religious minorities, and engaging in military exchange with imperial colonizers such as the US and Israel. When Orientalist logic is attuned more to an optics of cultural representation rather than an ethics of anti-imperialism, it risks being deployed by political projects of racial, religious, and caste supremacy—which are currently fueling genocide and ethnic cleansing against Indigenous people, Muslims, and lower-caste communities. Conclusively, a robust examination of the relationship between race and yoga must navigate these complexities. For yoga to be oriented toward a politics of racial justice, it must embody an ethics of anti-imperialism rather than a hollow politics of representation.

About the author

Sheena Sood, PhD (she/her), is a Philadelphia-based sociologist, writer, educator, and yoga teacher. Her research, "Omwashing Yoga: Weaponized Spirituality in India, Israel, and the US," investigates the growing incorporation of yoga and mindfulness by far-right law enforcement, military, and vigilante groups. Sheena is an Assistant Professor of Sociology at Delaware Valley University in Doylestown, Pennsylvania. She has written for *Jadaliyya*, *Race & Yoga*, and *Colorlines*. As an activist scholar, Sheena brings her research into praxis by curating "Decolonizing Yoga" workshops that challenge attendees to reckon with both yoga's oppressive layers and liberatory potential. She is also the founder of Yoga Warrior Tales, an interactive adventure-based educational program that teaches children yoga and mindfulness through a social justice lens.

Suggestions for further reading

In this book

See also chapters 51 (How has modern yoga developed around the world?) and 58 (What does yoga mean to Indians today?).

Elsewhere

Jain, Andrea R. *Peace Love Yoga: The Politics of Global Spirituality*. Oxford University Press, 2020.

Patankar, Prachi. "Ghosts of Yoga Past and Present." *Jadaliyya* (2014). https://www.jadaliyya.com/Details/30281.

Puri, Jyoti. "Sculpting the Saffron Body: Yoga, Hindutva, and the International Marketplace." In *Majoritarian State: How Hindu Nationalism Is Changing India*. Hurst, 2019.

Said, Edward. *Orientalism*. Vintage, 1978.

Soundararajan, Thenmozhi. *The Trauma of Caste: A Dalit Feminist Meditation on Survivorship, Healing and Abolition*. North Atlantic Books, 2022.

60 What is the relationship between yoga and capitalism?

Marissa Clarke

The relation between yoga and capitalism is not an assimilation of one static system (yoga) to another (capitalism); rather, the relation is a response to ever-changing socioeconomic developments. Like yoga, capitalism is a malleable concept with different historical forms, which means it is always context specific. For Karl Marx, the mechanisms of exploitation defined capitalism, particularly in the context of the means of production and employment of wage labor as surplus value, in the Industrial Revolution. For Max Weber, rational action defined the "spirit" of capitalism, emerging from the disruption of social relations and the ethos of self-control, during the Protestant Reformation. For Gilles Deleuze and Félix Guattari, any evolutionary account of capitalism should be rejected; hence they considered capitalism to be a contingent encounter between liquid wealth and deterritorialized labor power, which extracts surplus value from the differential flows of social relations. This entry explores the symbiotic socioeconomic relations between yoga and capitalism, using the examples of consumer culture, "emodities," and labor.

In contemporary discourse, it is common for scholars and practitioners to be critical of how yoga has become "commercialized" as a commodity in the "capitalist" consumer market. In her seminal text *Selling Yoga*, Andrea Jain argues that the rise of market capitalism, industrialization, and globalization in the late twentieth century, alongside the consequential dominance of consumer culture, helped shape yoga as a transnational commodity. Scholars such as Jeremey Carrette and Richard King criticized the commodification of yoga, among other spiritual products, for being inauthentic to traditional religious wares, suggesting that some pure, uncommodified form of yoga exists that is untarnished by socioeconomic forces like capitalism. However, Jain argues that such essentialist readings do not account for how contemporary yoga reflects the dominant non-dualist ontology and religio-philosophical paradigm of consumer culture, which links the self to the body. In other words, caring for the body through the consumption of yoga is synonymous with the transformative process of self-development. This relation is also viewed by Jain as an ideological one, insofar as the preoccupation with caring for the self is connected to the omnipresent logic of neoliberalism, whereby control over one's body and circumstances is perceived as a moral achievement in society. The behaviors synonymous with participation in yoga culture—such as exercise, healthy diets, emotional regulation, and "green" consumption patterns—fit well with the ethos of the autonomous, self-governing neoliberal subject. This relation is ideological because individualization is concomitant with privatization, which ultimately is a threat to the collective dimension of solving public problems, such as environmental devastation and social inequalities. To put it simply, social problems are translated into individual problems that the yoga social actor attempts to resolve through the "right" consumption choices, such as caring for one's body, buying sustainable products, or adopting ethical diets. Yet pervasive socioeconomic inequalities have implications on how *free* individuals really are to make the *right* choices.

This ideological relation between yoga and capitalism is also emotional. Eva Illouz asserts that the rise of consumer capitalism has intensified emotional life in the sense that life is guided by emotional projects like "finding inner peace" or "overcoming depression." Emotional life and consumption are intertwined, as commodities aid the expression/experience of emotions, and emotions are converted into commodities. Illouz terms this process as a coproduction of "emodities" (emotional commodities), which accounts for the fact that consumer capitalism has become a fundamental aspect of modern identity. Despite being a contemporary scholarly construct, emodity draws conceptual links to earlier Freudian perspectives of the "psyche" that helped inform the techniques of marketing science and branding. This is relevant for understanding the yoga economy, as practitioners buy yoga products and services not only for what they *do* but also for what they *mean* and how they help shape their sense of selfhood. The yoga class is an emodity of affective capitalism, considering that it operates in the spheres of the senses and experience; it is an intangible commodity experience that performatively produces emotional moods and bodily sensations. Yoga emodities are part of a larger health and well-being industry that targets the management of emotions, wherein the consumer has been socialized to coproduce, consume, and manage their emotionality. Emodity as a concept reveals that emotional authenticity and commodification happen simultaneously, aligning with the non-dualist metaphysics of consumer capitalism. Thus, the relation between yoga and capitalism can also be understood as a coproduction of emotionality.

The concept of "emodity" is significant for understanding yoga labor, especially when bearing in mind that critiques of labor are a common thread among Marxist, Weberian, and Deleuzoguattarian readings of capitalism. The yoga teaching profession is an example of "affective" or "immaterial" labor because it is centered on the creation and manipulation of affects encompassing sensations and emotions. The immaterial aspects of this labor relate to the rise of cognitive capitalism, whereby knowledge is a dominant mode of accumulation. The affective labor of the yoga teacher is the accumulation and transmission of knowledge, which becomes coproduced as an emodity experienced in the practitioner's body. The pursuit of yoga teacher trainings and professions is also representative of emotional and cognitive capitalism to the extent that emotional fulfillment guides rationality. People often pursue the yoga teaching profession not for the rational purpose of attaining economic ends but for the emotional value and meaning it brings to their lives, such as self-realization, fulfillment, freedom, friendships, and joy. A career in yoga may *feel* meaningful, but it still leaves many teachers scrambling for precarious work while also juggling various jobs with fewer rights in what is known as the "gig economy." This reveals how the pursuit of emotional fulfillment through work is intertwined with the capitalist mode of production. As Kathi Weeks argues, the problematization of work is not so much about the renunciation of labor—given its emotional forms of value. Rather, it is about refusing the valorization of work as a moral duty or proof of citizenship and refusing the exploitation of life for capital.

If life is exploited for the accumulation of capital, then it is also in the commons of life where potential for resistance to this exploitation can be discovered. There are various emerging yoga collectives that are seeking justice not just for precarious labor conditions in the yoga economy instilled by capitalist modes of production but also for the deep damages that capitalist extractivism inflicts upon the ecological, social, and biopolitical commons. The anti-capitalist struggle is also a struggle against other axes of domination; hence the struggle shares political alliances with feminist, antiracist, decolonial, queer, and anti-ableist movements. Although it is out of scope to do so for this volume, a full critique of capitalism requires an intersectional analysis that explores the threads that weave together production, social reproduction, political order, economy, and ecology. bell hooks emphasized the importance of intersectional activism in resisting intertwined systems of oppression, from imperialism, patriarchy, and white supremacy to capitalism. Perhaps the power of yoga's symbiotic socioeconomic relationship to capitalism lies in its potential to revolt against capitalist exploitation by building solidarities with the marginalized and strengthening the bonds of the common while seeking autonomy from capital through a politics of care.

About the author

Marissa Clarke is a PhD candidate at the University of Edinburgh (2021–2025) and visiting doctoral researcher at Universidade Federal do Rio Grande do Sul (2024). Her research explores the phenomenology of yoga, the body, and sound. She has an interdisciplinary background in marketing studies, religious studies, and health research. Her work is funded by the Scottish Graduate School for Arts & Humanities AHRC Doctoral Training Partnership.

Suggestions for further reading

In this book

See also chapters 26 (What life does the ideal yogi lead?) and 52 (Why did yoga start being practiced in the Western world?).

Elsewhere

Fraser, Nancy, and Rachel Jaeggi. *Capitalism: A Conversation in Critical Theory*. Polity Press, 2018.

Illouz, Eva. *Emotions as Commodities: Capitalism, Consumption and Authenticity*. Routledge, 2017.

Jain, Andrea R. *Selling Yoga: From Counterculture to Pop Culture*. Oxford University Press, 2014.

Lachmann, Richard. "The Origins of Capitalism." In *What Is Historical Sociology?* Polity Press, 2013.

Index

A

Abhidharma, 191, 193
abilities, 16, 77–79, 88, 89, 97, 194, 206, 227, 235
ableism, 97, 218
absorption, 48, 79, 116, 156
abuse, 61, 64, 85, 113, 160, 167, 200, 203, 204, 208, 218 (see also: sexual abuse)
academia, 66, 158, 213, 239–241
accessibility, 107, 111, 218, 222, 225
accountability, 61, 85
activism, 9, 102, 231, 245, 254, 258
adjustments, manual, 64, 65, 83, 84, 185
Advaita, 21, 22, 32, 48, 75, 230, 231
afflictions, 30, 57
ahiṃsā (see: nonviolence)
akṣara, 10, 41
alchemy, 77, 106
alignment, 88, 160, 218
Amanaska, 33, 55
Amaraugha, 49, 56, 57, 214
Amṛtasiddhi, 3, 29, 145, 214
Ananta (see: Śeṣa)
anatomy, 84, 88, 105, 133, 137, 138
aparigraha, 60, 63, 67, 68
Ashtanga Vinyasa Yoga, 85, 113, 125, 204, 213, 215, 218, 235, 236
aṣṭāṅgayoga, 59, 67–69, 79, 106, 116, 129, 141, 142
asteya, 60, 63, 67, 68, 111
Atharvaveda, 37, 128
ātman, 20, 42, 71, 142, 187
attachments, 39, 71, 72
austerities (see: tapas)
authenticity, 5, 113, 126, 166, 202, 245, 249, 257
authority, 7, 9, 10, 60, 64, 113, 165–167, 199, 202, 208
awareness, 53, 67, 117, 141, 142, 219, 227, 252
āyurveda, 7, 89, 101, 102, 104–107, 192, 249
AYUSH, 107, 249

B

balance, 87, 88, 101, 107, 114, 121, 137, 185, 206, 207
bandha, 117, 130, 156
bat penance, 118, 137, 138
beauty, 226, 227
belief, 16, 17, 19–22, 26, 85, 137, 158, 170, 198
Bengali, 38, 147, 239, 240
Bhagavadgītā, 16, 17, 34, 42, 48, 95, 142, 188, 231, 240
bhakti, 13, 16, 17, 22, 26, 76, 133, 196
bhaktiyoga, 16, 55, 95, 188, 214, 230
Bharatiya Janata Party (BJP), 107, 219, 248
bhāṣya, 96, 116, 117, 156
Bikram, 204, 215, 218
bindu, 42, 134, 138
biomedicine, 47, 48, 83–85, 160, 217, 227
bliss, 9, 74, 76, 203, 230
bodybuilding, 113, 121, 124, 221, 235, 245
brahmacarya (see: celibacy)
brahman, 20, 37, 41, 71, 75, 106, 142, 187, 192, 199
Brahmanism, 8, 24, 25, 37, 41, 63, 104, 132, 192, 233
British Wheel of Yoga, 184, 218
Buddha, 78, 128, 178, 253

C

cakras, 28, 84, 134, 143, 146, 150, 176
calisthenics, 124, 126, 253
caṇḍālī, 146, 147
capitalism, 9, 53, 200, 243, 244, 251, 252, 256–259
Carakasaṃhitā, 7, 105, 106
caste, 3, 37, 112, 159, 184, 254
celibacy, 60, 61, 63, 67–69, 71, 196, 204, 214
channels, 28, 120, 129, 130, 134, 146, 174, 175, 214 (see also: nāḍīs)
charisma, 101, 167, 170, 185, 198, 199, 207, 208

Christianity, 4, 5, 14, 18, 25, 26, 229–231
citta, 74, 142
cognition, 12, 75, 117, 132, 133, 141, 160, 258
colonialism, 17, 25, 104, 121, 125, 158, 243, 244, 249, 251–254
commodification, 17, 47, 200, 218, 244, 249, 251, 253, 256, 257
consent, 65, 204 (see also: adjustments, manual)
cosmology, 10, 41, 75, 133, 145, 146, 188, 248
counterculture, 104, 222, 229
cure, 47, 87, 88, 93, 107, 130, 221

D
Dattātreyayogaśāstra, 3, 111, 117, 155, 207, 214
death, 42, 48, 51, 56, 71, 76, 147, 175, 187, 202
decolonization, 159, 245, 253, 258
devotion, 13, 16, 22, 24, 51, 61, 68, 95, 133, 219
dhāraṇā, 59, 74, 79, 96, 116, 141–143, 176
dhyāna, 14, 59, 74, 76, 79, 95, 116, 141–143, 176, 217
discipline, 8, 48, 63, 64, 101, 102, 207 (see also: tapas)
disease, 8, 47, 87, 93, 105, 120, 122, 130, 137, 207
doṣa, 101, 105, 107
duḥkha, 8, 51

E
economics, 52, 53, 93, 170, 185, 226, 227, 249, 257, 258
effort, 24, 38, 52, 93, 117, 118, 120, 122, 163
effortlessness, 174, 207, 208
eightfold yoga (see: aṣṭāṅgayoga)
embodiment, 116, 117, 143, 150, 160, 204, 249, 254
emodity, 257, 258
emotion, 12, 17, 62, 141, 257, 258
enlightenment, 16, 43, 57, 133, 135, 199, 202–204
equanimity, 48, 135, 207
equipment, 122, 218
exploitation, 185, 200, 243–245, 251, 252, 256, 258, 259

F
fascia, 95, 97, 117
fasting, 65, 100
feminism, 227, 258
fixation of attention, 38, 40, 74, 79, 106, 135, 142
flexibility, 52, 72, 87, 88, 95–97, 101, 122, 223, 227
folklore, 65, 79, 177–179
force, 52, 65, 122, 128, 146, 147, 173, 213, 214

G
gender, 38, 67, 97, 102, 114, 130, 145, 159, 184, 225–227, 251
Gheraṇḍasaṃhitā, 13, 76, 87, 100, 112, 162
globalization, 34, 48, 117, 158, 215, 217, 231, 244, 245, 256
Gorakṣanātha, 33, 178, 189, 194–197, 240
Gorakṣaśataka, 48, 146, 189
gurukula, 37, 198–200
guru-śiṣya-paramparā, 169, 189, 198–200
gymnastics, 92, 113, 124–126, 215, 221, 226, 234, 235

H
hagiography, 113, 166, 170, 184, 233
hair, 112, 113, 188
harmonialism, 126
Haṭhābhyāsapaddhati, 96, 120, 121, 125, 137
Haṭhapradīpikā, 13, 34, 36, 72, 91, 96, 100, 120, 145, 162, 173–175, 214
heritage, 16, 41, 52, 166, 219, 242, 249
hierarchy, 159, 167, 200, 215, 251
Himalayas, 29, 113, 188
Hindi, 38, 162, 178, 213, 215, 240
Hindutva, 248, 249, 253
Hiranyagarbha, 187, 189
householders, 26, 61, 113, 185, 196, 233

I
ignorance, 71, 198
imbalance, 105, 207, 249
immortality, 56, 72, 78, 106, 195, 196, 214
impurities, 21, 87, 104, 118, 150
Indra Devi, 217, 226, 234
industry, 4, 60, 61, 83–85, 95, 167, 253, 257 (see also: capitalism)
initiation, 13, 69, 112, 126, 134, 171, 204, 229
injuries, 68, 84, 88
Instagram, 95, 102, 254
intentions of the practice, 9, 12, 13, 117, 118, 128, 142, 166, 244
International Day of Yoga, 219, 254
interoception, 117, 160

introspection, 60, 85, 143
inversion of the body, 118, 120, 137–139, 214
invisibility, 78, 177, 208
Islam, 4, 26, 249 (see also: Muslim)
īśvarapraṇidhāna, 21, 42, 60, 61, 68, 69
Iyengar, B. K. S., 65, 88, 113, 137–139, 166, 192, 215, 218, 222, 234–236

J
japa, 14, 42, 135
Japan, 14, 28, 219
Jivamukti Yoga, 101, 218
jīvanmukti, 42, 49, 51, 72, 75, 203, 204
jñānayoga, 16, 95, 187, 230
Jogpradīpakā, 92, 137, 138, 215
Jois, Pattabhi, 85, 113, 125, 156, 166, 192, 204, 208, 218, 234–236

K
kaivalya, 48, 75, 162, 202, 203
karmayoga, 16, 55, 63, 64, 95, 188, 200, 230, 231
Kaṭha Upaniṣad, 3, 42, 116, 141, 187
Kaulism, 79, 178, 195
khecarīmudrā, 175, 214
Khecarīvidyā, 33, 149, 150
Krishnamacharya, 92, 113, 124, 125, 135, 192, 199, 221, 226, 233–236
Kṛṣṇa, 17, 26, 34, 42, 49, 118, 142, 188
kumbhaka, 117, 173, 174, 214
kuṇḍalinī, 29, 56, 93, 134, 145–147, 175
Kundalini Yoga, 3, 134, 147, 204
Kuvalayananda, 160, 221

L
layayoga, 57, 76, 214
liberation (see: mokṣa)
lifestyle, 8, 9, 85, 102, 111–113, 184, 203, 217
limbs of yoga, 59, 60, 67, 74, 87, 129, 142, 176, 203
longevity, 138, 208
lotus pose, 57, 88, 95, 96, 112, 120, 122, 135

M
magic, 92, 104, 107, 132, 143, 179, 221
Mahābhārata, 7, 17, 34, 38, 63, 67, 78, 79, 96, 187
Maharishi Mahesh Yogi, 160, 200, 220
mahāsiddhas, 29, 177
mallakhamb, 124, 225
mantrayoga, 57, 133, 214
marketing, 52, 85, 102, 257
martial arts, 28, 124, 219, 225
masculinity, 125, 226, 248
massage, 28, 30, 97
materiality, 8, 10, 133, 203
Matsyendranātha, 33, 178, 189, 194–197
mayūrāsana, 121, 174, 206
medicine, 16, 28, 104–107, 192, 200, 217, 222, 249
memory, 12, 166, 185
menstruation, 122, 139
MeToo, 64, 204
militarization, 64, 124, 226, 248, 249, 254
mindfulness, 85, 160
mokṣa, 16, 36, 48, 51, 71, 75, 99, 104, 135, 187
monasticism, 4, 14, 26, 28, 61, 104, 155, 170, 229
morality, 8, 9, 21, 52, 101, 257, 258
motivations for practice, 47, 49, 68, 95, 118, 223
mudrā, 88, 93, 117, 135, 138, 145, 173, 175, 214
mukti (see: mokṣa)
Muslim, 4, 14, 25, 26, 178, 194, 254
Mysore, 92, 121, 124, 125, 135, 226, 233–236
mystics, 56, 74, 106, 143, 222, 249, 251, 253

N
nāda, 42, 76, 134
nādānusandhāna, 173, 175, 214
nāḍīs, 84, 129, 146
namaste, 13, 133, 253
Nāth, 3, 33, 107, 112, 133, 177, 178, 189, 196
nectar, 146, 195, 196, 214
neo-Hinduism, 17, 34, 231, 245
neoliberalism, 52, 53, 227, 249, 252, 257
Nepal, 72, 106, 194, 195
nirvāṇa, 48, 71, 202
niyama, 9, 52, 59–61, 67–69, 101, 111, 129, 241
non-dualist, 21, 22, 48, 75, 173, 203, 219, 257 (see also: Advaita)
nonstealing (see: asteya)
nonviolence, 9, 25, 60, 63–65, 67, 68, 99–101, 111

O
observances (see: yamas)
occult, 52, 217
oṃ, 10, 13, 21, 40–43, 49, 69, 132, 133, 135, 241

ontology, 7–10, 145, 257
oppression, 53, 230, 249, 252, 258
orality, 37–39, 105, 132, 163, 177, 191, 199, 235, 239, 248
Orientalism, 126, 158, 248, 251–254
orthodoxy, 7, 21, 22, 165, 233, 235

P
padmāsana, 57, 88, 95, 96, 120, 122
pain, 8, 30, 47, 65, 106, 122
Pakistan, 218, 247–249
Pali, 37, 78, 118, 121, 137, 239
paramparā (see: guru-śiṣya-paramparā)
Pārvatī, 33, 188, 189, 195
patriarchy, 18, 53, 61, 258
patronage, 112, 170, 234
pedagogy, 163, 183, 185, 208, 236
perfection, 52, 56, 72, 78, 87, 113, 129, 143, 177, 207
Persian, 25, 26, 239, 241
phenomenology, 42, 127, 159
philology, 59, 124, 158, 183, 185
pilgrimage, 92, 177, 229
poetry, 106, 132, 189, 194, 227, 240
postcolonialism, 243, 245, 248, 249, 251
post-lineage, 65, 167, 218
Prakrit, 37, 239
prakṛti, 8, 21, 48, 55, 75, 203
pramāṇa, 9, 156
praṇava, 41–43
pratyāhāra, 59, 116, 141, 176, 207
pūjā, 13, 17
Purāṇas, 7, 133, 188
purification, 17, 21, 36, 69, 93, 129, 130, 174, 206, 207
purity, 60, 100, 101, 252
puruṣa, 8, 21, 48, 55, 75, 142, 202, 203

R
racism, 159, 227, 249, 251–254
Raja Yoga, 189, 217, 230
rājayoga, 16, 52, 57, 76, 173, 175, 214, 230
Ramakrishna, 74, 75, 229–231
reformers, 25, 124, 125, 215, 221, 240
relaxation, 52, 88, 89, 95–97, 101, 206, 215, 223, 234
renunciation, 3, 61, 64, 71–73, 121, 177, 179, 225, 229, 258
restrictions, 9, 59, 67, 74, 75, 99, 100, 213
revival, 3, 75, 225, 226
Ṛgveda, 3, 20, 37, 38, 248
rope, 121, 225
ṛṣi, 30, 37, 187

S
sacrifice, 20, 41, 132
ṣaḍaṅgayoga, 79, 176
sādhakas, 56, 57, 107
sādhanā, 56, 93, 163
sādhus, 151, 163
safety, 58, 83–85
sages, 17, 33, 78, 121, 132, 166, 187, 188, 199
saints, 33, 43, 166, 192, 194
Śaivism, 25, 32, 72, 75, 146, 170, 177, 188, 194, 214
śakti, 72, 145, 146, 204
Śāktism, 32, 177, 195
salvation, 41, 175, 187, 202, 203
Sāṃkhya, 8–10, 21, 33, 48, 77–79, 106, 187, 191, 192
saṃnyāsins, 229, 230
sampradāya, 112, 169–171, 189, 196
saṃsāra, 20, 24, 48, 51, 71, 99, 206, 207
saṃskāra, 12, 71
saṃtoṣa, 60, 68
Śaṅkara, 21, 22, 96
sarvāṅgāsana, 137, 138
śāstras, 7, 10, 67, 128, 192
ṣaṭkarma, 105, 106, 174, 176
satya, 60, 63, 67, 68
Satyananda, 204, 205
śauca, 60, 68, 69
sculpture, 92, 183
semen, 69, 138, 195
Śeṣa, 34, 146, 192
sevā, 230, 231
sexual abuse, 64, 83, 85, 160, 200, 204
sexuality, 60, 61, 68, 69, 195, 196, 204, 214, 240, 251
siddha, 7, 106, 107, 133, 177–179
siddhi, 55–57, 78, 93, 106, 143, 149, 177, 194, 203, 240
Sikhism, 3, 25, 40, 43, 134, 148, 198
śīrṣāsana, 137, 138
śiṣya (see: guru-śiṣya-paramparā)
Śiva, 26, 33, 34, 112, 146, 149, 174, 177, 188, 195
Śivasaṃhitā, 33, 56, 87, 188, 189
sleep, 52, 67, 146, 207
soteriology, 42, 43, 55, 72, 126, 134, 147, 173, 179, 187
śramaṇa, 14, 20, 24, 99, 104, 202, 248

śruti, 32, 34, 37
standards, teaching, 61, 83, 202, 223, 227
strength, 38, 63, 72, 87–89, 96, 97, 113, 118, 121, 188
stretching, 28, 88, 96, 97
student-teacher relationships, 84, 165
Sufism, 14, 26, 40
sun salutations (see: sūryanamaskār)
supernatural powers (see: siddhi)
surrender, 17, 61, 69
sūryanamaskār, 121, 124, 125, 219, 225, 235, 253
sūtra, 9, 65, 68, 69, 74, 78, 116, 118, 156
svādhyāya, 9, 41, 60, 68, 69, 134, 241
Svātmārāma, 34, 72, 120, 162, 173–175, 214, 215

T
Tamil, 106, 239
tapas, 8, 13, 56, 65, 87, 91, 100, 118, 188, 213
tattva, 8, 48, 77
teacher training, 60, 88, 184, 218, 223, 240, 241
theology, 19, 52, 53, 159, 169
Theosophical Society, 60, 155, 221, 222
therapeutic benefits, 28–30, 48, 106, 107, 120, 122, 130, 160, 185, 235
Tibet, 14, 28–30, 113, 143, 147, 194, 233, 235, 239
trances, 48, 57, 74–76
transcendental meditation, 134, 143, 160, 200, 220

U
ujjāyī, 130, 156
union, 16, 17, 20, 48, 134, 203, 215
utkrānti (see: yogic suicide)

V
Vaiṣṇava, 7, 34, 79, 146, 159, 170, 178, 188, 206, 233
vajra, 29, 56
Vajrayāna, 7, 56, 146, 147
vajrolīmudrā, 175, 214
Vasiṣṭha, 33, 187
Vasubandhu, 191, 192
Vedānta, 22, 32, 75, 230, 231, 243
Vedanta Society, 4, 230
veganism, 9, 60, 101
vegetarianism, 60, 99–101
videhamukti, 49, 51, 175
viparītakaraṇī, 138, 175, 214
Viṣṇu, 17, 26, 34, 188
visualization, 21, 79, 132, 133, 135, 143
vitality, 69, 138, 227
Vivekamārtaṇḍa, 145, 189, 215
Vyāsa, 17, 67, 74, 129, 187, 191, 199

W
war, 222, 226, 249, 251
warriors, 37, 63, 64
wellness, 83, 126, 218
wisdom, 41, 56, 143, 200, 222
wrestling, 92, 121, 124, 225

Y
Yājñavalkya, 33, 187
Yajurveda, 37, 38
yamas, 9, 52, 59–61, 63, 67–69, 101, 111, 129
yantras, 29, 132
Yoga Alliance, 60, 61, 84, 218
Yoga Journal, 29, 95, 102, 223
Yogabīja, 33, 56, 57, 177, 215
Yogācāra, 3, 7, 55
Yogananda, 4, 126, 143
Yogendra, 113, 126, 160, 221, 226
Yogi Bhajan, 3, 134, 147, 204
yogic body, 56, 57, 133, 134, 146, 147, 150, 215
yogic suicide, 42, 76, 207
yoginī, 72, 149–152, 178, 188